AMERICAN BROADSIDES

AMERICAN BROADSIDES

Sixty
facsimilies
dated *1680* to *1800*
reproduced from originals
in the American
Antiquarian
Society

Selected & introduced by
Georgia B. Bumgardner

IMPRINT SOCIETY
Barre · Massachusetts · 1971

CONTENTS

INTRODUCTION

BROADSIDES contain some of the most fascinating material relating to life in early America. These single sheets of paper, usually printed on one side only, make it possible to view colonial society from a different vantage point than that usually afforded by the materials of military, political, and diplomatic history. Subject matter of these pieces of ephemera ranges from advertisements to the edifying warnings of criminals' confessions; official proclamations, instructions for school masters, comments on important contemporary events, information for immigrants, ballads and elegies—all found a convenient vehicle in the broadside during its heyday in the eighteenth century.

The American Antiquarian Society in Worcester, Massachusetts, has an excellent collection of broadsides which complements its collections of early American books, pamphlets, and newspapers. Other large collections can be found in most major libraries and historical societies.

The value of broadsides for the study of history was recognized at an early date at the American Antiquarian Society. In 1872, the librarian of the Society, Samuel F. Haven, made the following statement in his semiannual report: "There is another kind of historical supplies which it is equally desirable to collect and preserve in unlimited quantities, and which individuals are apt to gather as unconsciously and inexpensively and can spare quite as easily as [periodicals]. I refer to what are technically called *Broadsides*, embracing all sorts of posters, advertisements, notices, programmes, and indeed whatever is printed on one side of a sheet of paper, large or small. Ballads and proclamations usually come within the definition. They are the legitimate representatives of the most emphemeral literature, the least likely to escape destruction, and yet they are the most vivid exhibitions of the manners, arts, and daily life, of communities and nations. . . . They imply a vast deal more than they literally express, and disclose visions of interior conditions of society such as cannot be found in formal narratives."

The collection of broadsides has been formed over many years since it may be assumed that Isaiah Thomas was collecting them before he founded the American Antiquarian Society in 1812*. By that time, Thomas had become the foremost publisher as well as printer and seller of books in the United States. He had

---

*The Society has five broadsides printed in Charleston, South Carolina, between 1767 and 1769, years that Thomas was there working for Robert Wells. It seems probable that he presented them as part of his collection.

amassed a fortune and after retiring from active business in 1802 had the leisure to devote himself to the acquisition of books, newspapers, and other printed materials. He founded the Society to collect and preserve such printed matter for the future study of American history.

Broadsides were certainly not peculiar to American printing. The earliest one was printed by Gutenberg at Mainz in 1454 and was a letter of indulgence granted by Pope Nicholas V to aid John II against the Turks. As printing spread, so did the use of broadsides as a means of transmitting information. Soon after printing commenced in England, for example, Caxton issued broadsides from his press at Westminster. In England, as later in America, broadsides had as subject matter the startling descriptions of crimes and disasters in addition to relaying laws, proclamations, and news.

The first American broadside was "The Oath of a Free-Man," printed by Stephen Daye in Cambridge in 1639. Unhappily, no copy of this first piece of American printing survives, although the text is known from several sources. In the fifty years following the publication of "The Oath of a Free-Man," broadsides were generally official government proclamations and the Latin "Theses" and "Quaestiones" of Harvard College. By 1700, broadsides were issued more frequently and subject matter became more diverse to include elegies, oaths of allegiance, and a few religious documents.

The development of broadsides is closely related to that of newspapers in many ways. For the transmission of important news, weekly or semi-weekly newspapers were not fast enough [Plate 45]. Therefore, some of the most exciting news was published in broadside form or as an extra edition of the regular issue. It is important to realize also that space in newspapers was at a premium, whereas broadsides allowed for ample expression of emotion or opinion. They often served as a means of circulating poetry or countercurrents of thought [Plate 30]. What appears as a three line notice, or indeed what might not even appear in a paper, could be expanded to a full page broadside.

As daily newspapers became common after the Revolution, the broadside diminished in importance as a medium for news and opinion. After the early nineteenth century, although large numbers of broadsides were still issued, the quality of the typographical design declined. Uniformity of type-face and a too mechanical perfection elicit very little interest from us today when we see the variety of imaginative means employed by the colonial printer in the solution of typographical problems. In the nineteenth century, the subject matter of these single sheets is less diverse and less engrossing. Broadsides are still printed and used today, as a visit to a university campus will attest.

Once printed, broadsides were distributed and used in a variety of ways. The colophon of one tells us that they were sold "Very cheap to Travelling Traders." Peddlers apparently sold them in large numbers, particularly poems and ballads, along with their other wares. Nathaniel Coverly, for example, advertised in 1776 that he had available in his printing shop verses of popular interest "by the Groze or Dozen" [Plate 12]. Such items were very cheap, most being purchasable for pennies. Cheap and ready availability helps explain, of course, the wide distribution as well as the quite ephemeral nature of these sheets. It would not have been unusual for a broadside printed in Boston to have found its way to towns in New Hampshire or even New Connecticut and the frontier. Official American proclamations are recorded in large numbers in the Public Record Office in England. Information for immigrants was undoubtedly given wide circulation in England and on the Continent [Plate 6]. There is, however, a bias toward New England in the collection of the American Antiquarian Society and most of the items appear never to have left New England.

Other broadsides were distributed for definite purposes without cost. Official proclamations, especially, were sent to the ministers in each town with instructions that they should be read to the assembled congregations. Tax bills were sent annually to the town clerks by the governors. The report of a town meeting in Boston concluded by directing that the minutes be published and a copy sent to the free-holders of Boston and to the "Select-men of every Town in the Province; as also to the principal City or Town officers of the chief Towns in the several Colonies on the continent" [Plate 10]. While such broadsides were widely circulated, a small number could be printed for a limited circulation by the Sons of Liberty or other organizations.

Broadsides were also published for didactic purposes. "The Declaration, Dying Warning and Advice of Rebekah Chamblit" ends with a statement expressing "a desire that it may be publish'd to the World, and read at the Place of Execution"

[Plate 22]. The purpose was clearly to provide a warning to youth about the effects of sin. We might note parenthetically that this was a favorite subject of broadsides, as well as the object of the lesson found in most children's literature of the time.

Once distributed, broadsides were treated in much the same way as handbills are today. They were read once or twice, perhaps handed around to friends, and then were usually discarded. It is only by chance that many of these pieces are still in existence. Many, particularly ballads and proclamations, were probably pasted to walls or on boards and were destroyed by the passage of time. Although eighteenth century engravings like Paul Revere's "Boston Massacre" were often purchased already framed, this was not true of the cheap broadsides. Of those that did survive, an unfortunate number are torn, badly rubbed, and otherwise mutilated. Ironically, many were retained simply because of material written on the back, such as household accounts. Others were kept for sentimental reasons like the ballad ("On the Landing of the Troops in Boston, 1758") which was a gift from Samuel Byles to his sister in 1768.

Technically, broadsides are printed on only one side of a sheet of paper, as we have mentioned. If printed on both sides, they are called broadsheets. The size may vary; some are only three by five inches, while others are two by three feet. The average broadside is generally about ten by fifteen inches; the format of this book thus permits most facsimiles to be reproduced in the original size. In the mid-nineteenth century, circus advertisements sometimes reached the gigantic dimensions of eight by twelve feet. The quality of paper also varies a great deal. Official proclamations were usually printed on very white, heavy paper, whereas the inexpensive ballads appeared on soft paper which easily tore and was subject to rubbing. The paper was less likely to be pure white and often was brown or even grayish green. It is also possible that scraps of paper were used to print some of the items, particularly those small in size like Job Weeden's carrier's address [Plate 53].

The design of many broadsides was often naive but crudely handsome. When a large number of them are considered, embellishment or imaginative use of a variety of type faces is rare. On the other hand, Isaiah Thomas printed some very attractive broadsides. "A Monumental Inscription" [Plate 11] and his advertisement for *The Massachusetts Calendar* [Plate 42] both incorporate a variety of type faces with an illustration. Other attempts are less successful. "An Elegiac Poem" [Plate 38] and "The Tragedy of Louis Capet" [Plate 13] are adorned with enough cuts, but the overall impression is uncoordinated. The lack of concern about the esthetics of printing was not necessarily due to a lack of sophistication in America. English printing was usually superior, although it is possible to find examples which are less elegant than those produced in the colonies. The Society has an edition of "Father Abbey's Will" which was probably printed in London around 1780. At the head is a woodcut which is as crude as the worst American product.

Many printers of these broadsides also issued newspapers, periodicals, or almanacs. Such men as Robert Wells of Charleston, South Carolina, and Nutting P. Whitelock of Portsmouth, New Hampshire, issued very few books or pamphlets, concentrating their energies on newspapers. John Draper of Boston and Ezekiel Russell of Boston and Salem both printed a wide variety of books, pamphlets, and broadsides. Probably most printers were happy to issue broadsides since they provided a steady source of income, always a consideration for the printer. Sometimes, to save time and effort, the newspaper printer, using the same layout, reprinted an item which appeared in the newspaper.

The illustrations on American broadsides certainly deserve more comment than they have heretofore received. Most of these illustrations are anonymous, which makes the task more difficult. The earliest decoration of American origin was the official seal of the Massachusetts Bay Colony [Plate 29]. Executed by John Foster, it was used from 1675 until the end of the seventeenth century. Prior to 1718, the only other cuts in addition to official seals had been the "memento mori" found at the top of elegies [Plate 36]. The first true illustration related to the text appeared in 1718 on "Words of Consolation to Mr. Robert Stetson & Mrs. Mary Stetson, his Wife, On the Death of their Son Isaac Stetson, who Perished in the Mighty Waters, November 7th. 1718," a copy of which is in the Essex Institute, Salem, Massachusetts. The illustration and the text are not perfectly related, since the youth drowned after falling overboard from a sloop and not a galley as pictured on the broadside.

Printers had a number of illustrative "stock" cuts on hand which they gradually accumulated—coffins, skulls and crossed bones, Death with his scythe—which were reused many times without much regard for the text. This was due to simple economics and to the difficulty in finding an artist who could execute the design. The salability of broadsides depended on the speed with which they appeared. A printer just could not wait to issue a ballad about a contemporary event. If a printer could take the time to have an illustration specially made, the results were very effective, as we see on the "Account of the Wonderful Old Hermit's Death, and Burial" [Plate 59]. For the same economic reasons, few broadsides were published with copperplate engravings. Edes & Gill published "A Speech of the Rt. Hon. the Earl of Chatham" in Boston in 1771 with a copperplate engraving of William Pitt by Paul Revere. There are also broadside almanacs with elegant engravings. Except for these and a few other examples, this combination is rare.

The artistic quality of many of the woodcuts is poor, reflecting a lack of artistic talent available to many of the printers. To circumvent this problem, some printers executed their own illustrations. Jonathan Weatherwise [Plate 42] was cut by Isaiah Thomas around 1767 as a frontispiece to *The New Book of Knowledge* published by Zechariah Fowle in that year. Probably in reference to an earlier book, Isaiah Thomas wrote in his copy of *The New Book of Knowledge* at the Society: "Printed and Cuts Engraved wholly by I. Thomas then 13 years of age, for Z. Fowle when I.T. was his apprentice; bad as the Cuts are executed, there was not, at that time, an artist in Boston who could have done them much better. Some time before, and soon after, there were better Engravers in Boston." And so Jonathan Weatherwise kept appearing, even after Thomas used him again in 1772. On "Predictions for Year 1783," a copy of which is in the John Carter Brown Library, Providence, Rhode Island, Jonathan Weatherwise appears once again, this time in reverse. The printer, Ezekiel Russell, or one of his apprentices copied Thomas's illustration, and actually did rather poorly.

The use of woodcuts declined after 1800, probably because many of the better printers turned to the technically better illustrations engraved on end-grain wood, or to talented artists who engraved on copper and made aquatints. The woodcut-illustrated broadside, declining in importance, was more likely to be produced by a printer poor in means or provincial in location or attitude. Thus even such standard fare as the gallows scene became extremely crude. Another example of this decline is an 1815 edition of "The Grecian Woman," whose illustration is far less handsome and striking than the 1798 edition printed by Alden Spooner. In addition, the type is small and difficult to read. With the exception of special items such as carrier's addresses, it seems that there was less ingenuity and imagination in the design of broadsides after the early nineteenth century.

Selecting sixty broadsides from the American Antiquarian Society's large collection was a difficult task since there were so many which could not be included in this book. We have not, for example, included many of a distinctly political nature, although this was one of the important and frequent uses of broadsides. The printed record of the dispute over whether lawyers should be elected as assemblymen in New York in 1768 produced several handsome broadsides, but this topic is mainly of interest to historians. Other fascinating examples could not be included because too much of the text was obliterated. We have tried to concentrate on attractive examples which stress various aspects of society. They have been loosely arranged into eleven groups which by their very nature occasionally overlap. Some background information has been included, but hopefully the broadsides will speak for themselves.

The first group of broadsides stresses expansion—the growth of the nation northward, southward, and westward. Included are several broadsides about the slave trade during the 1700's and confrontations with the Indians, repercussions of territorial growth. Expansion also meant population growth, so two broadsides are included which advertise to Europeans the advantages to be found in migrating to South Carolina and New England. Another broadside outlining the excellent advantages of the Old Northwest Territory (the land between the Ohio and the Mississippi Rivers) was published twelve years after Congress passed the Northwest Ordinance. Here we see how the broadside was an efficient means by which official decisions were practically implemented.

Comments on contemporary events included both ballad and prose remarks on three of the most important political areas in which America was involved. The importation of the Seven Years' War to the North American continent was of tremendous significance to the British colonists. We have included in this respect a ballad which celebrated the defeat of the French at Montreal. Although there had been ballads heralding victories against Indians as early as 1675, the real deluge of this type of literature occurred during the French and Indian War when numerous ballads were issued. The American Revolution and the events leading up to it inspired many broadsides. Two in this group are straight prose reporting of two acts of political importance: the first announces the repeal of the Stamp Act in 1766 and describes the reaction of the London populace to this news, the second publishes the minutes of the Boston town meeting in 1767 which initiated a boycott of British goods. The evacuation of Boston by the British resulted in the publication of a ballad in 1776. Several years later appeared a poem commemorating the Boston Massacre as well as lamenting the release of Ebenezer Richardson from jail. The final broadside which comments on contemporary events has been included to emphasize the often underestimated importance of France in United States affairs both before, during, and after the Revolution. This commentary on the execution of Louis XVI brings together an emotional response to the regicide as well as indication of political feeling toward France.

Before the Revolution the spirit of patriotic sentiment was often expressed in ballads, such as those written during the French and Indian War. "Yankee Doodle" was a popular patriotic song during the Revolution, but was known as "The Yankey's Return from Camp." "The Sentiments of an American Woman," a very eloquent prose statement, was circulated and read a great deal. George Washington is the subject of two broadsides; the prominence of his role in the development of American patriotism was clearly without equal. The eulogies, both in printed image and verse, and oratory of which he was the subject after his death elevated him to a level of adulation matched perhaps only by Napoleon.

Many notable individuals believed that the hopes of the young nation relied on the proper education of youth. Two late eighteenth century broadsides have been selected to stress this view, as well as to emphasize the moral stance of government. Cotton Mather, nearly a century earlier, was concerned with the moral and religious development of the Negroes in Boston, as his "Rules for the Society of Negroes" indicate.

One of the largest groups of broadsides preserves in printed form the confessions and last words of repentance and warning of criminals about to be executed. To judge from the poverty and petty theft in contemporary London, the incidence of crime was probably less in the colonies than in Europe. Capital punishment for a repeated misdemeanor was not uncommon, and the moral of a life of crime was drawn clearly for all to see. The custom of issuing the last words of criminals in broadside form had long been popular in England. This type of literature must have appealed to a large number of people, much as tabloids have in recent years. The obvious intent of these broadsides was to inculcate morality by frightful example. In this vein we remark how an old Roman tale [Plate 28], while following the fashion of the late eighteenth century wave of Neo-classicism, nonetheless continues the theme of the ultimate triumph of moral virtue. "The True Account of a Young Lady" in all its comic aspects provides a needed counterpoint to the often dreary preachments on a life of crime.

Religion played a very important role in the lives of the colonists and permeated all aspects of life. Strange natural phenomena were interpreted in terms of divine favor or wrath; education was religious in nature; divine intervention was sought in the spring planting. This group of broadsides merely hints at some of these as well as presents two dialogues in which Death is the central character. A short poem by Samuel Sewall expresses in no uncertain terms the evangelistic fervor of the Puritans.

As the five elegies we have included show, broadside verse is not a genre of literature. Rather broadsides are merely vehicles. Many poems were circulated in manuscript form and never printed, others were issued as pamphlets or included in books of poetry. The composition of elegies was another long standing English custom, as was the practice of pinning them to the pall covering the casket of the deceased, as noted in several New England diaries. The first elegies to be printed possibly appeared in 1647, honoring Thomas Hooker and John Cotton. No copies are extant but Nathaniel Morton included them in his *New-Englands Memoriall* published in 1669. Elegies appeared very frequently from 1680 to 1730. Fewer were printed later although the practice continued as late as the mid-nineteenth century.

The issuance of broadside advertisements was for diverse purposes. Some were in the nature of a public service announcement, while others frankly peddled articles of various types. Of the latter, the broadside proclaiming the virtues of a patent medicine is fascinating. Presumably, these advertisements were posted in public meeting places where they were conspicuous.

Although life was difficult and busy for the Americans, record of their amusements is easily found in broadsides. Theater, songs, wild animals, reading, spectacles were all advertised in broadsides as well as in newspapers.

American humor is a peculiar topic to search for in the form of broadsides. The carrier's addresses have a touch of levity, but aside from them humorous verse is rare. We have a certificate of membership for one organization, The Idle Society, which is a whimsical response to the many societies founded for cultural and civic activities. However, having examined the many hundreds of broadsides in the Society's collection, we cannot help but conclude that men such as "Ephraim Eager" were indeed rare.

The final group is perhaps the most varied and intriguing. The American mind, although permeated by a sense of practicality and morality as well as its quest for self-identity, could still not resist the strange, the bizarre, the wonderful. Yet we today seize with as much eagerness such curiosities as a giant snake, a dark cloud, a drunken bicentenarian. Such is the continuing magnetic, evocative power of the broadside.

The measurements of the broadsides are in inches, width preceding height, and include the margins. Many items have had the margins trimmed, so our measurements will vary if compared to other copies. The Evans numbers refer to the entries in Charles Evans's *American Bibliography* (Chicago, 1904-1934, and Worcester, 1955) and to Roger P. Bristol's *Supplement to Charles Evans' American Bibliography* (Charlottesville, Virginia, 1970).

There are several other books to which I am indebted, particularly Ola E. Winslow's *American Broadside Verse From Imprints of the 17th & 18th Centuries* (New Haven, 1930) and Worthington C. Ford's *Broadsides, Ballads &c. Printed in Massachusetts, 1639-1800* (Boston, 1922). Sinclair Hamilton's *Early American Book Illustrators and Wood Engravings* (Princeton, 1958 and 1968) includes entries for a number of broadsides which are discussed with particular reference to the illustrations.

Marcus A. McCorison, director and librarian of the Society, has been most generous and cooperative in this attempt to present to a wider audience some of the treasures of the Society. I am indebted to Alden P. Johnson for suggesting this project and to David Godine for providing the handsome format. Finally, I want to thank my husband for his continual interest and assistance.

Georgia B. Bumgardner

EXPANSION

1. *Advertisement. Whereas the Proprietors of the Kennebeck Purchase from the late Colony of Plymouth.*
Boston, 1754.

In 1629 the Kennebec region in Maine was granted to Governor Bradford and his associates in the Plymouth Company. They retained the grant until 1640, when they ceded it to the Colony of New Plymouth. Since the Plymouth Colony was not strong or wealthy enough to govern such a large territory, the grant of land was sold to four individuals who became the Proprietors. A century later, strenuous efforts to settle the Kennebec Purchase began. Such advertisements as this with generous offers of land encouraged new settlers. Heavily forested land and the threat of Indian attacks made living in that area difficult.

Another broadside dated 1763 testifies to the progress of the settlements at Frankfort and elsewhere and advertises: "If any Protestant Families in Europe should incline to come over and settle a Part or the whole of any one or more of the said Townships, they may apply to Florentius Vassal, Esq; in Golden Square, London."

Evans 40712
8 ½ × 12 ¼

ADVERTISEMENT.

WHEREAS the Proprietors of the Kennebeck *Purchase from the late Colony of* Plymouth, *have made and are making divers Settlements on* Kennebeck-River, *particularly at* Frankfort *near* Richmond : *For the Encouragement whereof the said Proprietors have voted to make a Grant of One Hundred Acres of Land to every Family who shall settle there ; of which they hereby give publick Notice : And any Person or Persons inclining to settle may apply to the Committee of said Proprietors, who will shew them a Plan of said River and Land, and let them know the Conditions of Settlement :*

And to encourage People hereto, the said Committee hereby inform them, that at the said Town of *Frankfort,* there is a Saw-Mill & a Grist-Mill erected, and about Forty Families settled, who notwithstanding they went there so lately as in the Spring of 1752, have been able the past Year to raise nearly a Sufficiency of every Thing to maintain themselves ; and this present Year will stand in Need of no Assistance, having clear'd a considerable Quantity of Land, and found that it is capable of producing in great Plenty every Thing which this Climate is adapted to : And besides the Advantage of a rich Soil, is situated on a fine Navigable River, which has furnished the said Settlers with a Market for their Wood, by the Sale of which they have been paid considerable for their Labour in clearing the Land.

The Land intended to be granted is no Way inferior either in Respect of it's Quality or Situation to that already settled.

The Subscribers who are the Committee of the said Proprietors, may be treated with in *Boston.*

Boston,
Jan. 2. 1754.

Robert Temple,
Sylvester Gardiner,
Benjamin Hollowell, } Committee.
William Bowdoin,
James Bowdoin.

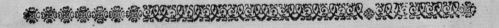

2. *By His Honour Spencer Phips, Esq; . . . A Proclamation. Boston: John Draper, 1755.*

Although the advertisement for the Kennebec Purchase omits any mention of Indians, this proclamation indicates that the Penobscot Indians must have been an obstacle to the growth of that territory. There had been numerous skirmishes between whites and Indians during the first half of the eighteenth century.

After the defeat of the French at Louisbourg, the Penobscot Indians attacked the English at Fort St. George several times between 1745 and 1747. Bounties were offered by the British at this time both for scalps and live captives. In 1749 a peace treaty supposedly terminated the hostilities. At the outbreak of the French and Indian War in 1755, the Penobscot Indians were to have been excluded from the declaration of war. Evidently, such was not the case. Incredibly enough, the Penobscots were not annihilated and members of that tribe still live in Maine.

Evans 40783
12 ½ × 15 ⅛

By His HONOUR

SPENCER PHIPS, Esq;

Lieutenant-Governour and Commander in Chief, in and over His Majesty's Province of the *Massachusetts-Bay* in *New-England*.

A PROCLAMATION.

WHEREAS the Tribe of *Penobscot* Indians have repeatedly in a perfidious Manner acted contrary to their solemn Submission unto His Majesty long since made and frequently renewed ;

I **have therefore, at the Desire of the House of Representatives, with the Advice of His Majesty's Council, thought fit to issue this Proclamation, and to declare the** Penobscot **Tribe of Indians to be Enemies, Rebels and Traitors to His Majesty King** GEORGE **the Second : And I do hereby require His Majesty's Subjects of this Province to embrace all Opportunities of pursuing, captivating, killing and destroying all and every of the aforesaid Indians.**

AND WHEREAS the General Court of this Province have voted that a Bounty or Incouragement be granted and allowed to be paid out of the Publick Treasury, to the marching Forces that shall have been employed for the Defence of the *Eastern* and *Western* Frontiers, from the *First* to the *Twenty-fifth* of this Instant *November* ;

I **have thought fit to publish the same ; and I do hereby Promise, That there shall be paid out of the Province-Treasury to all and any of the said Forces, over and above their Bounty upon Inlistment, their Wages and Subsistence, the Premiums or Bounty following,** viz.

For every Male *Penobscot* Indian above the Age of Twelve Years, that shall be taken within the Time aforesaid and brought to *Boston*, *Fifty Pounds*.

For every Scalp of a Male *Penobscot* Indian above the Age aforesaid, brought in as Evidence of their being killed as aforesaid, *Forty Pounds*.

For every Female *Penobscot* Indian taken and brought in as aforesaid, and for every Male Indian Prisoner under the Age of Twelve Years, taken and brought in as aforesaid, *Twenty-five Pounds*.

For every Scalp of such Female Indian or Male Indian under the Age of Twelve Years, that shall be killed and brought in as Evidence of their being killed as aforesaid, *Twenty Pounds*.

Given at the Council-Chamber in *Boston*, this Third Day of *November* 1 7 5 5, and in the Twenty-ninth Year of the Reign of our Sovereign Lord *GEORGE* the Second, by the Grace of GOD of *Great-Britain*, *France* and *Ireland*, KING, Defender of the Faith, *&c.*

By His Honour's Command,
J. Willard, Secr.

S. Phips.

GOD Save the KING.

BOSTON: Printed by *John Draper*, Printer to His Honour the Lieutenant-Governour and Council. 1755.

3. Charlestown, July 24th, 1769. To Be Sold, . . . A Cargo of . . . Negroes.
[Charleston, South Carolina, 1769.]

Slaves came early to the Americas: they replaced the native Indians, who died off rapidly after the earliest Spanish and Portuguese colonization in the West Indies and South America. The first slaves imported into the English colonies arrived in Virginia in 1619. By 1671 there were two thousand slaves in Virginia; a little over one hundred years later, three hundred thousand. Many slaves were imported from the West Indies, although most came directly from West Africa.

Growth and expansion of the colonies resulted in a chronic shortage of labor. The importation of indentured servants and apprentices never filled the demand since they all obtained their freedom after a specified number of years. Slavery, therefore, was instituted in all the colonies. Charleston was a major center for the slave trade from the eighteenth century until the Civil War.

Evans 41926
7 ⅝ × 12 ½

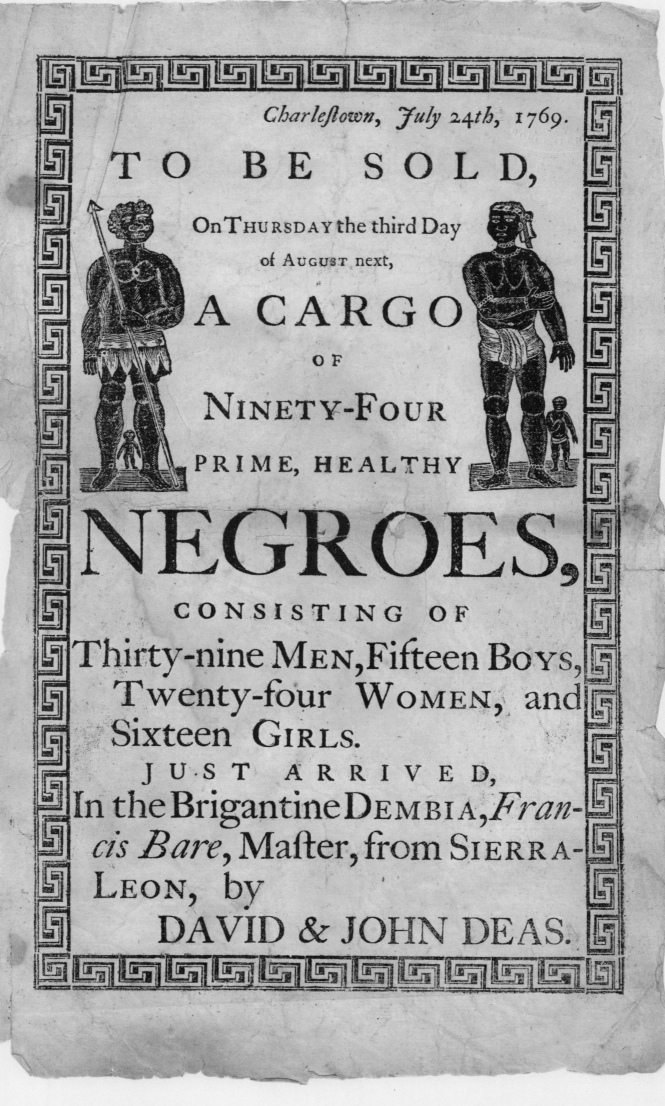

Charlestown, July 24th, 1769.

TO BE SOLD,

On THURSDAY the third Day
of AUGUST next,

A CARGO

OF

NINETY-FOUR

PRIME, HEALTHY

NEGROES,

CONSISTING OF

Thirty-nine MEN, Fifteen BOYS,
Twenty-four WOMEN, and
Sixteen GIRLS.

JUST ARRIVED,

In the Brigantine DEMBIA, *Francis Bare*, Master, from SIERRA-
LEON, by

DAVID & JOHN DEAS.

4. *Georgia. By the Honourable Lyman Hall, Esquire, . . . A Proclamation.*
[*Savannah*, 1783.]

In this proclamation, the Governor of Georgia requests that the rights of the Creek and Cherokee Indians be respected. That the State of Georgia issued this decree is very ironic since that state was the most rapacious of the thirteen in acquiring land from the Indians. Georgia was sparsely populated and was the buffer zone against the Spanish in Florida. By pushing the Indians westward, the government hoped to encourage immigration to strengthen the defenses against Spanish Florida.

In fulfilling this aim, the government was not particularly scrupulous. For example, in May of 1783, the government acquired a tract of land from the Cherokees only to discover it was actually Creek land. In November the government obtained the cession of the same tract from a few friendly Creek Indians. The rest of the tribe repudiated the treaty, although the state government persisted in acting as if the treaty had been signed with the entire Creek nation. The policy of the federal government had not yet been formulated, and therefore, the states had great latitude in dealing with the Indians.

Evans 44369
6 ½ × 12 ¼

Georgia.

BY THE HONOURABLE
LYMAN HALL, Esquire,

Captain General, Governor, and Commander in Chief, in and over the State aforesaid,

A Proclamation.

WHEREAS, in order to preserve peace, and maintain a friendly intercourse and a good understanding with the Indians of the Creek and Cherokee Nations, it is necessary to avoid any encroachments upon the lands allotted to them for their hunting grounds: And whereas many persons have, for some time past, made a practice of travelling over the lands, and marking the trees, on such their hunting grounds, whereby great offence hath been given to said Indians, and the peace and safety of the state thereby endangered:

I have therefore thought fit, by and with the advice of the Honourable Executive Council, to issue this my Proclamation, strictly forbidding all persons travelling over the lands, or marking the trees, on any of the said Indian hunting grounds, on any pretence whatever, within the boundary lines of this state, without special leave and license first had and obtained for that purpose: And all officers civil and military are hereby strictly required to take due notice of all persons offending in the premises, and them apprehend and secure, that they may be dealt with, according to the demerit of their offences, as the law directs.

Given under my hand, and the great seal of the said State, at Augusta, this thirteenth day of June, in the year of our Lord one thousand seven hundred and eighty-three, and of our Sovereignty and Independence the seventh.

LYMAN HALL.

By his Honour's command,
J. MILTON, Sec'ry.

GOD SAVE THE STATE.

5. *Information for Immigrants to the New-England States. Boston*, 1795.

Formed in 1793, the Massachusetts Society for the Aid of Immigrants was designed to assist and advise immigrants from Europe. The corresponding secretary, Jedidiah Morse, was the "father of American geography" and a Congregational clergyman. Various questions about New England's climate, agricultural possibilities, availability of land, wages, and taxes are answered quite candidly. For example, we remark the hideous inflation of fifty to seventy per cent which resulted from the scarcity of provisions due to the war in Europe.

Immigration in the late eighteenth century was stimulated by several factors. The industrial revolution put many artisans out of work. In England, the enclosure movement greatly affected small farmers. Finally, political upheavals, particularly in France, caused a number of émigrés to flee to America. At this time, few immigrants remained in Boston since that city was limited in its potential for growth for a variety of economic and geographical reasons. Many of the new arrivals went westward; others went to Philadelphia and New York which were growing faster than Boston and could absorb larger numbers of immigrants.

Evans 28321
14 ¼ × 19 ⅝

Information for Immigrants to the New-England States.

SINCE the commencement of the present unhappy war among the European nations, great numbers of people from France, Great-Britain, and their West-India islands, impelled by necessity, or prompted by a desire to avoid impending evils, have taken refuge in the United States. The principles of religion and humanity require the friendly attention of Americans to these strangers, many of whom arrive in circumstances of such wretchedness as to give pain to every feeling mind. It was in consequence of seeing among us, many immigrants of this description, to whom a little friendly advice and assistance would be acceptable, and useful, that a number of gentlemen in Boston, and its vicinity, associated at the close of the year 1793, under the name of "The Massachusetts Society for the aid of immigrants." Since the formation of this society, others have been instituted on similar principles in New-York, Philadelphia, and Charleston, (S. C.) ; at which places most of the immigrants arrive.

Not with design to *encourage* immigration, was our society formed ; for, in our opinion, the happiness of our country depends not on any *forced* increase of its population, its *natural* increase being sufficiently rapid, and more conducive to *uniformity* in principles, habits, and manners, the basis of political and social order and happiness ; but solely with a view to afford comfort and relief to such as voluntarily, and from real or supposed necessity, seek an asylum among us, to take such by the hand and direct them in the way to be useful to themselves, and to that country which protects and befriends them.

To promote the design of their institution, in the circulation of information, useful to foreigners, the society have thought proper to publish short answers to the following queries, proposed to them by an intelligent literary immigrant, and which appear to embrace most of the objects concerning which information is desired.

Quest. 1. Would it not be more advisable for farmers from Great-Britain, or other European countries, where agriculture has been carried to a high pitch of perfection, to settle in the *cultivated*, rather than in the *uncultivated* parts of America ?

Ans. Farmers from Europe will very probably find the *cultivated* parts of the United States more pleasant, and probably more agreeable to their views : For although the uncultivated parts offer the fairest prospect of laying the foundation for an estate for their posterity, yet in an unsubdued wilderness their business will be altogether new. The Americans are undoubtedly better calculated to subdue wild lands, than the English, who have been accustomed to a kind, mellow soil : So that though, with much spirit and enterprize, they may conquer many of the difficulties of settling a wild tract, yet, as their own knowledge will carry them most of the way, and a little information the rest, in managing improved farms, where they have considerable capital, preference is to be given to the latter.

Quest. 2. Are the difficulties of cultivating new land of long duration ? Would they not be almost insurmountable to an English farmer, who has always lived on land in a pretty high state of cultivation ?

Ans. The difficulties will be great, and of several years duration, to the English farmer, who will find every thing in the business a perfect contrast to the ease of cultivation in his own country, and have to encounter much hardship and toil ; whilst, however, the progressive improvement of his situation, and that of his neighbours, will from the first be a source of pleasure to him. In many parts, it has been found that the first settler of new lands clears it of the wood under the shelter of a hut only ; and after a short and imperfect cultivation of it, unable to pay for the soil, or influenced by a roving disposition, leaves it to a successor, who builds a small house and barn, and brings to the soil ; and he is often followed by a third occupier, purchasing his improvements, who brings the farm to a high state of cultivation. Yet this rotation cannot be said to be general in the New-England states, and seldom takes place but in case of the extreme poverty and rudeness of the first settler. The American farmer, who removes from old towns to new, generally increases his property faster by removal than he otherwise could ; and after a few years, gets into a comfortable way of living. In some instances, English farmers have succeeded in the uncultivated parts ; and where they have some property, need not be discouraged from making settlements in them.

Quest. 3. Can aliens hold lands in their own names in New-England ? If not, how can they purchase land with safety ?

Ans. They cannot hold lands in their own names, as the laws now stand. The state legislatures, who have power to regulate this business, may qualify aliens to hold lands in their own names, by act of assembly : But five years residence, by the last naturalization act, passed by Congress, are necessary to obtain citizenship.

Quest. 4. Can many farms be purchased at a reasonable rate in New-England, and particularly in Connecticut and Massachusetts ?

Ans. By prudent management in the application, there is no doubt that many good farms may be purchased at reasonable rates. The price has been raised in consequence of the present war in Europe, which has increased the price of provisions ; but when a peace takes place, farms will probably revert to their former value.

Quest. 5. Are Connecticut and Massachusetts overstocked with inhabitants ? Are the people obliged to migrate from those states ? Is there not still room for farmers, who have been used to land in a higher state of cultivation than Connecticut and Massachusetts ?

Ans. They are not over-stocked with inhabitants. This is evident from observing in our towns, where the numbers increase, that individual affluence increases proportionally. The young people migrate, not from necessity, but in expectation of getting larger estates. In consequence, partly, of this disposition to migrate, many excellent tracts may be purchased in old settled towns, which will suit good farmers, and be found capable of great improvement.

Quest. 6. Is wheat blighted, or destroyed by the Hessian fly ?

Ans. It is a received opinion, that wheat is subject to blight within 30 or 40 miles from the sea ; but in the interior parts, no such complaint is made, and it is generally raised. The Hessian fly is almost unknown in New-England.

Quest. 7. Is the land in Connecticut and Massachusetts pretty good ? Is it better adapted for grazing than grain ?

Ans. Probably as good as in any part of America, excepting new land. It is hilly and stony, and well watered. The western counties of Massachusetts, and the middle and eastern parts of Connecticut, are esteemed very good. Many parts are equally fitted for grazing and grain ; it is preferable for the former to the southern states : Yet the average produce of all sorts of grain in New-England exceeds that of the southern states.

Quest. 8. Can produce be easily conveyed to market ?

Ans. There are so many navigable rivers in the New-England states, that few situations are more than 50 miles distant from water conveyance ; as may be seen by recurring to maps. Connecticut river, particularly, lies convenient to a great extent of the New-England states. By these and other rivers, by several canals now cutting ; by the post roads, which are pretty good, though far inferior to those in England ; and by the snow in winter, the conveyance of produce to market is rendered generally easy.

Quest. 9. Do different sorts of fruit come to perfection ?

Ans. All sorts of English fruit come to perfection in New-England, and some which do not commonly grow in England. Orchards are universal in this country, except in the eastern parts of Maine.

Quest. 10. Are the eastern states as healthful as the middle and southern states ? the people as virtuous and well informed ? education as good, cheap, and convenient ?

Ans. We are not subject, except from some local, temporary cause, to the fever and ague in New-England ; though consumptions, and other diseases known in England, prevail. The inhabitants here are more robust, and live to a greater age, generally, than at the southward. It is well known that the body of the people are better informed, more industrious and temperate ; education better provided for, by schools, which are established, by law, in all the settled parts of New-England.

See Amer. U. Geog. Vol. I. p. 310, 311, 314, 315, 316.

Quest. 11. Does slavery exist in New-England ?

Ans. It does not exist in Massachusetts ; and in the other New-England states, efficacious measures have been adopted for its certain, but gradual abolition.

Quest. 12. What religious sects are there in New-England ? What sect is most numerous ?

Ans. The same sects as in England ; and a few of American growth. Congregationalists are by far the most numerous.

See Amer. U. Geog. p. 378.

Quest. 13. Are the people inclined to persecute each other for religious or political opinions ?

Ans. A persecuting *power* is not known in America, but a persecuting *spirit* is not extinguished. Zeal for religious opinions sometimes, and for wild democracy in opposition to rational republicanism, often manifests itself by abusive and inflammatory writings and speeches only ; for the laws effectually restrain opposite sects and parties from injuring one another.

Quest. 14. How are the Clergy and Schoolmasters supported ?

Ans. Every town, consisting of 50 householders, is obliged, by law, to maintain a Schoolmaster ; whom they select and contract with voluntarily ; and whose salary is paid either by annual assessments on the property of the inhabitants of the town or parish, or voluntary contributions. Pew rents, assessments of the property of the inhabitants of the parish, parsonages, monies at interest, and voluntary contributions, are the principal means of supporting the Clergy.

Quest. 15. How are the poor maintained ?

Ans. Every town is obliged, by law, to support its poor inhabitants ; which are not numerous. The paupers, who are not inhabitants of any particular town, are maintained by the state.

Quest. 16. Are the people in general well affected to the federal government ?

Ans. They are in general ; for they consider the national prosperity connected with it.

Quest. 17. Is the expense of living moderate ?

Ans. Since the present European war, the price of living has been dear, having increased from 50 to 70 per cent. When the war is over, it will probably be much diminished.

Quest. 18. Are the taxes moderate ?

Ans. Yes. The expenses of government are less, by much, in proportion to numbers and wealth, than in any nation on the old continent.

Quest. 19. Are servants scarce, and wages high ?

Ans. Common labourers and servants of both sexes are much wanted. Women's wages, in the sea ports, are from 25 to 50 dollars per annum, and considerably less in the country. Men's wages are from 60 to 120 dollars per annum, in the maritime towns ; and somewhat less in the country.

Quest. 20. Are mechanics scarce, and wages high ?

Ans. House-carpenters and masons are much wanted at present. Their common wages are from 80 to 125 cents per day ; 100 cents being a dollar. Mechanics of sober character, and skilled in their trades, of almost every kind, may find employment, and wages equal to their support ; but particularly sail-cloth weavers and flax-dressers, and workers in iron.

Quest. 21. Can manufactures be as advantageously established in New-England as in the southern and middle states ?

Ans. Almost every attempt to establish manufactures in the southern states, has failed ; whereas, in Massachusetts, several important manufactures have been brought to perfection. Wood and water, those powerful and necessary agents in manufactures, are every where plenty ; but the high price of labour is a great obstacle to the success of this branch of business.

Quest. 22. Is the climate of Connecticut and Massachusetts as temperate as that of the middle and southern states ?

Ans. Our winters are generally longer and colder, though the winter is often as severe in Pennsylvania as in the eastern states. Our summers are not so hot, and our hot days are succeeded by cool nights, which render them more tolerable. Sudden changes of temperature are probably more frequent here ; but still our climate is more healthful.

Quest. 23. Of what extraction are the people of New-England ?

Ans. They are very generally of English extraction, and resemble the English in their character, manners, and habits.

PUBLISHED *by Order of the* IMMIGRANT SOCIETY *in* BOSTON.

Thomas Russell, President.

Jedidiah Morse, Corresponding Secretary.

BOSTON, *October* 27, 1795.

6. *Information, To those who are disposed to migrate to South-Carolina.*
Charleston, South Carolina: [Markland & M'Iver?], 1795.

Another society to encourage and to aid immigrants from Europe was formed in Charleston, South Carolina. This detailed and informative broadside describes the commerce, agriculture, and various manufacturing possibilities of South Carolina. Rather than being merely promotional, these organizations were quite honest in their descriptions. Many interesting points are raised, including the similarity of the inland region to Devonshire in England and Languedoc in France. Charleston's harbor receives special notice as it is "open all the winter, and its contiguity to the West-Indian islands, gives the merchants superior advantages for carrying on a peculiarly lucrative commerce."

Evans 28411
10 ⅜ × 16 ½

INFORMATION,

To those who are disposed to migrate to South-Carolina.

SOUTH-CAROLINA lies between the 31st and 34th degrees of north latitude, and between the 78th and 81st degrees of west longitude from London. In form it nearly resembles a triangle, the base of which extends along the sea above two hundred miles. Georgia on the south, and North-Carolina on the north side thereof, approximate to each other about three hundred miles from the sea coast, so as nearly to form an angle enclosing the whole of the state. Hence more than nineteen in twenty of its inhabitants are perfectly secure from the incursions of Indians; and none are at all exposed to them, but a few residing in a single angle of the state, at the foot of the mountains. For eighteen years past there has been no war between any tribe of Indians and the people of South-Carolina, and there is little probability of any in future: but should such an event take place, the dangers to be apprehended from it will be truly inconsiderable, and these will be daily diminishing. Within the state of South-Carolina, are millions of acres of good plantable land, comparatively useless for want of cultivation; these would afford employment and subsistence to ten times the number of all its present inhabitants. The country along the coast, and for eighty or an hundred miles to the westward, is generally low and flat, and abounds more or less, especially on and near the rivers, with swamps or marshes; these when cleared and cultivated, yield, in favorable seasons, on an average, to the planter, an annual income of from twenty to forty dollars from each acre, and often much more: but this species of soil cannot be cultivated by white men, without risquing both health and life. Though a residence in or near these swamps is very injurious to health, yet it has been satisfactorily ascertained, that, by moving three miles therefrom, into the pine lands, which occupy the middle ground between the rivers, an exemption from autumnal fevers may be obtained. These swamps do not cover an hundredth part of the land in South-Carolina, yet as they are most productive, and have been first and longest cultivated, they have given to the whole state the name of being unhealthy; though it is well known, that in Charleston, and in the high dry pine or fir lands of the low country, and in the whole of the back country, and in every part of the state, not contiguous to swamps, marshes, or stagnant water, the inhabitants enjoy as great a portion of health as is usual in most parts of the world.

Near the sea coast, rice, indigo, hemp, Indian corn, every species of pulse and potatoes, rye, oats, and cotton, are raised with ease and great plenty. From experiments which have been made, it is well ascertained, that olives, silk, and madder may be as abundantly produced in South-Carolina, as in the South of France. On and near the many rivers, which water the state, lumber of all kinds may be cut to great advantage. The woods abound with pine trees, ash, maple, beach, tupelow, cypress, red and white cedar, juniper, poplar, walnut, hickory, sycamore, chesnut, mulberry, gum, sassafras, wild cherry, chinquopin, laurel, bay, locust, sumach, dogwood, and all the variety of oaks; the live oak in particular, so useful in ship building, and the palmeto grow in great plenty on the sea islands, and lands adjacent.

In the vicinity of Charleston, firewood, when brought to market, though abundant and easily conveyed by water, will sell for five times the first cost of the lands from which it is cut; and the land, after it is so cleared, will sometimes command a higher price than before.

About a hundred miles from the coast, the swamps terminate; the land is high and dry, and from thence to the western extremity of the state is beautifully diversified with hills and vallies, affording most agreeable prospects, resembling Devonshire in England, or Languedoc in France. In this part of South-Carolina, the country is remarkably healthy---In the warmest season the heat of the day is far from being excessive, and the nights are pleasantly cool---land can be there safely cultivated by white men, and is so for the most part; and though it can be purchased by the acre for a price varying from half a dollar to four dollars, it will yield, in good seasons, to the industrious cultivator, an annual income of from five to fifteen dollars from every acre that is carefully planted. The winters are so short, and mild, that two crops, one of barley and one of corn, or one of wheat and one of corn have been frequently obtained from the same ground within a twelve month. And in the low country numerous herds of cattle and hogs may be maintained throughout the winter, as well as summer, by feeding on the spontaneous productions of the earth; and even in the most western parts of the state, they do not require to be fed more than three or four months in the year. The adjacent ocean and rivers abound with fish.---Trout, bream, mullets, whiting, blackfish, bass and rockfish, are common. Shad and herring are so abundant in their season, that they may be caught with facility in great quantities. The country is well stocked with wild geese, ducks, turkies, and pigeons, with plovers, woodcocks, snipes and partridges. Deer are so easily procured, that the flesh of one, full grown, may be purchased, in many parts of the state, for a dollar, and no game laws exist to restrain the inhabitants from availing themselves of the means of support, which the woods, the air, and the waters afford.

In the upper country, indigo, wheat, Indian corn, rye, barley, oats, tobacco hemp, flax, and cotton are profitably raised; and from late experiments it has been ascertained that vines may be cultivated, and wine made to great advantage: Snakeroot, pinkroot, and a variety of medicinal herbs grow spontaneously: also ginseng on and near the mountains. The silk worm might be easily and extensively propagated, and silk raised to great advantage in every part of the state.

A canal from Santee to Cooper river, is now more than half done, and seven hundred labourers are constantly employed thereon. When this is compleated, which it probably will by the end of the year 1796, it will bring navigation to the doors of a great proportion of the inhabitants of the state, and leave none in the most inland situation, fifty miles removed from the benefits of conveying by water, to market, the fruits of their industry.

A monied capital may be employed to great advantage in South-Carolina, in various ways, viz.

First, In commerce. The sea ports are Beaufort, Georgetown and Charleston. Beaufort is noted for its excellent harbor and healthy situation. Georgetown is advantageously situated at the confluence of several rivers, connected with an extensive back country of both the Carolinas, and bids fair to be a place of importance. Charleston is by far the most considerable city on the sea coast, for an extent of six hundred miles. From it are annually exported about the value of two millions and a half of dollars, in native commodities; and it supplies, with imported goods, a great part of the inhabitants of North-Carolina and Georgia, as well as those of South-Carolina. The harbor thereof is open all the winter, and its contiguity to the West-India islands, gives the merchants superior advantages for carrying on a peculiarly lucrative commerce. A waggon road of only fifteen miles is all that is wanted, to open a communication with the inhabitants of the south western territory of the United States. Knoxville, the capital of that territory, is one hundred miles nearer to Charleston, than to any other considerable seaport town on the Atlantic ocean.

Secondly, A monied capital may be profitably employed, in erecting mills, for making paper, for sawing lumber, and especially for manufacturing wheat flour. There are hundreds of valuable mill seats unimproved, and the woods abound with pine trees. A bushel of wheat may be purchased in South-Carolina for half a dollar, which will make as good flour, as that which in the vicinity of proper mills, sells for double that price. Such is the cheapness and fertility of the soil, that half a dollar a bushel for wheat, would afford a great profit to the cultivators thereof.

Thirdly, In tanning and manufacturing leather---cattle are raised with so much ease, in a country where the winters are both mild and short, that hides are remarkably cheap. The profits of tanners and shoemakers must be considerable, when it is a well known fact, that the hides of full grown cattle, and a single pair of shoes sell for nearly the same price.

Fourthly, In making bricks. These now sell for nine dollars a thousand, and the call for them, is so great, that the bricklayers are not fully supplied.

Fifthly, In making pot-ash. The ashes that might be collected in Charleston, and from the woods burnt in clearing new lands in the country, would furnish the means of carrying on the manufacture of pot-ash to great advantage.

Sixthly, Those who do not choose to engage in active business, may put out their money on interest, at the rate of seven per cent. per annum, and under circumstances that would afford unquestionable security for the punctual payment of both principal and interest. The existing laws impose no tax, whatever, on money at interest.

Mechanics in every branch of business, though aliens, may, immediately on their arrival, set up their respective trades, under the same legal protection as the oldest inhabitants. Bricklayers, carpenters, mill-wrights, shoemakers, taylors, blacksmiths, and labourers of all kinds, cannot fail of meeting with ready employment, and good wages, varying from half a dollar to two dollars a day. But the cultivators of the earth, above all others, will find in South-Carolina, an opportunity of turning their money and industry to the greatest advantage.

The constitution of South-Carolina, makes the most ample provision for the full enjoyment of civil and religious liberty. Every congregation associated for the worship of the deity, has equal protection, and can easily obtain incorporation, which gives it the rights of holding real & personal estates; of prosecuting its claims in the courts of justice, and every other right attached to a body known and recognised by the laws; but no one can lord it over another. In the constitution it is declared, "that the free exercise of religious profession and worship, without discrimination, or preference, shall forever hereafter, be allowed within the state to all mankind," and that "all power is originally vested in the people, and that all free governments are founded on their authority, and are instituted for their peace, safety and happiness." In conformity to these principles, the only laws which govern, are those which are enacted by the representatives of the people, freely and fairly chosen. To favor the cause of republicanism and natural justice, laws made since the revolution have abolished the rights of primogeniture, and have ordained an equal distribution of the estates of intestate persons, without any preference of males, or of the first born. There is also something peculiar in the manner of constituting juries in South-Carolina; the names of the individuals that compose them, are drawn by a child indiscriminately out of a box, containing numerous lists of the taxable citizens. This precaution puts it out of the power of the sheriff, or of any other person, whatever, to make a selection of any men favorable to one party, or one side of the cause in controversy.

To all who intend to migrate to South-Carona, it is recommended to order matters so, that they may arrive in the month of November, or soon after, if they intend to live near the sea coast, they will then be accustomed to the climate before the heat of summer commences: if they intend to reside in the upper country they may, for some months after their arrival, pass without danger, through the maritime settlements to the hilly country westward, where they may enjoy as great a degree of health, as usually falls to the lot of man, in any part of the world.

Charleston, South-Carolina, March 26, 1795. } *Published by order of the South-Carolina Society, for the information and assistance of persons emigrating from other countries.*

JOHN RUTLEDGE, President.
DAVID RAMSAY, } *Vice Presidents.*
JOHN BEE HOLMES, }
JOHN SPLATT CRIPPS, Treasurer.
JOHN MITCHELL, Secretary.

COMMITTEE OF CORRESPONDENCE.

HENRY WILLIAM DESAUSSURE,
CHARLES G. CORRE,
DAVID RAMSAY,
ADAM TUNNO,
WILLIAM CRAFTS,
CASPER C. SCHUTT,
RICHARD FURMAN,
CHARLES COTESWORTH PINCKNEY,
THOMAS MORRIS,
JOHN F. KERN,
JOHN RUTLEDGE, Junior,
JAMES DELAIRE,
NATHANIEL RUSSELL,
DANIEL O'HARA.

7. *New Ohio Lands, and Title Indisputable.*
Providence, Rhode Island: [*John Carter, Jr.*], 1799.

Sylvester Fuller was one of several speculators who purchased land in the Northwest Territory. This broadside praises Ohio for its agricultural promise and its abundance of natural resources, particularly trees for naval stores. The natural fecundity of the land is a very important point with all land speculators, since many of the immigrants were farmers.

It is informative to compare this advertisement to a later account. In 1812 Timothy Alden, a minister from New York, traveled to Cincinnati to view Ohio for himself. In a pamphlet for two speculators named Griffith and Wallace, he states: "The quality of the soil is generally excellent, admitted on all hands to be equal, if not superiour, to any of equal extent in Pennsylvania. In point of situation, they are not surpassed by any interior lands in the United States, for healthfulness, good and abundant waters, and choice of markets for their rich products." Timothy Alden was sufficiently impressed that he moved to Meadville, Pennsylvania, where he established Allegheny College. He later moved to Pittsburgh and to Cincinnati.

Evans 35526

12 × 16 ½

NEW OHIO LANDS,

AND TITLE INDISPUTABLE.

THE Subscriber having lately purchased a Tract of 21,401 Acres of Land, lying on the Waters of the Elk River, one of the Sources of the Great Kanhaway and Ohio River, in the County of Randolph, State of Virginia, reputed one of the best Countries for Land in that extensive State; a Part of which Tract of Land, the Subscriber has already disposed of to Persons in the State of Rhode-Island, some of which declare their Intention of going on immediately and making Settlements—and wishing to dispose of a few Thousand Acres more, takes this public Method to inform those who wish to remove to a luxuriant Soil and a Climate mild and healthy, that they may be supplied (if applied for soon) with Tracts for Farms at a very reasonable Price.

Many Authors identically characterise this Part of the Western Country as the best calculated to furnish the Comforts of Life with Ease, of any Part of the United States; and all agree that it will produce from 60 to 100 Bushels of good Corn to the Acre; and that the first Rate Land is too rich for Wheat, till it is reduced by four or five Years Cultivation. A Gentleman of Veracity affirmed to the Subscriber that he had experienced the Production of small Grain, 35 Bushels of Wheat and 50 Bushels of Rye, per Acre; and the Subscriber himself witnessed in the Year 1789 (when in that Country) the Measure of upwards of two Hundred Bushels of Indian Corn, from two Acres of Land. The Rivers which are large and numerous produce Plenty of excellent Fish and Fowl, and the Forests abound with Buffalo, Deer and vast Quantities of other Game; there is Plenty of Cane, which fattens Cattle; where no Cane grows, there is Abundance of wild Rye, Clover, Orchard, Spear, Peavine, Buffalo, and other Grass, covering vast Tracts of Country, and affording excellent Food for Cattle; the Fields are likewise covered with Plenty of wild Herbage not common to other Countries.

Col. Gordon, in his Journal, has the following Observations:—

"The Country on the Ohio is every where pleasant, with "large level Spots of rich Land, and every where remarka-"bly healthy; one general Remark of this Nature, will "serve for the whole Tract of the Globe comprized between "the Western Skirts of the Alleghany Mountains; running "thence South-Westwardly to the Distance of 500 Miles to "the Ohio, then crossing them Northerly to the Head Riv-"ers that empty themselves into the Ohio, thence East along "a Ridge that separates the Lakes and Ohio Streams to "French Creek. This Country may, from a proper Knowl-"edge, be affirmed to be the most healthy, most pleasant, "and the most commodious Spot of Earth known to the "European People."

The following just and judicious Observations were addressed to the Earl of Hillsborough in the Year 1770, when Secretary of State for the North American Department.—

"No Part of North America will require less Encouragement for the Production of Naval Stores, and raw Materials for Manufactories in Europe, and for supplying the West-India Islands with Lumber, Provisions, &c. than the Country of the Ohio; and for the following Reasons:—1st. The Lands are excellent, the Climate temperate, the Grapes, Silk-Worms and Mulberry-Trees, abound every where; Hemp, Hops, and Rye grow spontaneously in the Vallies and low Lands; Lead and Iron Ore are found in Plenty in the Hills; Salt Springs are innumerable, and no Soil is better adapted to the Culture of Tobacco, Flax and Cotton, than that of the Ohio.—2dly. The Country is well-watered by several navigable Rivers communicating with each other.—3dly. The River Ohio is, at all Seasons of the Year, navigable for large Boats, like West Country Barges, rowed by four or five Men, and from the Month of Febru-ary to April large Ships may be built on the Ohio and sent to Sea, laden with Hemp, Iron, Flax, Silk, Tobacco, Cotton, Pot-Ash, Beef, Flour, Corn, Ship-Plank, &c."

The Lands on the various Streams abovementioned, are all interspersed with a Variety of Soil which conduces to Pleasantness of Situation, and lays the Foundation for the Wealth of an agricultural and manufacturing People. Large level Bottoms, or natural Meadows, from 20 to 50 Miles in Circuit are every where found, bordering the Rivers and variegating the Country in the interior Parts; these afford as rich a Soil as can be imagined, and may be reduced to proper Cultivation with very little Labour; it is said that in many of these Bottoms a Man may clear an Acre a Day fit for planting with Indian-Corn, there being no Underwood; and the Trees growing very high and large but not thick together, need nothing but girdling. Springs of excellent Water abound in every Part of this Territory, and small and large Streams for Mills and other Purposes are actually interspersed as if by Art, that there may be no Deficiency in any of the Conveniences of Life.

"Very little waste Land is to be found in any of this Tract of Country, there are no Swamps but such as may be readily drained and made into arable and meadow Land; and though the Hills are frequent they are gentle and swelling no where high or incapable of Tillage, they are of a deep rich Soil covered with a heavy Growth of Timber, and well adapted to Wheat, Rye, Indigo, Tobacco, Cotton, &c."

[Morse's Geography.]

With respect to the Climate, Snow seldom falls deep or lays long; the Winter, which begins about Christmas, is never longer than three Months, and is commonly but two, and is so mild that Cattle can live well with very little Fodder, and all the Year, excepting the Winter Months, the Plains, Vallies and Forests are adorned with a Variety of Flowers of the most admirable Beauty. Here is also found the beautiful Tulip bearing Magnolia tree, which has an extensive Smell, and continues to blossom and seed for several Months together.

The Subscriber wishes to observe, that to point out the many Advantages to be experienced by Settlers in the Western Country requires more Space than can possibly be comprized in an Advertisement, which is already large; he must therefore refer those who wish to purchase, to the Geographers for an Account of that delightful Region.

SYLVESTER FULLER.

N. B. Elk-River has at this Time many Settlements; and below its Mouth at the Mouth of the Great Kenhaway Settlement, in the Year 1785, a large Settlement was formed called Kenhaway Settlement, and since, opposite the Great Kenhaway River, another one called the Galliopolis Settlement, which, when the Census was taken contained 1000 Inhabitants; the County of Randolph, 951, besides Slaves; Kenhaway County 6015, besides Slaves; Greenbrier which is adjacent 6015, besides Slaves. Elk River as per Scale of Morse's U. Geography, is distanced 60 Miles from Marietta upon the Muskingum, and in another Direction 70 Miles from Morgan's Town, a large trading County Town upon the Monongalia River, a Western Branch of which runs close to the Head of Elk. The County of Monongalia in 1790, had 4768 white Inhabitants, and a Number of Slaves. In a Word the rapid Population of the Western Country has not only astonished America itself, but it must amaze Europe; the first Settlement on the Western Waters by the English, was in 1760, and the Inhabitants on these Waters some Years ago, were estimated at 400,000—upwards of 10,000 Emigrants were known to arrive in the State of Kentucky alone, in one Year.

[Imlay.]

Providence, May 11, 1799.

CONTEMPORARY EVENTS

8. *Canada Subjected. A New Song.*
[*No place*, 1760.]

Many of the broadsides were occasioned by outbursts of patriotism and enthusiasm after victorious battles and campaigns. "Canada Subjected" celebrates the successful siege of Montreal which ended the French and Indian War in North America. Many other ballads originated in this war, including several on the death of General Wolfe at Quebec in 1759.

The woodcut at the top of the broadside was designed to be used on an earlier broadside—"Earthquakes Improved"—which was printed in Boston by John Green in 1755 after an earthquake in New England. Its use on this broadside suggests that "Canada Subjected" was printed immediately after the news was received without wasting time to make an appropriate illustration for it. The other two cuts represent two themes of the song: armed, savage heathenry and the peaceful rest of "The blushing Morn" and "honest husbandry."

Evans 41027
8 × 12 ⅞

CANADA
SUBJECTED.

---A New Song.---

BRAVE Soldiers all, both far and near,
  Lay by your Swords and never fear:
For now the Battle being o'er
The thund'ring Cannon ceaſe to roar.

Lay by the Trumpet and the Drum;
For joyful Days at laſt are come,
And CANADA is all our own,
And ſubject to great GEORGE's Throne.

The *Savages* lay down their Arms.
The *French* do ceaſe to raiſe Alarms.
Now CANADA is fallen down
Before the Troops of GEORGE's Crown.

Great was the Day of our Succeſs,
When Heav'n our Hoſts was pleas'd to bleſs
When proud *Quebec* and *Montreal*
A Prey to *Engliſh* Troops did fall.

Let martial Muſic ſound no more;
We have no Foes upon the Shore:
But now we joyfully will ſing,
And drink a Health to GEORGE our King.

We'll beat our Swords into Plough-ſhares,
And into Pruning-hooks our Spears;
And bloody Fighting we'll deny,
And follow honeſt Huſbandry.

Rejoice, O *Youth!* the riſing Age,
May you not need in War 't engage;
May ev'ry Thing ſucceed ſo well,
That Peace with you may ever dwell!

Behold the bloody Sons of *Gaul!*
Rejoice with Trembling at their Fall.
The Blood which cruelly they ſhed
Has fall'n on their own guilty Heads.

Some Time ago their Joy was loud,
And CANADA grew very proud;
While we were mourning in Diſtreſs.
With Widows and the Fatherleſs.

We've took their Towns, and ſo poſſeſs
Their Paſtures and the Wilderneſs.
Triumphant News ſpreads thro' the Land,
That we have got the Upper-hand.

Ye holy Prophets now rejoice,
And ye GOD's Saints that hear his Voice;
Becauſe the Lord hath ſaved you
From Inſults of the *Popiſh* Crew.

With them was found the Blood of Slain,
And on their Robes there was a Stain;
They drunken were with Chriſtian Blood,
Which flowed down like as a Flood.

Hail, happy Day!---the bluſhing Morn
With Pleaſure may our Souls adorn,
When proud *Montreal* became a Prey;
We'll ever bleſs the glorious Day!

O! when will come the happy Hour,
Which will deſtroy all *Babel*'s Pow'r!
When will the bleſſed Morning come,
When *Babylon* receives her Doom!---

The Time in Haſte is coming on,
The End of haughty *Babylon*:
The joyful Cry ſhall quickly be,
" She's like a Stone ſunk in the Sea!"

The Time will come, when Pope and Fry'r
Shall both be roaſted in the Fire;
When the proud *Antichriſtian* Whore
Will ſink, and never ariſe more.

9. *Glorious News. Boston, Friday 11 o'clock, 16th May 1766. Boston: Drapers, Edes & Gill, Green & Russell, and Fleets, 1766.*

The repeal of the Stamp Act in 1766 was greeted with general rejoicing among the colonists. As soon as Boston received the news by ship from London, this broadside was printed by the publishers of four Boston newspapers, none of which was issued on a daily basis. This broadside also reveals that the repeal was "glorious news" not only to the colonists, but also to the English merchants and, to judge by the "huzzaing, clapping Hands," the populace of London.

Similar broadsides exist which announced to the public the declaration of war by Great Britain against France, news of Washington's victory at the battle of Princeton, and the end of the American Revolution. Daily newspapers were not common until after the Revolution, so that broadsides such as these were necessary to convey important news as soon as it was received.

Evans 10317

8 × 13

Glorious News.

BOSTON, Friday 11 o'Clock, 16th *May* 1766.

THIS Instant arrived here the Brig Harrison, belonging to *John Hancock*, Esq; Captain *Shubael Coffin*, in 6 Weeks and 2 Days from LONDON, with important News, as follows.

From the LONDON GAZETTE.

Westminster, March 18th, 1766.

THIS day his Majesty came to the House of Peers, and being in his royal robes seated on the throne with the usual solemnity, Sir Francis Molineux, Gentleman Usher of the Black Rod, was sent with a Message from his Majesty to the House of Commons, commanding their attendance in the House of Peers. The Commons being come thither accordingly, his Majesty was pleased to give his royal assent to

An ACT to REPEAL an Act made in the last Session of Parliament, intituled, an Act for granting and applying certain Stamp-Duties and other Duties in the British Colonies and Plantations in America, towards further defraying the expences of defending, protecting and securing the same, and for amending such parts of the several Acts of Parliament relating to the trade and revenues of the said Colonies and Plantations, as direct the manner of determining and recovering the penalties and forfeitures therein mentioned.

Also ten public bills, and seventeen private ones.

Yesterday there was a meeting of the principal Merchants concerned in the American trade, at the King's Arms tavern in Cornhill, to consider of an Address to his Majesty on the beneficial Repeal of the late Stamp-Act.

Yesterday morning about eleven o'clock a great number of North American Merchants went in their coaches from the King's Arms tavern in Cornhill to the House of Peers, to pay their duty to his Majesty, and to express their satisfaction at his signing the Bill for Repealing the American Stamp-Act, there was upwards of fifty coaches in the procession.

Last night the said gentleman dispatched an express for Falmouth, with fifteen copies of the Act for repealing the Stamp-Act, to be forwarded immediately for New York.

Orders are given for several merchantmen in the river to proceed to sea immediately on their respective voyages to North America, some of whom have been cleared out since the first of November last.

Yesterday messengers were dispatched to Birmingham, Sheffield, Manchester, and all the great manufacturing towns in England, with an account of the final decision of an august assembly relating to the Stamp-Act.

When the KING went to the House of Peers to give the Royal Assent, there was such a vast Concourse of People, huzzaing, clapping Hands, &c. that it was several Hours before His Majesty reached the House.

Immediately on His Majesty's Signing the Royal Assent to the Repeal of the Stamp-Act the Merchants trading to America, dispatched a Vessel which had been in waiting, to put into the first Port on the Continent with the Account.

There were the greatest Rejoicings possible in the City of London, by all Ranks of People, on the TOTAL Repeal of the Stamp-Act,—the Ships in the River displayed all their Colours, Illuminations and Bonfires in many Parts. — In short, the Rejoicings were as great as was ever known on any Occasion.

It is said the Acts of Trade relating to America would be taken under Consideration, and all Grievances removed. The Friends to America are very powerful, and disposed to assist us to the utmost of their Ability.

Capt. Blake sailed the same Day with Capt. Coffin, and Capt. Shand a Fortnight before him, both bound to this Port.

It is impossible to express the Joy the Town is now in, on receiving the above, great, glorious and important NEWS—The Bells in all the Churches were immediately set a Ringing, and we hear the Day for a general Rejoicing will be the beginning of next Week.

PRINTED for the Benefit of the PUBLIC, by *Drapers, Edes & Gill, Green & Russell*, and *Fleets*.

The Customers to the Boston Papers may have the above gratis at the respective Offices.

10. *At a Meeting of the Freeholders and other Inhabitants of the town of Boston, . . . 28th of October* 1767.
[*Boston,* 1767.]

This is one of many broadsides relating the minutes of the town meetings held in the colonies. This particular Boston town meeting initiated the boycott against imports from Great Britain in response to the Townshend duties. The colonists resolved to encourage the manufacture of many items in Massachusetts, particularly glass and paper, and to "prevent the unnecessary Importation of European Commodities, the excessive Use of which threatens the Country with Poverty and Ruin."

Accounts of meetings such as this one were also printed in the newspapers. In comparison to the newspaper versions, the broadside was easier to read and cheaper to distribute to the other colonies. In fact this town meeting recommended that the minutes be printed and circulated to other colonies.

Evans 10564

8 × 12 ⅞

At a Meeting of the Freeholders and other Inhabitants of the Town of *Boston*, legally assembled at *Faneuil*-Hall, on Wednesday the 28th of *October*, 1767.

THE Town then took into Consideration the Petition of a Number of Inhabitants, " That some effectual Measures might be " agreed upon to promote Industry, Oe- " conomy, and Manufactures ; thereby " to prevent the unnecessary Importation of Euro- " pean Commodities, which threaten the Country " with Poverty and Ruin :" Whereupon in a very large and full Meeting, the following Votes and Resolutions were passed Unanimously.

Whereas the excessive Use of foreign Superfluities is the chief Cause of the present distressed State of this Town, as it is thereby drained of its Money ; which Misfortune is likely to be increased by Means of the late additional Burthens and Impositions on the Trade of the Province, which threaten the Country with Poverty and Ruin :

Therefore, *VOTED*, That this Town will take all prudent and legal Measures to encourage the Produce and Manufactures of this Province, and to lessen the Use of Superfluities,& particularly the following enumerated Articles imported from Abroad, viz. *Loaf Sugar, Cordage, Anchors, Coaches, Chaises and Carriages of all Sorts, Horse Furniture, Men and Womens Hatts, Mens and Womens Apparel ready made, Houshold Furniture, Gloves, Mens and Womens Shoes, Sole-Leather, Sheathing and Deck Nails, Gold and Silver and Thread Lace of all Sorts, Gold and Silver Buttons, Wrought Plate of all Sorts, Diamond, Stone and Paste Ware, Snuff, Mustard, Clocks and Watches, Silversmiths and Jewellers Ware, Broad Cloths that cost above 10s. per Yard, Muffs Furrs and Tippets, and all Sorts of Millenary Ware, Starch, Womens and Childrens Stays, Fire Engines, China Ware, Silk and Cotton Velvets, Gauze, Pewterers hollow Ware, Linseed Oyl, Glue, Lawns, Cambricks, Silks of all Kinds for Garments, Malt Liquors and Cheese.*——And that a Subscription for this End be and hereby is recommended to the several Inhabitants and Housholders of the Town ; and that *John Rowe*, Esq; Mr. *William Greenleafe, Melatiah Bourne*, Esq; Mr. *Samuel Austin*, Mr. *Edward Payne*, Mr. *Edmund Quincy*, Tertius, *John Ruddock*, Esq; *Jonathan Williams*, Esq; *Joshua Henshaw*, Esq; Mr. *Henderson Inches*, Mr. *Solomon Davis, Joshua Winslow*, Esq; and *Thomas Cushing*, Esq; be a Committee to prepare a Form for Subscription, to report the same as soon as possible ; and also to procure Subscriptions to the same.

And whereas it is the Opinion of this Town, that divers new Manufactures may be set up in America, to its great Advantage, and some others carried to a greater Extent, particularly those of Glass & Paper

Therefore, *Voted*, That this Town will by all prudent Ways and Means, encourage the Use and Consumption of Glass and Paper, made in any of the British American Colonies ; and more especially in this Province.

[*Then the Meeting adjourn'd till 3 o'Clock Afternoon.*]

III o'Clock, *P. M.*

THE Committee appointed in the Forenoon, to prepare a Form for Subscription, reported as follows.

WHEREAS this Province labours under a heavy Debt, incurred in the Course of the late War ; and the Inhabitants by this Means must be for some Time subject to very burthensome Taxes :——*And as our Trade has for some Years been on the decline, and is now particularly under great Embarrasments, and burthened with heavy Impositions, our Medium very scarce, and the Balance of Trade greatly against this Country :*

WE therefore the Subscribers, being sensible that it is absolutely necessary, in Order to extricate us out of these embarrassed and distressed Circumstances, to promote Industry, Oeconomy and Manufactures among ourselves, and by this Means prevent the unnecessary Importation of European Commodities, the excessive Use of which threatens the Country with Poverty and Ruin—DO promise and engage, to and with each other, that we will encourage the Use and Consumption of all Articles manufactured in any of the British American Colonies, and more especially in this Province ; and that we will not, from and after the 31st of *December* next ensuing, purchase any of the following Articles, imported from Abroad, viz. *Loaf Sugar,* and all the other Articles enumerated above.——

And we further agree strictly to adhere to the late Regulation respecting Funerals, and will not use any Gloves but what are Manufactured here, nor procure any new Garments upon such an Occasion, but what shall be absolutely necessary.

The above Report having been considered, the Question was put, Whether the same shall be accepted ? *Voted unanimously in the Affirmative.* —And that said Committee be desired to use their best Endeavours to get the Subscription Papers filled up as soon as may be. Also, *Voted unanimously,* That the foregoing Vote and Form of a Subscription relative to the enumerated Articles, be immediately Published ; and that the Selectmen be directed to distribute a proper Number of them among the Freeholders of this Town ; and to forward a Copy of the same to the Select-Men of every Town in the Province ; as also to the principal City or Town Officers of the chief Towns in the several Colonies on the Continent, as they may think proper.

Attest,

William Cooper, *Town-Clerk.*

Then the Meeting was Adjourn'd to the 20th Day of November next.

11. *A Monumental Inscription on the Fifth of March.*
[Boston: Isaiah Thomas, 1772.]

The Boston Massacre was frequently commemorated in broadsides as well as in sermons during the revolutionary period. This piece recalls the Massacre and inveighs against the release of Ebenezer Richardson from jail. Richardson was a despised customs official who had killed Christopher Seider on February 22, 1770, while a mob was gathered outside his door. He was tried for manslaughter, pronounced guilty, but was never sentenced. Richardson was released from prison on March 10, 1772. In *The Massachusetts Spy* for March 5, 1772, Isaiah Thomas printed the summary of events in the same type and layout, and this broadside was undoubtedly printed within a few days of that newspaper issue.

The woodcut of the Boston Massacre was executed by Paul Revere and was first used in Thomas's *The Massachusetts Calendar* for 1772. This small woodcut differs substantially from Revere's larger and more famous engraving of the Massacre.

An early manuscript note on this copy of the broadside identifies the allusions to "Lines," "Ropes," "Cushing," and "Bridge of Tories" (Trowbridge) as the judges in the trial.

Evans 12302
11 ⅞ × 19 ½

A MONUMENTAL INSCRIPTION

ON THE

Fifth of March.

Together with a few LINES

On the Enlargement of

EBENEZER RICHARDSON,

Convicted of MURDER.

AMERICANS!
BEAR IN REMEMBRANCE
The HORRID MASSACRE!
Perpetrated in King-street, Boston,
New-England,
On the Evening of March the Fifth, 1770.
When FIVE of your fellow countrymen,
GRAY, MAVERICK, CALDWELL, ATTUCKS,
and CARR,
Lay wallowing in their Gore!
Being *basely*, and most *inhumanly*
MURDERED!
And SIX others badly WOUNDED!
By a Party of the XXIXth Regiment,
Under the command of Capt. Tho. Preston.
REMEMBER!
That Two of the MURDERERS
Were convicted of MANSLAUGHTER!
By a Jury, of whom I shall say
NOTHING,
Branded in the hand!
And *dismissed*,
The others were ACQUITTED,
And their Captain PENSIONED!
Also,
BEAR IN REMEMBRANCE
That on the 22d Day of February, 1770.
The infamous
EBENEZER RICHARDSON, Informer,
And tool to Ministerial hirelings,
Most *barbarously*
MURDERED
CHRISTOPHER SEIDER,
An innocent youth!
Of which crime he was found guilty
By his Country
On Friday April 20th, 1770;
But remained *Unsentenced*
On Saturday the 22d Day of February, 1772.
When the GRAND INQUEST
For Suffolk county,
Were informed, at request,
By the Judges of the Superior Court,
That EBENEZER RICHARDSON's *Case*
Then lay before his MAJESTY.
Therefore said *Richardson*
This day, MARCH FIFTH! 1772,
Remains UNHANGED!!!
Let THESE things be told to Posterity!
And handed down
From Generation to Generation,
'Till Time shall be no more!
Forever may AMERICA be preserved,
From weak and wicked monarchs,
Tyrannical Ministers,
Abandoned Governors,
Their Underlings and Hirelings!
And may the
Machinations of artful, *designing* wretches,
Who would ENSLAVE THIS People,
Come to an end,
Let their NAMES and MEMORIES
Be buried in eternal oblivion,
And the PRESS,
For a *SCOURGE* to Tyrannical Rulers,
Remain FREE.

AWAKE my drowsy Thoughts! Awake my muse!
　　Awake O earth, and tremble at the news!
　　In grand defiance to the laws of God,
The Guilty, Guilty murd'rer walks abroad.
That city mourns, (the cry comes from the ground,)
Where law and justice never can be found:
Oh! sword of vengeance, fall thou on the race
Of those who hinder justice from its place.
O MURD'RER! RICHARDSON! with their latest breath
Millions will curse you when you sleep in death!
Infernal horrors sure will shake your soul
When o'er your head the awful thunders roll.
Earth cannot hide you, always will the cry
Of Murder! Murder! haunt you 'till you die!
To yonder grave! with trembling joints repair,
Remember, SEIDER's corps lies mould'ring there;
There drop a tear, and think what you have done!
Then judge how you can live beneath the Sun.
A PARDON may arrive! You laws defy,
But Heaven's laws will stand when KINGS shall die.
Oh! Wretched man! the monster of the times,
You were not hung " by reason of *old Lines,*"
Old Lines thrown by, 'twas then we were in hopes,
That you would soon be hung with *new made* Ropes
But neither *Ropes nor Lines*, will satisfy
For SEIDER's blood! But GOD is ever nigh,
And guilty souls will not unpunish'd go
Tho' they're excus'd by judges here below!
You are enlarg'd but cursed is your fate
Tho' *Cushing*'s eas'd you from the prison gate
The ╬ Bridge of Tories, it has borne you o'er
Yet you e'er long may meet with HELL's dark shore.

* "Lines"- the name of one of the judges
※ Name of another Judge no way amiss
† Do. of another of the Judges
╬ Trowbridge another Judge

12. *A Poem On the Late distress of the Town of Boston. By E[lisha] R[ich].*
Chelmsford: N. Coverly, 1776.

The Evacuation of Boston by the British Army on March 17, 1776, is celebrated in this poem by Elisha Rich whose initials may be found in the last verse. The poet alludes to the Stamp Act, the closing of the Port of Boston, and Bunker Hill. The last nine stanzas are an impassioned plea to Americans not to commit the sins of the British Government when they undertake self-government.

   The woodcut on this broadside was previously used by Nathaniel Coverly on a ballad celebrating the skirmish at the Light House in 1775, "Poetical Remarks Upon the Fight at the Boston Light House," also by Elisha Rich. This explains in some way why the iconographic elements of the boat, cannon and light house have little relation to the main images of the poem: the bramble and cedar tree, Boston town and Bunker Hill.

Evans 15061

9 ¾ × 15 ½

A POEM

On the late distress of the
TOWN of
BOSTON

With some Remarks of the sudden Flight of the MINISTERIAL Troops, after plundering and Destroying the Property of the Worthy Inhabitants, they left the town in the greatest confusion imaginable, not allowing themselves time to take with them great part of their Warlike Stores, In short, they fled like Murderer's pursued by the Hand of Justice.

COME shout AMERICANS with Joy,
And let God's praise your tongues employ,
Who did our foes designs destroy,
That would our Liberties annoy.

Your officers and soldiers brave,
By God's kind hard, your land doth save,
While britons seeking to inslave,
Sink deeper down into their grave.

Britanna's glory once was high,
While she sought peace and liberty;
Her fame around the earth did fly,
And King's her greatness did envy.

She might still greater glory see:
Her Princes, sons of nobles be,
Had she have let her Sons been free,
And never crown'd the bramble-tree.

This bramble so in pride did rise,
So void of love and pitying eyes,
He would not hear the oppressed crys,
But did their humble suits despise.

My pow'r unlimitted, I say
Shall over the whole Realm bear sway:
My taxing power they shall obey,
Through the whole North-America.

My Parliament espouse my cause,
Men of true merit and applause;
My Commoners enforce my laws,
And from my help there's few withdraws:

Tall Cedars in America,
Shall bend their lofty tops to me,
And from taxes shall not be free,
Yet represented here shan't be.

AMERICANS could not endure
To fall beneath a tyrant's power;
And tho' his wrath would them devour,
Yet they submit not for one hour.

While they request superior aid;
They do refuse the bramble shade,
And while his laws are not obey'd,
They of his frowns are not afraid.

His wrath doth first on BOSTON fall;
He stops our Ports and Harbour's all,
Then for his bloody troops doth call
For to inslave or murder all.

Thus stoping our Commerce and trade,
The Town of BOSTON they invade,
And in her streets they do parade,
Till it a den of thives is made.

Her Liberty for to confound,
With fleets and armies her surround;
With trenches they threw up her ground,
While tyrants Drums and Trumpets sound.

In BOSTON they dominion bare,
It's owners treasure they don't spare,
But like blood-hounds that hungry were,
They rob and pillage every where.

This Town their garrison they make,
While it's true owner's hearts do ake:
At length the Town, they must forsake,
To other Town's for safety take.

Before hostilitie's commence't,
They have the Town for their defence,
Their Cannon mounted to dispence,
Destruction to AMERICANS.

When they this Town had fortified,
With strong defence on every side:
There's now no Bridle to their pride,
They think none can their force abide.

They then begin their murderers theme,
Well pleas'd with their curs't plot they seem,
Their victory now a plercing cream,
Till justice ev'rthrows their scheme.

AMERICANS this murder see,
And could no longer silent be,
But with one mind and heart agree,
To set unhappy BOSTON free,

In Seventy-Five this war began,
With fighting while the year was run,
With Cannon, bayonet and Gun,
While blood on either side did run,

Our Colonies unite as one,
Commanded by brave WASHINGTON,
Who to our help together run,
Whose branded swords and armour shone.

Brave WASHINGTON is valiant found,
His Men our tyrant foes surround,
Their cruel Plot he doth confound,
And is at last with victory crown'd.

Our foes through fear did melt away,
To see our Forts rise night and day:
The ADMIRAL to How did say,
These Rebels Drive, or I'll not stay.

These bloody Troops to memory call,
How they on BUNKER's HILL did fall,
They have no courage left at all,
They run away Torries and all.

They quit their Fort on BUNKER's HILL,
Tho' bitterly against their will,
They fear to stay, least they see hell,
Adue, BOSTON, BOSTON farewell.

On Seventeenth of March they flee,
Since there they could no safety see;
Left BOSTON to it's owner free,
And trust the mercy of the sea,

With shame the City they resign'd,
And left much of their store's behind,
Nor could they in our Harbour find,
A shelter from the stormy wind.

GOD grant these troops may never more,
Have footing on New-England shore,
To lay her Sen's in bloody gore,
To set up an oppressive pow'r.

By sea they oft defeated were,
Before their transports came a shore,
And lost much of their warlike stor,
And many were laid in their gore.

Britanna now consider well,
Thy forces that us'd to excel,
By sad defeats doth plainly tell,
The cause they'r in is black as hell.

By slaughter in AMERICA,
Doth not blood's gilt upon the lay,
Then bid farewel to peace for aye,
Unless blood clences, blood's gilt away.

Bloods gilt doth call for blood again,
Nought else can wash away it's stain,
If than thy murderer's are not slain,
You draw your swords for war in vain.

You that in BOSTON dwellers were,
And have been scattered here and there,
How doth your hearts rejoice to hear,
Your City of those murderer's clear.

Give glory to the LORD most high,
Who did defeat thine enemy,
That so few of thy son's did die,
Or went into captivity.

Some that were neighbour's once to you,
That joined with this bloody crew,
Through fear and shame, are now withdrew,
And those that stay'd, their deeds may rue.

Should you 'gain your Lard pofefs,
And GOD should you increase and bless:
Avoid all luxereus excefs,
Lest GOD bring still greater distress.

AMERICANS consider all,
What fate on British tyrants fall,
And pattern not by them at all,
Lest you in vain for helpers call,

While you behold God's wond'rous hand,
In garding thee by sea and land:
Truft in his Name and as a friend,
He will thy glorious cause defend.

All covetous desires disdain,
Nor judge amifs for lukers gain,
But lovers of true peace remain,
And you'l not find God's promise vain.

Oppress not in Religion still;
Tax none to Priest's against their will,
For this will peace and friendship kill,
And the whole state with tumult fill,

For as in things of GOD we see,
Men's conscience's are wholly free,
True sons of peace cannot agree,
That worldly mastership should be.

Christ's Kingdom here hath true defence;
From the true Gospel influence:
Nor needs it fines or prisonments,
Or robing to bear it's expence.

Can Patriots for Liberty,
Against a civil tyrants cry,
And not give equal Liberty,
To ev'ry diff'rent sectery.

Then let AMERICA be free,
And love true peace and Liberty;
That GOD our lasting friend may be,
To the latest posterity.

If these afflictions should be blest
And many should releave th' oppresst,
That we in GOD may find true rest,
Thy friend E. R. hath his requeft.

CHELMSFORD: Printed and Sold at N. Coverly's Printing-Office. Where may be had, Verses by the Groze or Dozen. M,DCCLXXVI.

13. *The Tragedy of Louis Capet.*
Springfield: Edward Gray, 1793.

American feelings on the French Revolution were mixed, if indeed not contradictory. On the one hand, there was a natural sympathy between the young republics with their ideals of Roman virtue and hatred of absolute rule. Not a few American patriots would have rejoiced at the news that the French Republic had declared war against "all monarchies," particularly the coalition led by England and Spain. On the other hand, it shocked and grieved the former colonists to learn that Louis XVI had been executed in January of 1793. For, it was Louis and the nobles of the *ancien régime* who had given at least tacit support to the fledgling American Republic in its struggle against Great Britain. Sympathy was naturally extended to Marie-Antoinette, who was to survive her husband for some eight months.

This broadside from Massachusetts would seem to indicate that although Americans were in support of other peoples in their fight for freedom from tyranny, the spectre of regicide, "when Mobs triumphant seize the reins/ And guide the Car of State", was more than they could tolerate. There was increasing disillusionment on this side of the Atlantic with a "nation, *once* polite". Within five years, the affair of the "X Y Z despatches" and the quasi-war on the sea had diminished most of the feeling of fraternity between the two nations.

Evans 26273
16 ⅝ × 20 ¾

THE TRAGEDY OF LOUIS CAPET:

Being a True and Authentic NARRATIVE of the horrid and barbarous EXECUTION of the late unfortunate MONARCH, LOUIS XVIth of France, who was beheaded, on the Twenty first of January, 1793, conformably to a Decree of the NATIONAL CONVENTION on Suspicion of TREASON.—Which bloody Transaction (it is thought by every true friend to American Revolution) will eternally disgrace the Annals of the French Nation: And may his Death be as sincerely lamented by every honest and grateful AMERICAN, as it is by the Majority of the Citizens of France.——This Narrative, with the Poetry annexed, is published in this Form at the Request of many true Republicans, and recommended to be preserved as a Memorial of that shocking and melancholy Event.

[Translated from a FRENCH GAZETTE.]
PARIS, (Capital of FRANCE) Jan. 22, 1793.

LOUIS CAPET KING of FRANCE. Æ 41

CONFORMABLY to the arrangement made by the Executive-Council, LOUIS CAPET was yesterday put to death at the Place de la Revolution.—Twenty five citizens, of known principles, acquainted with the manual exercise, and having each 16 rounds of shot were chosen from each section, to form a guard of 1200 men, who accompanied the unfortunate MONARCH to the place of Execution.—Strong detachments from the different legions were posted in the streets through which the ROYAL PRISONER was to pass, and also in all the avenues leading to the Place de la Revolution, to prevent confusion; and each section had a body in reserve, ready to move at a moments notice, to maintain the public order, should any attempt have been made to disturb it.—Cannon were also distributed in every quarter, where it was thought they would be any way serviceable, had events made it necessary to employ them; for even to the last moment, the sanguinary faction, who pronounced the death of the unfortunate MONARCH, manifested symptoms of fear that some attempts might be made to rescue him.

Between eight and nine o'clock in the morning LOUIS proceeded from his appartments in the Temple, and got into the Mayor's carriage, who accompanied him, as did also M. Escheveaux de Fermont, an Irish Priest, whom he requested might attend him.——LOUIS was dressed in a brown great coat, white waistcoat, black breeches and stockings; his hair was dressed.

The procession, commanded by Marefchal Santere, proceeded along the Boulevards to the Place de Revolution: One hundred Gendarmes on horseback formed an advanced guard to the procession.—The rear guard was composed of one hundred national guards from the military school, also mounted.—Various referves of cavalry lined the procession and patroled the outskirts of the city.

The unfortunate MONARCH arrived at the foot of the scaffold at twenty minutes past ten.—He mounted the scaffold with firmnefs and dignity: He appeared defirous of addreffing the people; but even this laft wifh was denied him: Drums and trumpets gave the fignal, at 22 minutes paft 10 his head was fevered from his body.—The Place de la Revolution was fo ftrongly guarded by troops, that no perfon was fuffered to pafs after the KING had entered it; thofe, however, who had previoufly entered, and got near enough the fcaffold, notwithftanding the indecent noife of drums, & trumpets, heard him plainly pronounce thefe words, "CITIZENS, I FORGIVE MY ENEMIES, AND I DIE INNOCENT!"

After his death, the neareft fpectators divided what of his hair had been cut off by the ftroke of the gurlotine! and feveral perfons were fo inhuman as to dip their handkerchiefs and buttons in his blood, which they carried about, crying, Behold the blood of a Tyrant!——When the Executioners fhewed his head to the people, cries of Vive la Nation! Vive la Ripublique! were heard on all fides; and feveral gropes made ufe of the following expreffions, We always wifhed well to him, but we never wifhed well to us. Many however, fhewed emotions of a different nature, but which they were obliged to conceal as much as poffible, for their own perfonal fafety.

Occafioned by the DEATH of LOUIS XVIth.

WHEN Mobs triumphant
  feize the reins,
And guide the Car of State;
Monarchs will feel the galling chains,
  And meet the worst of fate,
For inftance, view the Gallic fhore,
  A nation, once polite;
See what confufion covers o'er
  A Star, that fhone fo bright.
Then from the fcene recoil
  with dread,
  For LOUIS is no more!
The barb'rous Mob cut of his head,
  And drank the fpouting gore.
Shall we, the Sons of Freedom dare,
  Againft fo vile a Race?
Unlefs we mean ourfelves to bare,
  The palm of their difgrace.
No! GOD forbid, the man who feels
  The force of pity's call,
To join thofe Brutes, whofe fentence feals,
  Whofe hearts are made of gall.

On the Decolation of LOUIS 16.

LOUIS the great is dead!
  ah what a found!
It muft all grateful hearts
  fincerely wound;
He to America did lend his aid,
And fent affiftance in the time
  of need.
Led to the block, oh mournful
  fight to fee
That beft of Kings a facrifice
  to be!
His enemies with hardened
  hearts they ftood,
"And dip'd their buttons in
  their MONARCH's blood."
He is beheaded! what a difmal
  thing!
He was a generous and a mighty
  King.
Full blooming in the flower of
  youthful age,
He fell a Victim to his Country's
  rage.
Unhappy QUEEN! what forrows rend thy breaft,
Thou art a ftranger to all peace
  and reft;
A tender OFFSPRING, mid a
  lawlefs Band,
Soon to be banifh'd from
  his native Land.

THE QUEEN'S LAMENTATION

For the DEATH of her BELOVED LOUIS.

"As a Man falleth before wicked Men,
  "fo felleft Thou."

O Woe is me, poor QUEEN of FRANCE!
  Ye Females hear my call;
Both high and low come weep with me,
  For I'm bereft of all.

II.

Cruel and fierce their anger was,
  A horrid, fpiteful Clan;
Their malice and their hatred curs'd,
  In which they flew a Man.

III.

Ah! had I been of meaner Birth,
  Nor doom'd a CROWN to wear,
Perhaps I might efcaped death,
  But I my fate muft bear.

IV.

The name of CAPET is no more,
  Then weep ye friends to men;
The wants of all he did deplore,
  Ah! wail his cruel end.

V.

Is LOUIS gone? the Friend of Man;
  Will none his fate bemoan?
Oft did his heart relent at woe,
  And footh'd the wretch that groan'd.

VI.

Such Piety fo feldom feen
  Among the Crowned Great;
But black defigns of bloody Men,
  Have brought him to his fate.

VII.

The Widow and the Orphan's tear
  Shall the fad tale relate,
Whofe hearts he did vouchfafe to chear,
  In cyprefs mourn his fate.

VIII.

The crafty Prieft and Statefman check'd,
  Their wily fchemes deftroy'd;
The honeft Man met his refpect,
  But Knaves he e'er annoy'd.

IX.

To tell his num'rous good acts wro't,
  Would fwell my Sheet to large,
But ah! the horrid cruel thought!
  They him with Treafon charge.

X.

The FRIEND to bold COLUMBIANS all,
  A Friend in time of need;
I know they will regret his fall,
  And curfe the horrid deed.

XI.

Poor LOUIS! ah! thy Shades adieu!
  No more in life fhall fee!
No more my SIRE and LOVER too,
  Unhappy is poor me!

XII.

His SISTER's fate alarms each tho't,
  Her danger is fo great,
Left fhe be to the Scaffold bro't,
  And fhare a cruel fate.

XIII.

But ONE who reigns above the fky,
  Maintains her innocence,
And when upon the Scaffold high,
  Will prove her beft defence.

XIV.

My DAUPHIN's fate bewail and mourn,
  All ye who feel for woe,
Left he be fnatched in his turn,
  Tho' fcarce alone can go.

XV.

Ah! little Infant! haplefs YOUTH!
  Ill fated was your Birth,
Ah! muft I tell a folemn truth,
  You'll foon return to earth.

XVI.

Fain would I leap thefe fable walls,
  Could I obtain a fight
Of him who was my all in all,
  My charmer and delight.

XVIII.

But we fhall meet where none moleft,
  Where all in love do dwell;
Where Kings and Beggars are at reft,
  Then all things will be well.

Springfield: Printed and Sold by Edward Gray, 1793.

PATRIOTISM

14. *The Yankey's return from Camp.*
[*No place, 1775.*]

This familiar ballad became, of course, the most popular American patriotic song. Judging from the number of different editions and various titles, "Yankee Doodle" was just as popular during the Revolution as now. The origins of the song are not definitely known, but the earliest version probably dated from the French and Indian War. No copy of that version is still in existence. The lyrics for the present broadside were in all probability inspired by a visit to the patriots' camp in Cambridge in 1775. The illustrations were also used on "The Farmer and his Son's return from a visit to the CAMP," another contemporary issue of "Yankee Doodle."

8 5/8 × 10 3/8

The YANKEY's return from CAMP.

FATHER and I went down to camp,
  Along with Captain Gooding,
There we fee the men and boys,
  As thick as hafty pudding.
          Yankey doodle keep it up,
Chorus.   Yankey doodle, dandy,
      Mind the mufic and the ftep,
          And with the girls be handy.
And there we fee a thoufand men,
  As rich as 'Square David ;
And what they wafted every day,
  I wifh it could be faved.
          Yankey doodle, &c.
The 'laffes they eat every day,
  Would keep a houfe a winter :
They have as much that I'll be bound
  They eat it when they're a mind to.
          Yankey doodle, &c.
And there we fee a fwamping gun,
  Large as a log of maple,
Upon a ducid little cart,
  A load for father's cattle.
          Yankey doodle. &c.
And every time they fhoot it off,
  It takes a horn of powder—
It makes a noife like father's gun,
  Only a nation louder.
          Yankey doodle, &c.
I went as nigh to one myfelf,
  As 'Siah's underpining ;
And father went as nigh again,
  I tho't the deuce was in him.
          Yankey doodle, &c.
Coufin Simon grew fo bold,
  I tho't he would have cock'd it :
It fcar'd me fo, I fhrink'd it off,
  and hung by father's pocket.
          Yankey doodle, &c.
And captain Davis had a gun,
  He kind of clapt his hand on't,

And ftuck a crooked ftabbing iron
  Upon the little end on't.
          Yankey doodle, &c.
And there I fee a pumpkin fhell
  As big as mother's bafon,
And ev'ry time they touch'd it off,
  They fcamper'd like the nation.
          Yankey doodle, &c.
I fee a little barrel too,
  The heads were made of leather,
They knock'd upon't with little clubs,
  And call'd the folks together.
          Yankey doodle, &c.
And there was captain Wafhington,
  And gentlefolks about him,
They fay he's grown fo tarnal proud,
  He will not ride without 'em.
          Yankey doodle, &c.
He got him on his meeting clothes,
  Upon a flapping ftallion,
He fet the world along in rows,
  In hundreds and in millions.
          Yankey doodle, &c.
The flaming ribbons in their hats,
  They look'd fo taring fine, ah,
wanted pockily to get,
  To give to my Jemimah.
          Yankey doodle, &c.
I fee another fnarl of men
  A digging graves, they told me,
So tarnal long, fo tarnal deep,
  They 'tended they fhould hold me.
          Yankey doodle, &c.
It fear'd me fo, I hook'd it off,
  Nor ftop'd, as I remember,
Nor turn'd about 'till I got home,
  Lock'd up in mother's chamber.
          Yankey doodle, &c.

15. *The Sentiments of an American Woman.*
[*Philadelphia: John Dunlap*, 1780.]

This eloquent testimony to the pride and spirit of the American people during the Revolution was discovered in a bound volume of the *Pennsylvania Packet*, a Philadelphia newspaper. This address was widely circulated at the time and was often read by ministers to their congregations.

Although several women like Molly Pitcher and Margret Corbin actually fought in the Revolution, most females expressed their patriotism in quieter, more symbolic gestures. Many wore homespun, refused to drink imported tea, and renounced European finery. The reverse of this broadside suggests a very practical plan by which American women could put in effect their noble sentiments. Cash could be donated to a fund which General Washington would dispose of "in the manner he shall judge most advantageous to the Soldiery." With typical eighteenth century delicacy, the American women desire that the money be used "to render the condition of the Soldier more pleasant, and not to hold place of the things which they ought to receive from the Congress, or from the States," particularly clothing and arms.

Evans 16992
8 ½ × 13 ⅜

THE SENTIMENTS of an
AMERICAN WOMAN.

ON the commencement of actual war, the Women of America manifested a firm resolution to contribute as much as could depend on them, to the deliverance of their country. Animated by the purest patriotism, they are sensible of sorrow at this day, in not offering more than barren wishes for the success of so glorious a Revolution. They aspire to render themselves more really useful; and this sentiment is universal from the north to the south
of the Thirteen United States. Our ambition is kindled by the fame of those heroines of an-
tiquity, who have rendered their sex illustrious, and have proved to the universe, that, if
the weakness of our Constitution, if opinion and manners did not forbid us to march to glory by the same paths as the Men, we should at least equal, and sometimes surpass them in our
love for the public good. I glory in all that which my sex has done great and commendable.
I call to mind with enthusiasm and with admiration, all those acts of courage, of constancy and patriotism, which history has transmitted to us: The people favoured by Heaven,
preserved from destruction by the virtues, the zeal and the resolution of Deborah, of Judith,
of Esther! The fortitude of the mother of the Macchabees, in giving up her sons to die before her eyes: Rome saved from the fury of a victorious enemy by the efforts of Volumnia,
and other Roman Ladies: So many famous sieges where the Women have been seen forget-
ing the weakness of their sex, building new walls, digging trenches with their feeble hands,
furnishing arms to their defenders, they themselves darting the missile weapons on the enemy, resigning the ornaments of their apparel, and their fortune, to fill the public treasury,
and to hasten the deliverance of their country; burying themselves under its ruins; throwing
themselves into the flames rather than submit to the disgrace of humiliation before a proud
enemy.

Born for liberty, disdaining to bear the irons of a tyrannic Government, we associate ourselves to the grandeur of those Sovereigns, cherished and revered, who have held with so much
splendour the scepter of the greatest States, The Batildas, the Elizabeths, the Maries, the Ca-
tharines, who have extended the empire of liberty, and contented to reign by sweetness and
justice, have broken the chains of slavery, forged by tyrants in the times of ignorance and
barbarity. The Spanish Women, do they not make, at this moment, the most patriotic sacrifices,
to encrease the means of victory in the hands of their Sovereign. He is a friend to the French
Nation. They are our allies. We call to mind, doubly interested, that it was a French Maid
who kindled up amongst her fellow-citizens, the flame of patriotism buried under long mis-
fortunes: It was the Maid of Orleans who drove from the kingdom of France the ancestors
of those same British, whose odious yoke we have just shaken off; and whom it is necessary
that we drive from this Continent.

But I must limit myself to the recollection of this small number of atchievements. Who
knows if persons disposed to censure, and sometimes too severely with regard to us, may not
disapprove our appearing acquainted even with the actions of which our sex boasts? We are
at least certain, that he cannot be a good citizen who will not applaud our efforts for the relief
of the armies which defend our lives, our possessions, our liberty? The situation of our soldiery
has been represented to me; the evils inseparable from war, and the firm and generous spirit
which has enabled them to support these. But it has been said, that they may apprehend, that,
in the course of a long war, the view of their distresses may be lost, and their services be forgotten. Forgotten! never; I can answer in the name of all my sex. Brave Americans, your
disinterestedness, your courage, and your constancy will always be dear to America, as long
as she shall preserve her virtue.

We know that at a distance from the theatre of war, if we enjoy any tranquility, it is the
fruit of your watchings, your labours, your dangers. If I live happy in the midst of my family;
if my husband cultivates his field, and reaps his harvest in peace; if, surrounded with my
children, I myself nourish the youngest, and press it to my bosom, without being affraid
of seeing myself separated from it, by a ferocious enemy; if the house in which we dwell; if
our barns, our orchards are safe at the present time from the hands of those incendiaries, it is
to you that we owe it. And shall we hesitate to evidence to you our gratitude? Shall we hesitate
to wear a cloathing more simple; hair dressed less elegant, while at the price of this small privation, we shall deserve your benedictions. Who, amongst us, will not renounce with the highest
pleasure, those vain ornaments, when she shall consider that the valiant defenders of America will be able to draw some advantage from the money which she may have laid out in these;
that they will be better defended from the rigours of the seasons, that after their painful toils,
they will receive some extraordinary and unexpected relief; that these presents will perhaps
be valued by them at a greater price, when they will have it in their power to say: *This is
the offering of the Ladies.* The time is arrived to display the same sentiments which animated
us at the beginning of the Revolution, when we renounced the use of teas, however agreeable to our taste, rather than receive them from our persecutors; when we made it appear to
them that we placed former necessaries in the rank of superfluities, when our liberty was interested; when our republican and laborious hands spun the flax, prepared the linen intended
for the use of our soldiers; when exiles and fugitives we supported with courage all the evils
which are the concomitants of war. Let us not lose a moment; let us be engaged to offer the homage of our gratitude at the altar of military valour, and you, our brave deliverers, while mer-
cenary slaves combat to cause you to share with them, the irons with which they are loaded, receive with a free hand our offering, the purest which can be presented to your virtue,

BY AN AMERICAN WOMAN.

16. *Procession.*
Boston, Oct. 19, 1789.

One aspect of American life just after the Revolution which must not be ignored is patriotism. Much excitement was generated by a presidential visit to a town. For this visit by George Washington, a procession was arranged and a large triumphal arch was erected.

Apart from the patriotic aspect of this document, it is interesting to note the variety of artisans and tradesmen in Boston in 1789. Their protocol is also noteworthy. Rather than listing the various trades in order of importance, the organizers of the procession had to resort to an alphabetical arrangement so that no one trade would feel slighted.

Evans 21701
10 ⅛ × 15 ¾

Procession.

BOSTON, OCT. 19, 1789.

AS this town is shortly to be honoured with a visit from THE PRESIDENT of the United States: In order that we may pay our respects to him, in a manner whereby every inhabitant may see so illustrious and amiable a character, and to prevent the disorder and danger which must ensue from a great assembly of people without order, a Committee appointed by a respectable number of inhabitants, met for the purpose, recommend to their Fellow-Citizens to arrange themselves in the following order, in a

PROCESSION.

IT is also recommended, that the person who shall be chosen as head of each order of Artizans, Tradesmen, Manufacturers, &c. shall be known by displaying a WHITE FLAG, with some device thereon expressive of their several callings—and to be numbered as in the arrangement that follows, which is alphabetically disposed, in order to give general satisfaction.---- The Artizans, &c. to display such insignia of their craft, as they can conveniently carry in their hands. That uniformity may not be wanting, it is desired that the several Flag-staffs be SEVEN feet long, and the Flags a YARD SQUARE.

ORDER OF PROCESSION.

MUSICK.

The Selectmen,		Goldsmiths and Jewellers,	No. 17.
Overseers of the Poor,		Hair-Dressers,	No. 18.
Town Treasurer,		Hatters and Furriers,	No. 19.
Town Clerk,		House Carpenters,	No. 20.
Magistrates,		Leather Dressers, and Leather-Breeches Makers,	No. 21.
Consuls of France and Holland,		Limners and Portrait Painters,	No. 22.
The Officers of his Most Christian Majesty's Squadron,		Masons,	No. 23.
The Rev. Clergy,		Mast-makers,	No. 24.
Physicians,		Mathematical Instrument-makers,	No. 25.
Lawyers,		Millers,	No. 26.
Merchants and Traders,		Painters,	No. 27.
Marine Society,		Paper Stainers,	No. 28.
Masters of vessels,		Pewterers,	No. 29.
Revenue Officers,		Printers, Book-binders and Stationers,	No. 30.
Strangers, who may wish to attend.		Riggers,	No. 31.
Bakers,	No. 1.	Rope-makers,	No. 32.
Blacksmiths, &c.	No. 2.	Saddlers,	No. 33.
Block-makers,	No. 3.	Sail-makers,	No. 34.
Boat-builders,	No. 4.	Shipwrights, to include Caulkers, Ship-Joiners, Head-builders and Sawyers,	No. 35.
Cabinet and Chair-makers,	No. 5.	Sugar-boilers,	No. 36.
Card-makers,	No. 6.	Tallow-Chandlers, &c.	No. 37.
Carvers,	No. 7.	Tanners,	No. 38.
Chaise and Coach-makers,	No. 8.	Taylors,	No. 39.
Clock and Watch-makers,	No. 9.	Tin-plate Workers,	No. 40.
Coopers,	No. 10.	Tobacconists,	No. 41.
Coppersmiths, Braziers and Founders,	No. 11.	Truckmen,	No. 42.
Cordwainers, &c.	No. 12.	Turners,	No. 43.
Distillers,	No. 13.	Upholsterers,	No. 44.
Duck Manufacturers,	No. 14.	Wharfingers,	No. 45.
Engravers,	No. 15.	Wheelwrights,	No. 46.
Glaziers and Plumbers,	No. 16.	Seamen,	

N. B.—In the above arrangement, some trades are omitted—from the idea, that they would incorporate themselves with the branches mentioned, to which they are generally attached. For instance—it is supposed, that under the head of *Blacksmiths*, the Armourers, Cutlers, Whitesmiths and other workers in iron, would be included; and the same with respect to other trades.

EACH division of the above arrangement is requested to meet on such parade as it may agree on, and march into the Mall—No. 1 of the Artizans, &c. forming at the South-end thereof. The Marshals will then direct in what manner the Procession will move to meet the President on his arrival in town. When the front of the Procession arrives at the extremity of the town, it will halt, and the whole will then be directed to open the column—one half of each rank moving to the right, and the other half to the left—and then face inwards, so as to form an avenue through which the President is to pass, to the galleries to be erected at the State-House.

IT is requested that the several School-masters conduct their Scholars to the neighbourhood of the State-House, and form them in such order as the Marshals shall direct.

THE Marine Society is desired to appoint some persons to arrange and accompany the seamen.

17. *The Launch. A Federal Song.*
[*Boston*, 1789.]

Patriotic sentiments were expressed very strongly in the songs of the people. "The Launch" was composed, appropriately enough, for the launching of the *Merrimack* on October 12, 1798. Her maiden voyage to the Windward Islands was made to protect American merchantmen during the naval conflict with France during John Adams' administration. In June of 1799, the American vessel captured her first prize, *L'Magicienne* (sic), which the French had seized from the American Navy in November of 1798. The *Merrimack* served in the Caribbean until 1801, when she returned to Boston and was sold by the Navy.

Evans 48501
10 ¼ × 17 ⅝

THE

Launch,

A FEDERAL SONG.

YE Sons of COLUMBIA, your ardour display,
    With true Federal Spirit, on this joyful day;
When the MERRIMACK, in speed is bending her course,
The Trade of COLUMBIA, to protect by main force.

Let true Federal mirth be seen in each face,
No *Jacobin* or *Traitor* your company disgrace;
But shew your dislike to such characters as these,
And tell them they're welcome to the *Fraternal Squeeze*.

See the Eagle assuming her right for to reign,
Her wings on a flutter, those rights to maintain;
While commerce denotes the pursuits we explore—
The Seas of the World from America's shore.

See *Justice*, the guide by which we'll maintain
Our *rights* on the Land, and our *claim* on the Main—
By Justice we make all *our* actions to square,
Whether Peace be our fortune, or destiny—WAR.

With *Barry* and *Nicholson*, and brave Captain *Brown*,
We've nothing to fear from *Talleyrand's* frown;
His millions demanded—we'll pay in a scroll,
Well tinctur'd with Powder, and display'd by a Ball.

Let the French & the Dutch, their own contracts attend,
And *Talleyrand* with *rescriptions* his *associates* befriend;
While ADAMS and WASHINGTON stands at the helm,
We'll mind our own business, and leave their's to them.

To confide in the wisdom of patriots thus try'd,
(Tho the French and all Europe, their virtues deride)
Is the duty of all, whose wish is to share
A right in the glory of COLUMBIA so fair.

The Directory of France, with all their deceit,
May sound false alarms—our spirits to defeat;
Still we've men at the helm, who with wisdom can shi[e]
And track them in Council, as well as in field.

Our Constitution and laws, by our father's design'd
To render us happy—and useful and kind;
We'll freely support—with our lives and estates,
Without hesitation or lengthy debates.

By three captur'd Frenchmen, safe lodg'd on our sho[re]
Some pence is recover'd, to replenish our store;
Tho' millions beside have been robb'd from our land,
We'll make them to tremble, *and refund cash in hand.*

No peace with such robbers, 'till down on their knees,
They beg of us pardon—and pay for the SQUEEZE;
'Till all their proud hearts are melted as one,
And promise us treble for mischief they've done.

And now, my brave friends, let's each one unite,
In wishing the MERRIMACK a sure and quick flight;
From the cradle to that element—design'd for her station,
To bravely oppose the proud foes of our Nation.

FINIS.

18. *A Proclamation. By the President of the United States of America.*
[Boston]: Young & Minns, 1800.

If Washington was admired and revered during his lifetime, this devotion became even more intense after his death. This broadside reprints the official proclamation which made February 22, Washington's birthday, a day of public mourning. There was a great number of public addresses given thereafter on this date, for over one hundred of these were printed and are still in existence.

Evans 37921

14 ⅞ × 19 ¼

A Proclamation.

By the President of the United States of America.

WHEREAS the Congress of the United States have this day Resolved, "That it be Recommended to the People of the United States to assemble on the *twenty-second day of February next*, in such numbers and manner, as may be convenient, publickly to testify their Grief for the Death of Gen. GEORGE WASHINGTON, by suitable Eulogies, Orations, and Discourses, or by Public Prayers:" and, "That the President be requested to issue a Proclamation for the purpose of carrying the foregoing Resolution into effect." Now, Therefore, I, JOHN ADAMS, President of the United States of America, do hereby Proclaim the same accordingly.

Given under my Hand and the Seal of the United States, at Philadelphia, the sixth day of January, in the year of our Lord, one thousand eight hundred, and of the Independence of the said States the twenty-fourth.

JOHN ADAMS.

By the President,
TIMOTHY PICKERING, *Secretary of State.*

Commonwealth of Massachusetts.

In Senate, January 14, 1800.

RESOLVED, 1*st*, That an Oration on the Sublime Virtues of Gen. GEORGE WASHINGTON be delivered before the *Lieutenant-Governor*, the *Council*, and the two Branches of the *General Court*, in the Old-South-Meeting-House, in *Boston*, [with consent of the Proprietors thereof] by such Person, and at such time, as His Honor the *Lieutenant-Governor*, the *President* of the *Senate* and the *Speaker* of the *House* of *Representatives* shall appoint for that purpose; and that the *Chaplain* of the *General Court* be requested to introduce the Exercises with Prayer to the Throne of Grace. *N. B. The first Resolve need not be communicated*

2d, That the *Lieutenant-Governor*, the *Council*, and the two Branches of the *General Court*, will, in compliance with the Recommendation of Congress, in their Resolve of the 30th of December last, "testify our Grief for the Death of General GEORGE WASHINGTON," by uniting in Public Solemn Worship of the Deity in the Church in Brattle-Street in *Boston*, [with consent of the Proprietors] on *Saturday the twenty-second day of February next*, at eleven of the Clock in the Forenoon, (if the General Court shall then be in Session) and will then bow in humble Adoration and Prayer before the Supreme Disposer of all Events, and to attend upon a Discourse to be adapted to the occasion; that we will suspend our usual business for this purpose; and that the *Chaplain* of the *General Court* be requested to deliver that Discourse, and to lead in the other Religious Exercises of the Day.

AND we have confidence, that our Fellow Citizens, of all denominations, throughout the Commonwealth, will then unite in like Services, so that the whole People, with one Heart and one Voice, may, at the same time, duly express their Sensations on this Mournful Occasion.

Sent down for Concurrence,

SAMUEL PHILLIPS, *President.*

In the House of Representatives, Jan. 14, 1800. Read and Concurred,

EDWARD H. ROBBINS, *Speaker.*

January 14, 1800. By the Lieutenant-Governor Approved,

MOSES GILL.

A True Copy—Attest,

JOHN AVERY, *Secretary.*

PRINTED BY *YOUNG & MINNS*, PRINTERS TO THE STATE.

EDUCATION

19. [*Cotton Mather*] *Rules For the Society of Negroes.* 1693.
[*Boston: Bartholomew Green, 1706-1713.*]

In Cotton Mather's diary for December 1693, there is the following entry:
"Besides the other praying and pious Meetings, which I have been continually
serving, in our Neighbourhood, a little after this Time [October 10, 1693, was
previously mentioned], a company of poor Negroes, of their own Accord,
addressed mee, for my Countenance, to a Design which they had, of erecting
such a Meeting for the Welfare of their miserable Nation that were servants
among us." Mather continues, describing the meeting and listing the several
points on which he counseled them. The rules were probably printed soon
after the meeting in 1693. The present broadside is a later edition, for Cotton
Mather only lists eight rules in his diary. The ninth one makes a reference
to a book which Mather wrote in 1706, *The Negro Christianized*, so this
broadside must have been printed after 1706. On the back of it, there is a note
in the hand of Samuel Sewell: "Left at my house for me, when I was not
at home, by Spaniard Dr. Mather's Negro; March 23. 1713/14."

There may well be more sincerity in this piece than apparent condescension
since Mather also wrote at the same time a set of nine rules for a religious
society of young men in Boston. They were published in *Early Religion,
Urged in a Sermon* (Boston, 1694).

Evans 1653
7 ½ × 12 ¼

RULES
For the Society of
NEGROES. 1693.

WE the Miserable Children of *Adam*, and of *Noah*, thankfully Admiring and Accepting the Free-Grace of GOD, that Offers to Save us from our Miseries, by the Lord Jesus Christ, freely Resolve, with His Help, to become the Servants of that Glorious LORD.

And that we may be Assisted in the Service of our *Heavenly Master*, we now Join together in a SOCIETY, wherein the fallowing RULES are to be observed.

I. It shall be our Endeavour, to Meet in the *Evening* after the *Sabbath*; and *Pray* together by Turns, one to Begin, and another to Conclude the Meeting; And between the two *Prayers*, a *Psalm* shall be Sung, and a *Sermon* Repeated.

II. Our coming to the Meeting, shall never be without the *Leave* of such as have Power over us: And we will be Careful, that our Meeting may Begin and Conclude between the Hours of *Seven* and *Nine*; and that we may not be *unseasonably Absent* from the Families whereto we pertain.

III. As we will, with the Help of God, at all Times avoid all *Wicked Company*, so we will Receive none into our Meeting, but such as have sensibly *Reformed* their Lives from all manner of Wickedness. And therefore, None shall be Admitted, without the Knowledge and Consent of the *Minister* of God in this Place; unto whom we will also carry every Person, that seeks for *Admission* among us; to be by Him Examined, Instructed and Exhorted.

IV. We will, as often as may be, Obtain some Wise and Good Man, of the *English* in the Neighbourhood, and especially the Officers of the Church, to look in upon us, and by their Presence and Counsil, do what they think fitting for us.

V. If any of our Number, fall into the Sin of *Drunkenness*, or *Swearing*, or *Cursing*, or *Lying*, or *Stealing*, or notorious *Disobedience* or *Unfaithfulness* unto their Masters, we will *Admonish* him of his Miscarriage, and Forbid his coming to the Meeting, for at least *one Fortnight*; And except he then come with great Signs and Hopes of his *Repentance*, we will utterly Exclude him, with Blotting his *Name* out of our List.

VI. If any of our Society Defile himself with *Fornication*, we will give him our *Admonition*; and so, debar him from the Meeting, at least *half a Year*: Nor shall he Return to it, ever any more, without Exemplary Testimonies of his becoming a *New Creature*.

VII. We will, as we have Opportunity, set our selves to do all the Good we can, to the other *Negro-Servants* in the Town; And if any of them should, at unfit Hours, be *Abroad*, much more, if any of them should *Run away* from their Masters, we will afford them *no Shelter*: But we will do what in us lies, that they may be discovered, and punished. And if any *of us*, are found Faulty, in this Matter, they shall be no longer *of us*.

VIII. None of our Society shall be *Absent* from our Meeting, without giving a *Reason* of the Absence; And if it be found, that any have pretended unto their *Owners*, that they came unto the *Meeting*, when they were otherwise and elsewhere Employ'd, we will faithfully *Inform* their Owners, and also do what we can to Reclaim such Person from all such Evil Courses for the Future.

IX. It shall be expected from every one in the Society, that he learn the *Catechism*; And therefore, it shall be one of our usual Exercises, for one of us, to ask the *Questions*, and for all the rest in their Order, to say the *Answers* in the *Catechism*; Either, The *New-English* Catechism, or the *Assemblies* Catechism, or the Catechism in the *Negro Christianized.*

20. *Pennsylvania. By the President and Supreme Executive Council of the Commonwealth of Pennsylvania, A Proclamation.*
[Philadelphia]: Francis Bailey, [1782].

This Pennsylvania Proclamation represents an attempt to suppress "vice, profaneness and immorality" by legislation. Similar laws were enacted by other states at the same time. Whether these acts had any effect is debatable. In Pennsylvania the legislature was ready to amend the law by 1793. In that year a group of clergymen from Philadelphia petitioned the legislature to extend the law against vice and immorality to include a prohibition of the theater.

The emphasis in the broadside and in the 1793 movement against the theater was that youth was easily affected by evil influences. The ministers stated in 1793 "and they [youth], moreover, form that part of the community who should have their principles guarded by the most solicitous care." The broadside also stresses the resulting moral benefits of good and careful education.

Evans 17664

13 × 16 ¼

PRINTED BY   FRANCIS BAILEY.

PENNSYLVANIA, *ſſ*.

By the PRESIDENT and SUPREME EXECUTIVE COUNCIL of the Commonwealth of *Pennsylvania,*

A PROCLAMATION.

AS the beſt and greateſt of Beings commanded mankind into exiſtence with a capacity for happineſs, beſtowing upon them underſtanding and many "*good gifts*"; ſo when they, by an abuſe of the bleſſings thus intruſted, had involved themſelves in guilt and miſery, his compaſſion was extended towards them, and in "*his tender mercies,*" not only "*ſeed time and harveſt, and cold and heat, and ſummer and winter, and day and night,*" were continued unto them, but "*the eternal purpoſes*" were revealed, and the heavenly treaſuries opened, to reſtore the human race to the tranſcendent privilege from which by tranſgreſſion they were fallen: AND in this "*marvellous work,*" the laws of righteouſneſs have been with ſuch infinite wiſdom adjuſted, and united to the obligations of nature, that while they jointly tended to promote the felicity of men in a future ſtate, they evidently co-operate to advance their welfare in the preſent, and to offend againſt the ſanctions of revelation, or the dictates of reaſon and conſcience, is aſſuredly to betray the joys of this life, as well as thoſe of another:

WHEREFORE, as we are entirely perſuaded that juſt impreſſions of the Deity are the great ſupports of morality, AND AS the experience of ages demonſtrates, that regularity of manners is eſſential to the tranquillity and proſperity of ſocieties, AND the aſſiſtance of the ALMIGHTY, on which we rely, to eſtabliſh the ineſtimable bleſſings our afflicted country is contending for, cannot be expected without an obſervance of his holy laws; We eſteem it our principal and indiſpenſable duty to endeavour, as much as we can, that a ſenſe of theſe intereſting truths may prevail in the hearts and appear in the lives of the inhabitants of this ſtate; AND THEREFORE have thought proper to iſſue this Proclamation, ſincerely deſiring that they, ſeriouſly meditating on the many ſignal and unmerited benefits of public and private import conferred upon them, the affecting invitations and munificent promiſes of divine goodneſs, and the "*terrors ſet in array*" againſt the diſobedient, may be urged to exert themſelves in avoiding, diſcountenancing, and ſuppreſſing all vice, profaneneſs and immorality, and feeling a due gratitude, love, and veneration for their moſt gracious, all-wiſe, and omnipotent Benefactor, Sovereign, and Judge, and a correſpondent temper of reſignation to the diſpenſations of his Supreme Government, may become a people "*truſting in him, in whom they live and move, and doing good.*"

AND TO THE INTENT that theſe deſireable ends may be forwarded, all perſons are hereby fervently exhorted, to obſerve the LORD's DAY, commonly called Sunday, and thereon conſtantly to attend the worſhip of GOD, as a ſervice pleaſing to him who is, "*a hearer of prayer,*" and condeſcends to "*inhabit the praiſes of his people,*" and profitable to themſelves; a neglect of which duty has, in a multitude of inſtances, been the beginning of a deviation into the ways of preſumption, that at length have led into the deepeſt diſtreſſes and ſevereſt ſorrows:

AND AS the education of youth is of ſo much moment to themſelves and to the commonwealth, which cannot flouriſh unleſs that important point be diligently regarded, the ſentiments, diſpoſitions, and habits being then generally formed that pervade the reſt of their lives, all parents, guardians, maſters, and tutors are hereby ſtrenuouſly called upon, to diſcharge the high truſt committed to them, and for which they muſt account, by a faithful attention; that thoſe under their care may be nurtured in piety, filial reverence, ſubmiſſion to ſuperiors in age or ſtation, modeſty, ſincerity, benevolence, temperance, induſtry, conſiſtency of behaviour, and a frugality regulated by an humble reliance on Providence, and a kind reſpect for others; that their inexperienced minds may be by wholeſome inſtructions fully convinced, that whatever employment they are deſigned for, virtue will be a chief promoter of ſucceſs, and irregularity of conduct the greateſt obſtacle to it; that the intellectual faculties are aided by moral improvements, but weakened by illicit courſes; and, in brief, that Religion is the friend of their peace, health and happineſs; and that to diſpleaſe their Maker, or to treſpaſs againſt their neighbour, is inevitably to injure themſelves.

AND we expect and hereby require, that all well diſpoſed perſons, and eſpecially thoſe in places of authority, will by their converſation and demeanor encourage and promote piety and virtue, and to their utmoſt contribute to the rendering theſe qualities truly laudable and honourable, and the contrary practices juſtly ſhameful and contemptible; that thus the influence of good men, and the dignity of the laws, may be combined in repreſſing the follies and inſolencies of ſcorners and profligates, in directing the weak and thoughtleſs, and in preſerving them from the pernicious contagion of evil examples: AND for further promoting ſuch reformation, it is hereby enjoined, that all magiſtrates, and others whom it may concern, be very vigilant and exact in diſcovering, proſecuting, and puniſhing all perſons who ſhall be guilty of profanation of the LORD's DAY, commonly called Sunday, blaſphemy, profane ſwearing or curſing, drunkenneſs, lewdneſs, or other diſſolute or immoral practices; that they ſuppreſs all gaming houſes, and other diſorderly houſes; that they put in execution the act of General Aſſembly, entitled, "*An Act for the ſuppreſſion of Vice and Immorality,*" and all other laws now in force for the puniſhing and ſuppreſſing any vice, profaneneſs or immorality: AND for the more effectual proceeding herein, all Judges and Juſtices, having cognizance in the premiſes, are directed to give ſtrict charges at their reſpective Courts and Seſſions, for the due proſecution and puniſhment of all who ſhall preſume to offend in any of the kinds aforeſaid; and alſo of all ſuch as, contrary to their duty, ſhall be remiſs or negligent in putting the laws in execution: And that they do at their reſpective Courts and Seſſions cauſe this Proclamation to be publicly read, immediately before the charge is given: AND every Miniſter of the Goſpel is requeſted ſtrongly to inculcate in the reſpective congregations where they officiate, a love of piety and virtue, and an abhorrence of vice, profaneneſs, and immorality.

GIVEN in Council, under the hand of the Preſident, and the Seal of the State, at Philadelphia, this twentieth day of November, in the year of our Lord one thouſand ſeven hundred and eighty two.

ATTEST.   **JOHN DICKINSON.**

T. MATLACK, SECRETARY.

GOD SAVE THE COMMONWEALTH.

21. *Recommendations to the Schoolmasters, . . . Boston, the 15th of October* 1789.
[*Boston,* 1789.]

On September 15, 1789, the Town Clerk of Boston called for a meeting of the freeholders and other inhabitants of the Town at Faneuil Hall on September 23 "to consider the Proposals of a large number of respectable Inhabitants of the Town, for the instruction of the Youth of both sexes; and for reforming the present system of public education." A pamphlet, "The System of Public Education Adopted by the Town of Boston," and this broadside resulted from the meeting.

The description of treatment of students and of the values which the teachers were supposed to inculcate in their young charges make this "Recommendations to the Schoolmasters" of more than passing interest. Educators in the early years of the Republic were optimistic about the future of the country and believed that education should play a large role. Noah Webster asserted in 1790 that "the education of youth is, in all governments, an object of the first consequence. The impressions received in early life usually form the characters of individuals, a union of which forms the general character of a nation."

Evans 45443
8 ⅛ × 11 ½

RECOMMENDATIONS to the SCHOOLMASTERS,

by the Committee appointed to carry into execution the System of public Education, adopted by the Town of BOSTON, the 15th of October 1789.

THAT the Schoolmasters consider themselves as in the place of Parents to the children under their care, and endeavour to convince them by their mild treatment, that they feel a parental affection for them.

That they be sparing as to threatnings or promises, but punctual in the execution of the one and the performance of the other.

That they never make dismission from school, at an earlier hour than usual, a reward for attention or diligence ; but endeavour to lead the children to consider being at school as a privilege, and dismission from it as a punishment.

That they never strike the children on the head, either with the hand or any instrument ; nor authorize one scholar to inflict any corporal punishment on another.

That, when circumstances admit, they suspend inflicting punishment 'till some time after the offence committed, or conviction of the offence.

That, as far as is practicable, they exclude corporal punishment from the schools ; and, particularly, that they never inflict it on females.

That they introduce such rewards as are adapted to stimulate the ingenuous passions of the children.

That they inculcate upon the scholars the propriety of good behaviour, during their absence from school.

That they frequently address their pupils on moral and religious subjects ; endeavouring to impress their minds with a sense of the being and providence of God, and the obligations they are under to love, serve, and pray to him ; their duty to their parents and masters ; the beauty and excellence of truth, justice, and mutual love ; tenderness to brute creatures, and the sinfulness of tormenting them and wantonly destroying their lives ; the happy tendency of self-government and obedience to the dictates of reason and religion ; the duty which they owe their country, and the necessity of a strict obedience to its laws ; and that they caution them against the prevailing vices, such as sabbath-breaking, profane cursing and swearing, gaming, idleness, writing obscene words on the fences, &c.

That, for the sake of uniformity, in the government of the schools, the Masters, in conference together, form systems of rules for the observance of the children, and present them to the Committee for their approbation ; which, being approved, shall be considered as the standing Laws of the Schools.

CRIMINALS

22. *The Declaration, Dying Warning and Advice of Rebekah Chamblit.*
Boston: S. Kneeland & T. Green, [1733].

This confession of Rebekah Chamblit is one of the earliest examples of its type in the colonies. One purpose of these confessions was to warn youth against the evils of a life devoted to crime.

This broadside was published immediately after the execution. In the *Boston Weekly News-Letter* for September 27, 1733, appears an announcement of the publication of the broadside which was issued according to the express wishes of the dying woman. The law which she violated was entitled "An Act to prevent the destroying and murdering of Bastard Children." This same Declaration was appended to a sermon, "Lessons of Caution to Young Sinners," delivered by Thomas Foxcroft.

The type used for Rebekah Chamblit's name in the title is very different from the type commonly used in America during the early eighteenth century. Rather, it is very similar to French sixteenth century italic type.

Evans 3639
12 ¼ × 15 ⅜

The Declaration, Dying Warning and Advice of

Rebekah Chamblit

A Young Woman Aged near Twenty-seven Years, Executed at *Boston* September 27th. 1733. according to the Sentence pass'd upon her at the Superiour Court holden there for the County of *Suffolk*, in *August* last, being then found Guilty of *Felony*, in concealing the Birth of her spurious Male Infant, of which she was Deliver'd when alone the Eighth Day of *May* last, and was afterwards found Dead, as will more fully appear by the following Declaration, which was carefully taken from her own Mouth.

BEING under the awful Apprehensions of my Execution now in a few Hours; and being desirous to do all the Good I can, before I enter the Eternal World, I now in the fear of GOD, give this Declaration and Warning to the Living.

I Was very tenderly brought up, and well Instructed in my Father's House, till I was Twelve Years of Age; but alass, my Childhood wore off in vanity. However, as I grew in Years, my Youth was under very sensible Impressions from the SPIRIT of GOD; and I was awakened to seek and obtain Baptism, when I was about Sixteen Years of Age; and lived for some time with a strictness somewhat answerable to the Obligations I was thereby brought under. But within two or three Years after this, I was led away into the Sin of Uncleanness, from which time I think I may date my Ruin for this World. After this, I became again more watchful, and for several Years kept my self from the like Pollutions, until those for which I am now to suffer.

And as it may be necessary, so doubtless it will be expected of me, that I give the World a particular account of that great Sin, with the aggravations of it, which has brought me to this Shameful Death: And accordingly in the fear of GOD, at whose awful Tribunal I am immediately to appear, I solemnly declare as follows;

That on Saturday the Fifth Day of *May* last, being then something more than Eight Months gone with Child, as I was about my Houshold Business reaching some Sand from out of a large Cask, I received considerable hurt, which put me into great Pain, and so I continued till the Tuesday following; in all which time I am not sensible I felt any Life or Motion in the Child within me; when, on the said Tuesday the Eighth Day of *May*, I was Deliver'd when alone of a Male Infant; in whom I did not perceive Life; but still uncertain of Life in it, I threw it into the Vault about two or three Minutes after it was born; *uncertain,* I say, whether it was a living or dead Child; tho', I confess its probable there was Life in it, and some Circumstances seem to confirm it. I therefore own the Justice of GOD and Man in my Condemnation, and take Shame to my self, as I have none but my self to Blame; and am sorry for any rash Expressions I have at any time uttered since my Condemnation; and I am verily persuaded there is no Place in the World, where there is a more strict regard to Justice than in this Province.

And now as a Soul going into Eternity, I most earnestly and solemnly Warn all Persons, particularly YOUNG PEOPLE, and more especially those of my own Sex, against the Sins which their Age peculiarly exposes them to; and as the Sin of Uncleanness has brought me into these distressing Circumstances, I would with the greatest Importunity Caution and Warn against it, being perswaded of the abounding of that Sin in this Town and Land. I thought my self as secure, a little more than a Year ago, as many of you now do; but by woful Experience I have found, that Lust when it has conceived bringeth forth Sin, and Sin when it is finished bringeth forth Death; it exposes the Soul not only to Temporal, but to Eternal Death. And therefore as a Dying Person, let me call upon you to forsake the foolish and live: Do not accompany with those you know to be such, and if Sinners entice you do not consent. I am sensible there are many Houses in this Town, that may be called Houses of Uncleanness, and Places of dreadful Temptations to this and all other Sins. O shun them, for they lead down to the Chambers of Death and Eternal Misery.

My misspence of precious Sabbaths, lies as a heavy burden upon me; that when I might have gone to the House of GOD, I have been indifferent, and suffer'd a small matter to keep me from it. What would I now give, had I better improv'd the Lord's Day! I tell you, verily, your lost Sabbaths will sit heavy upon you, when you come into the near prospect of Death and Eternity.

The Sin of Lying I have to bewail, and wou'd earnestly caution against; not that I have took so great a pleasure in Lying; but I have often done so to conceal my Sin: Certainly you had better suffer Shame and Disgrace, yea the greatest Punishment, than to hide and conceal your Sin, by Lying. How much better had it been for me, to have confess'd my Sin, than by hiding of it to provoke a holy GOD, thus to suffer it to find me out. But I hope I heartily desire to bless GOD, that even in this way, He is thus entring into Judgment with me; for I have often thought, had I been let alone to go on undiscovered in my Sins, I might have provok'd Him to leave me to a course of Rebellion, that would have ripen'd me for a more sudden, and everlasting Destruction; and am fully convinc'd of this, that I should have had no solid ease or quiet in my mind, but the Guilt of this undiscover'd Sin lying upon my Conscience, would have been a tormenting Rack unto me all my Days; whereas now I hope GOD has discover'd to me in some measure the evil of this, and all my other Sins, and enabled me to repent of them in Dust and Ashes; and made me earnestly desire and plead with Him for pardon and cleansing in the precious Blood of the REDEEMER of lost and perishing Sinners: And I think I can say, I have had more comfort and satisfaction within the Walls of this Prison, than ever I had in the ways of Sin among my vain Companions, and think I wou'd not for a World, nay for ten Thousand Worlds have my liberty in Sin again, and be in the same Condition I was in before I came into this Place.

I had the advantage of living in several religious Families; but alass, I disregarded the Instructions and Warnings I there had, which is now a bitterness to me; and so it will be to those of you who are thus favoured, but go on unmindful of GOD, and deaf to all the Reproofs and Admonitions that are given you for the good of your Souls. And I would advise those of my own Sex especially, to chuse to go into religious Families, where the Worship and Fear of GOD is maintained, and submit your selves to the Orders and Government of them.

In my younger Years I maintain'd a constant course of Secret Prayer for some time; but afterwards neglecting the same, I found by experience, that upon my thus leaving GOD, He was provoked to forsake me, and at length suffer'd me to fall into that great and complicated Sin that has brought me to this Death: Mind me, I first left GOD, and then He left me: I therefore solemnly call upon YOUNG PEOPLE to cherish the Convictions of GOD's Holy SPIRIT, and be sure keep up a constant course of fervent Secret Prayer.

And now I am just entring into the Eternal World, I do in the fear of GOD, and before Witnesses, call upon our YOUNG PEOPLE in particular, to secure an Interest in the Lord JESUS CHRIST, and in those precious Benefits He has purchased for His People; for surely the favour of GOD, thro' CHRIST, is more worth than a whole World: And O what Comfort will this yield you when you come to that awful Day and Hour I am now arriving unto. I must tell you the World appears to me vain and empty, nothing like what it did in my past Life, my Days of Sin and Vanity, and as doubtless it appears now to you. Will you be perswaded by me to that which will yield you the best Satisfaction and Pleasure here, and which will prepare you for the more abundant Pleasures of GOD's Right Hand for evermore.

Sign'd and Acknowleg'd in the Presence of divers Witnesses, with a desire that it may be publish'd to the World, and read at the Place of Execution.

Rebekah Chamblit.

September 26th.
1733

BOSTON: Printed and Sold by *S. Kneeland* and *T. Green*, in Queen-street.

23. *Mr. Occom's Address to his Indian Brethren.* *[No place, 1772.]*

Samson Occom was an Indian who became an ordained minister and a missionary to the Indians. Rather than preach theology to the Indians, he preferred to exhort them to righteous behavior, as is emphasized in this poem.

Moses Paul, the criminal, was born in Barnstable, Massachusetts, in 1742 and became a member of the Provincial Regiment under Colonel Putnam. Later he went to sea in the service of merchants. After the murder, he was duly tried, sentenced and executed. Occom also preached a sermon on the execution day which was printed in about twenty editions. There are several other broadside editions of this poem which are still extant.

Evans 42362a

8 ½ × 13 ⅝

Mr. Occom's Addreſs

TO

HIS

INDIAN

BRETHREN.

On the Day that MOSES PAUL, an Indian, was executed at NEW-HAVEN, on the 2d of SEPTEMBER, 1772, for the Murder of MOSES COOK.

I.

MY kindred Indians, pray attend and hear,
With great attention and with godly fear;
This day I warn you of that curſed ſin,
That poor, deſpiſed Indians wallow in.

II.

'Tis drunkenneſs, this is the ſin you know,
Has been and is poor Indians overthrow;
'Twas drunkenneſs that was the leading cauſe,
That made poor Moſes break God's righteous Laws.

III.

When drunk he other evil courſes took,
Thus hurried on, he murdered Moſes Cook;
Poor Moſes Paul muſt now be hang'd this day,
For wilful murder in a drunken fray.

IV.

A dreadful wo pronounc'd by God on high,
To all that in this ſin do lie;
O deviliſh beaſtly luſt, accurſed ſin,
Has almoſt ſtript us all of every thing.

V.

We've nothing valuable or to our praiſe,
And well may other nations on us gaze;
We have no money, credit or a name,
But what this ſin does turn to our great ſhame.

VI.

Mean are our houſes, and we are kept low,
And almoſt naked, ſhivering we go;
Pinch'd for food and almoſt ſtarv'd we are,
And many times put up with ſtinking fare.

VII.

Our little children hovering round us weep,
Moſt ſtarv'd to death we've nought for them to eat;
All this diſtreſs is juſtly on us come,
For the accurſed uſe we make of rum.

VIII.

A ſhocking, dreadful ſight we often ſee,
Our children young and tender, drunkards be;
More ſhocking yet and awful to behold,
Our women will get drunk both young and old.

IX.

Behold a drunkard in a drunken fit;
Incapable to go, ſtand, ſpeak, or ſit;
Deform'd in ſoul and every other part,
Affecting ſight! enough to melt one's heart.

X.

Sometimes he laughs, and then a hideous yell,
That almoſt equals the poor damn'd in hell;
When drown'd in drink we know not what we do,
We are deſpiſed and ſcorn'd and cheated too.

XI.

On level with the beaſts and far below
Are we when with ſtrong drink we reeling go;
Below the devils when in this ſin we run,
A drunken devil I never heard of one.

XII.

My kindred Indians, I intreat you all,
In this vile ſin never again to fall;
Fly to the blood of CHRIST, for that alone
Can for this ſin and all your ſins atone.

XIII.

Though Moſes Paul is here alive and well,
This night his ſoul muſt be in heaven or hell;
O! do take warning by this awful ſight,
And to a JESUS make a ſpeedy flight!

XIV.

You have no leaſe of your ſhort time you know,
To hell this night you may be forc'd to go;
Oh! do embrace an offer'd CHRIST to-day,
And get a ſealed pardon while you may.

XV.

Behold a loving JESUS, ſee him cry,
With earneſtneſs of ſoul, "Why will ye die?"
My kindred Indians, come juſt as you be,
Then Chriſt and his ſalvation you ſhall ſee.

XVI.

If you go on and ſtill reject Chriſt's call,
'Twill be too late, his curſe will on you fall;
The Judge will doom you to that dreadful place,
In hell, where you ſhall never ſee his face.

24. *The Last Words and Dying Speech of Levi Ames, . . . 21st Day of October*, 1773.
Boston, [1773].

The trial and execution of Levi Ames for burglary aroused much comment in Boston. Both his youthfulness and the fact that the others involved in the crime were not sentenced to death stimulated interest in the case. Ames' errant, larcenous youth was the subject of sermons and broadsides. Three poems—"The Dying Groans of Levi Ames", "An Exhortation to Young and Old . . .", and "The Speech of Death to Levi Ames"—are recorded in the collection of the Historical Society of Pennsylvania.

The account in the American Antiquarian Society is notable for the vivacious narrative presentation of Ames' career. A typical mixture of fact and ideal is discernable. One can readily see that the populace was as attracted by the accumulated details of crime as it was repulsed by the concept of it. If Levi's case left the good citizens of New England all the more convinced of the necessity of leading a virtuous life and resisting temptation, it also provided them with the practical admonition to keep their "doors and windows shut on evenings and secured well to prevent temptation."

The incomplete paragraph reads: "Some time last fall I saw Tho. Clark who told me he had seven pounds of plate hid, viz. a tankard, a number of table spoons, and one soup ditto; these he dug up while I was with him; we carried them away from that place and hid them in a stone wall, near a [barn] close to the sign of the bell on Wrenthan road, but he never informed me where he got them, or how he came by them; he offered me one half if I would dispose of them, but I was afraid to do it."

Evans 42401
14 ⅞ × 19 ¼

...or a small [parcel] of tea-spoons, with [...]
two pair of sugar tongs. I also stole from Mr. *Keith* at *Natick*,
two coats and jackets, with which I dressed myself when I came
to *Boston*; I gave *John Battle* twenty dollars to make up the matter with Mr. *Keith*, being part of the money I stole from Mr.
Hammond of *Waltham*. I stole ten or eleven dollars from Mr.
Symonds of *Lexington*, whose son in law Mr. *Meriam*, while I was
in prison, informed me where the money was and how to get it,
but he never received any of it; I supposed he gave me this information thro' envy against his father in law, thro' whose means
he was then confined for debt. I stole a pair of saddle bags at *Leaton's*
tavern in *Waltham*; the buckles were marked I. D. which I delivered to a man at *Marlborough*, a blacksmith, to make up with
him for some stockings I took from him; his name I do not remember. I twisted a padlock and enter'd the cellar of a Minister's house at *Marlborough*, I then went up the cellar stairs, light-
ed a candle in order to get some victuals. I have several times
taken sundry articles off of lines, hedges, fences, bushes, apple-
trees, grass, &c. but cannot recollect the owners. I stole two
great coats and sold them. I have left three shirts and
stole two pair of stockings at *Newbury-Port*: I
several pair of flockings at *Scipio Burriam's* at *Newbury-Port*: I
stole an ax out of
a cart and hid it in a stone wall between *Watertown* and *Boston*,
(the night before I took the money from Mr. *Hammond* in *Little-
Cambridge*, near to Mr. *Dana's* tavern, there I left it with a design
to sell it when I came back. I broke open the house of Mr. *Rice*
in *Marlborough*, on the Lord's day, while the people were gone to
public worship, having been advised to it by *Daniel Cook*, when we
were in *Concord* Goal; was taken in the house, and returned the
things to the owner.

Some [time last] fall I saw *Thos. Cook* who told me he had seven
[silver spoons?] [...] hid, viz. a tankard, a number of table spoons,
[and soup] ditto; these he dug up while I was with him; we
[carried them] away from that place and hid them in a stone wall,
[in a b]arn, close to the sign of the bull on *Wrentham* road, but
[neith]er informed me where he got them, or how he came by
them; he offered me half if I would dispose of them, but I was
afraid to do it.

Last *June* an Irishman who called his name *Thomas Smith*, of
middle feature, much marked with the small-pox, told me that he
knew of a watch which was taken from his excellency some time
ago, and I suspected that he was the person who stole it, because
he said he knew the governor's house well: He also assured me
that his Excellency had a considerable quantity of money in the
house, and asked me to go with him to get it. I denied,
knowing that the governor had many servants, which I urged as
a reason why I would not join him. He said he had one to assist him, whose name he would not tell me, unless I would be one
of the party. He further declared that he should go well armed
with swords and pistols. Upon this I absolutely refused, because
I never thought of murdering any man, in the midst of all my
scene of thieving. He thought to prevail on me by telling me that
there was a chest of dollars in the house but I would not go with
them.

In the same month, (*June*) I lodged at a tavern in *Killingsley*
or *Pomfret* in *Connecticut* government, on the Lord's day, where

to the desk, which we broke open with the chizels, [...]
led out the first drawer, and said there was small change in it,
which was all we could find. As he was going away, I pulled out
another drawer, in which I found a bag of silver coin.—After
that we came out, and went to fox-hill, near the powder-house,
where we hid the place, which we had kept in our pockets while
we were at supper, and when we entered Mr. *Bicker's* house. The
small change in silver, which *Atwood* took were equally divided,
tho' the gold which *Atwood* had then secreted I knew nothing of, nor did he ever give me any of it. Before supper I saw him at Mr. *Bell's*, when he informed me that a
warrant was out for me; he went with me to *Winisimit*, and advised me to go over the ferry, promising to meet me at *Portsmouth*
the Wednesday following at the house in which he was taken. I
returned again to *Boston* to see if any of my cloaths were done,
which I had bespoke; on Saturday I was taken by Mr. *Bicker* and
saw *Atwood* no more till I saw him in the
prison yard after he was apprehended.

Thus have I given an account of that shocking manner in which
I have filled up a short life, and of which I am now ashamed.
May God forgive me my dreadful wickedness, committed both
against him, and many worthy men, of whom also I would ask
forgiveness, it being not in my power to make restitution, which
if it was I would readily do it.—I also forgive from my heart *Joseph Atwood*, who swore on my tryal that I entered the house of
Mr. *Bicker* first, and let him in, when he knows in his conscience,
that he entered first and let me in. I die in charity with all mankind. But though I lived such a wicked life, it was not without
some severe checks of conscience. For, after I had stolen, I have
been so distressed at times, as to be obliged to go back, and throw
the stolen goods at the door, or into the yard, that the owners
might have them again.—And not long before I was taken
for this last robbery, I passed the gallows on *Boston* neck
with some stolen goods under my arm; when my conscience ter-
ribly smote me, and I tho't I should surely die there, if I did not
leave off this course of life. What I then feared, is now come
upon me.—

Having thus given an account of my dreadful life of wickedness, I would also mention the manner in which I have conducted,
and my mind has been exercised during my confinement in goal,
since the awful sentence of DEATH was pass'd upon me.

At first I had secret hopes of escape; that I should by some
means get out of prison. When I saw that it was impossible, I
endeavoured to reconcile myself as well as I could. My conscience made me uneasy—I thought I had been so wicked that I
should certainly go to Hell. And when I considered how short
my time was, I knew I could not do good works to go to Heaven.
To Hell then I was sure I should go. And I seemed to have
such an awful fight of Hell and the Grave, that I was very much
terrified indeed—I then took to drinking strong liquor in order
to drown my sorrow. But this would not do—I left that off and
took to reading my bible; my conscience became so uneasy, that
I could have no rest. O! a wounded conscience who can bear?
I tried to pray; but it came into my mind that the prayers of the
wicked would not be heard. Yet I could not help crying for

[...] 2. Parents and masters I entreat who have any concern for [...]
connection with children, to have an eye over their actions; and
to take special care for their precious and immortal souls.

3. All Persons whether old or young, who may see these lines,
spoke as it were by a poor, dying, sinful man, now bound in
chains, and who has but a short space of time before he must
launch into an endless eternity; guard against every temptation
to sin. If at any time you are tempted to do any thing like the
poor soul who now speaks to you, earnestly pray to God for
strength to resist the temptation, as well as for repentance for
your past sins.

The youth more especially I would solemnly caution against
the vices to which they are most inclin'd.—Such, as *bad Women*,
who have undone many, and by whom I also have suffered much;
the unlawful intercourse with them I have found by sad experience, leading to almost every sin. I also warn them to guard a-
gainst the first temptation to *disobedience to parents*. Had I regarded the many kind intreaties and reproofs of my tender Mother,
I had never come to this shameful and untimely death.

Profane *cursing and swearing* I also bear my dying testimony a-
gainst, as a horrid sin, and very provoking to God.

Nor must I omit to mention *gaming*, to which young people
are much inclin'd, and which at this day prevails to the ruin of
many. For when a youth hath gamed away all his money, he
will be tempted even to steal from his master or parents, in order
to get at it again. Besides, this sin leads to *drunkenness*; another
dreadful vice.

There is one sin more that I must warn all persons against, and
that is, *a profanation of the Lord's day, and of public worship*. Oh!
how many such days have I despised, and while others have been
engaged in serving God, I have been employed in wickedness,
which I now confess with grief of heart.

4. I have one request more to make from the borders of the
grave, a compliance, with which is earnestly desired by a poor dying
mortal: which is, That no person, old or young, would ever reflect on my poor dear Mother, or Brother, or any of my relations,
on account of my shameful and untimely death, who could not
prevent my wickedness, and have trouble too much to be borne,
by the life I have lived, and the death I am to die.

I desire sincerely to thank all the good ministers of the town,
who have taken great pains with me ever since the sentence of
death was past upon me, to convince me of my unhappy situation,
of my lost and undone condition by nature, of my aggravating
sins by practice, and of the infinitely free rich grace and mercy
of God, only thro' the merits and mediation of my dear Saviour
Jesus Christ. I also thank all the good people both of town and
country, who, I have reason to think, have offered up many
prayers at the throne of grace for me. I also thank Mr. *Otis*,
the goal-keeper and his family, who have all been very kind to
me during my confinement in Gaol.

And now may Jesus Christ forgive me, the worst of sinners, as
he did the thief on the cross, if h does not, I am forever undone
in soul and body!

Attest, JOSEPH OTIS,   *Levi Ames.*
Dept. Goal-Keeper.

BOSTON: Printed and Sold at the Shop opposite the Court-House in Queen-Street.

The last WORDS and Dying SPEECH of
L E V I A M E S,

Who was Executed at Boston, on Thursday the 21st Day of October, 1773, for BURGLARY.

Taken from his own Mouth, and Published at his desire, as a solemn Warning to all, more particularly Young People.

There is a Way that seemeth right unto a Man, but the End thereof are the Ways of Death.   Prov. 14. 12.

I LEVI AMES, aged twenty-one years, was born in *Groton*, in *New-England*, of a credible family, my father's name was *Jacob Ames*, who died when I was but two years old. I am the first of the family who was ever disgraced. My prevailing fin, and that for which I am soon to suffer death was *Thievings* to practice which I began early and pursued it constantly; except at certain intervals when my conscience made me uneasy, and I resolv'd to do so no more.

My first thefts were small. I began this awful practice by stealing a couple of eggs, then a jack-knife, after that some chalk. But being detected and reproved for the crime, I thought to repent and reform ; but found myself powerfully urged to repeat this wickedness, by the temptations of the devil ; with which I again complied. My tender Mother seeing me take such horrid courses, and dreading the consequences, often entreated and pleaded with me to turn from my evil ways, and I as often assured her that I would. Had I followed her good advice and counsel, I should never have come to this shameful and untimely end. But obedience to my parent ! God will not let disobedient children pass unpunished.

Having got from under my mother's eye, I fell went on in my old way of stealing ; and not being permitted to live with the person I chose to live with, I ran away from my master, which opened a wide door to temptation, and helped on my ruin ; for being indolent in temper, and having no honest way of supporting myself, I robbed others of their property.

About this time I stole a gun at *Woburn*, from *Josiah Richardson*, and a large silver spoon from one Mr. *Howard* of the same town. I then broke open the shop of Mr. *Edward Hammond*, in the county of *Plymouth*, and took out a piece of broad-cloth, and some money. I stole between twenty and thirty dollars from another person, whose name I have forgot. I broke open the shop of Mr. *Jonas Cutler*, of *Groton*, and took from him a good [...] [...] a quantity of silk, mire, and several pieces [...]

eat and drank and went off without paying. A few evenings after, I returned shoved up the window, and put in my hand and stole a box with a johannes, some small change, a pair of knee-buckles, and sleeve buttons, for which I was apprehended, confessed the fact, returned the goods, was punished and set at liberty. The same night as above I took a horse out of *Killingsley*, and rode him down to the county of *Worcester*, where I broke a shop open about day light, and took a quantity of coppers, and a remnant of fatin : The owners have got them again. I also robbed a baker at *Rhode-Island* of a quantity of coppers which I found in three baskets, and spent them.

As for *Atwood*, in company with whom I committed that theft for which I am soon to die, my acquaintance with him began in the following manner—I was standing at a countryman's cart, in the market at *Boston*, asking the price of a turkey ; *Atwood* came up to me, and we fell into conversation, he asked me to walk with him to Beacon-Hill, which I did.—We asked each other about the place of resort. I told him that I lodged at Capt. *Dickey's*. He asked him where he belonged ? He said he was born in an Island in the West-Indies, and that his parents lived in Rhode-Island. I asked him where he had been ? he told me that he lately came from *Portsmouth*. I told him that since he had no money, if he would go with me to my lodgings, I would give him some dinner—I asked him what he would do with some silver plate, if he had any to dispose of ? He told me he knew of a goldsmith who would take it, because he had sold some to him before. I told him I knew where there was some, and if he would go with me, we would get it ; to which he consented. We then went to *Menzoeny*, and found it hid in a stone wall. We kept it about us till next Morning. He told me he knew of a Vendue master in *Boston*, with whom he had lived, who had a large sum of money by him, and if I would join him, we would get it. I asked who it was ; he said Mr. *Bicker*. We accordingly agreed to steal it. At night, after we had slept, we went to a joiner's shop, into which I [...]

mercy. I was at times ready to despair of the mercy of God. But the ministers who visited me, assured me that the mercy of Christ was sufficient to cleanse me from all fin, which gave me a little encouragement to go on crying to God. I now began to understand something of that law of God which I had broken, as condemning me for the wickedness of my heart as well as life—I saw that I was undone, that my heart and life were bad beyond all account. I saw that if God should damn me a thousand times he would be just, and I should have nothing to say. In this condition I was a week before the time first fixed for my execution The loss of body and foul made me tremble ; though I could not freely tell all that I felt to, all who came to see me. I thought that if I should be executed in this condition, I must be dragged like a bullock to the slaughter.

But God's name be blessed forever ; that on Friday evening, the 8th instant, I turned over a little book which was put into my hands, in which I saw, Ezek. 36. 26, 27. *A new heart will I give you, and a new spirit will I put upon you ; and I will take away the stony heart out of your flesh, and I will give you a heart of flesh. And I will pour out my spirit upon you, &c.* This at once surprized me : I knew that I wanted this new heart ; and could not help looking on this as God's gracious promise to me : and I tho't that as I knew God could not lie, if I would not believe this, I would believe nothing : my mind at once felt easy. I now saw that I had sinned against God all my life with as much envy, as ever I killed a snake ; which I always hated.

After this I had, and now have such a view of the way of salvation by Christ, that I feel and do feel my foul rest on him as my only hope of salvation. Since which I have found peace of mind, anger against myself for fin, and a desire to be made holy. At times the terrors of death seem to be removed : at other times I am full of fears lest I should deceive myself. Yet I cannot but hope that Christ has freely pardoned me. On him I desire to rest living and dying ; and to give him all the praise.

And now as a dying man I mention the following things, viz. [...]

25. *The Last Words of William Huggins and John Mansfield
. . . June 19th, 1783, at Worcester, . . .*
[*Worcester*, 1783.]

In this broadside it is interesting to note that Huggins and Mansfield were
not the proper names of the criminals. The two men wanted to die using
their aliases to protect their families from shame. As is usual with this type
of narrative, the account ends with an admonition and encouragement to
youth to "forsake the paths of vice and immorality, and seek the road to
virtue and happiness."

The cut on this broadside had already been used by Isaiah Thomas, the
printer, on another broadside which he published in 1779 on the execution of
Robert Young for rape. For this one, Thomas added an extension to the cut
to represent the second figure. Such practical ingenuity was common among
American printers.

Evans 17994
19 × 22 ⅜

which have brought me to this unfortunate condition.

At length I went to *Stockbridge*, in the Common-wealth of *Massachusetts*, where I lived a considerable time, and worked at the farming business, but spent what money I earned as fast as I could procure it, to no good purpose.

I continued in *Stockbridge* until the latter part of the last summer, at which time I first became acquainted with *Mansfield*; we soon became very intimate, and agreed to set off together for *Salem*, in order to take a voyage to sea. As we were both destitute of money, and were very poorly clothed, and had no inclination to work to procure what we wanted in an honest way, we dishonourably and unhappily determined to take property from others, which we had no right to, and thereby broke that great command of the Almighty, which he delivered upon *Mount Sinai*, THOU SHALT NOT STEAL.

In a short time after I became acquainted with *Mansfield*, we set off from *Stockbridge*, and committed several robberies, the most capital of which was one in *Pelham*, at the house of Mr. *Gray*, and another in *Harvard*, at the house of Mr. *Parkhurst*: For the last

On my arrival at *Halifax*, I was put on board a prison-ship in the harbour, where I remained a long and tedious winter, and until the twenty-fifth day of May following, destitute of the comforts of life: I then made my escape from the prison-ship, but was almost naked, and without money or friends. My intention was then to have gone home to my parents, and for that purpose, after getting on shore, took to the woods, and sat out for *Annapolis-Royal*, which, I was told, was above one hundred miles from *Halifax*. I had neither shoe nor stocking. For five days and

quainted. We found each others circumstances to be somewhat familar; and after some consultation, we agreed to go to *Salem* together, and look out for a vessel and take a voyage to sea. In order to fit ourselves out with clothing and other necessaries, and to furnish us with money to purchase some things to carry with us to trade with, as a venture, we came to the fatal determination of supplying ourselves with money, or other property which would fetch it, in any way or manner that should offer; and to rob and steal from others what we thought would be sufficient for our purpose.

Having come to this resolution we left *Stockbridge*, and both of us being without money, we sometimes begged victuals on our way from that place to *Pelham*; where being arrived, we went in the evening to the house of Mr. *Gray*; we knocked at the door, and were told to walk in: Finding only Mr. *Gray*, his wife and a few small children in the house, all of whom we could manage, we cruelly took Mr. *Gray* and bound him, and laid him on his bed: Mrs. *Gray*, we put down the cellar, giving her at her request, her clothes and a light: We then rifled the house, and took a watch and some articles of clothing, and made off. For this action, I, with *Huggins*,

From *Harvard* we went to *Concord*, where we were pursued, taken up, examined, and committed to gaol, in that town: In about thirteen days afterwards we were removed to the gaol in *Worcester*. When we were taken, we delivered up all the articles we robbed Mr. *Gray* and Mr. *Parkhurst* of, excepting *Six Dollars*, to one Mr. *Butler* of *Concord*. We sincerely beg the forgiveness of Mr. *Parkhurst*, and all others whom we have any ways injured, and are sorry that it is not in our power to give them better satisfaction.

JOHN MANSFIELD.

HAVING given the foregoing accounts of our lives, one of which is signed *William Huggins*, and the other *John Mansfield*, we would here observe, that *William* and *John* are our proper christian-names, given to us by our parents; but the sir-names *"Huggins"* and *"Mansfield"* are only names which we took to ourselves to prevent our real ones from being known. As we have been tried, found guilty, and received sentence of death under those names;

plying us with clothing and other necessary things.

We pray that our unhappy fate may be a solemn WARNING to YOUTH, and induce them to forsake the path of vice and immorality, and seek the road to virtue and happiness. We earnestly intreat you to be obedient to your parents, and hearken to their good advice. Avoid idleness as the mother of sin, and the inventor of evil deeds. Flee the drunkard's company; and may all those who are addicted to the crimes which we have committed, and which have brought us to close our lives with infamy, view the awful prospect which will soon be exhibited to their fight at the place where our bodies are destined to suffer, and by forsaking their evil ways avoid our miserable death.

As we draw nigh for forgiveness, so we really forgive all who may have injured us.

In a few hours more, O eternal all-gracious JEHO-VAH! we must quit our existence on earth, and join the world of spirits: And do thou, most merciful GOD, we humbly beseech thee, receive into the blessed mansions of immortality our never-dying souls!

WILLIAM HUGGINS,
JOHN MANSFIELD.

Worcester-Gaol, June 18, 1783.

MANSFIELD's SOLILOQUY! Or an Elegy on the Execution of HUGGINS and MANSFIELD for BURGLARY.

AWAKE ye Mufes of the Cypress grove,
To scenes of publick justice! and improve
Those moments lent me by impending fate,
That sternly hails me to an unknown state!
Had not primeval sin stamp'd on our race
A mark of frailty, error and disgrace,
Ye ne'er would find occasion to appear,
And drop with us the keen lamenting tear;
But since, alas! our natures are betray'd
By wiles fallacious, and satannick aid,
We're all consign'd to err, mistake the road,
And trample heedless on the laws of God.
Oft have we brav'd the foe in martial fray,
And earn'd the laurels of a well-fought day,
Have vanquish'd foes, been vanquish'd by their hand,
Nor will the landfhip of an Eden's grove,
Could bring contentment to the human breaft,

But rear'd new thoughts, ambitious to be bleft.
We by the tumults of a giddy mind
O'erturn'd our reason, gave it to the wind;
Blinded the eyes of conscience in the soul,
Whereby our actions she could not control;
And thus equip'd with diabolick shield,
We stalk'd nocturnal to the vicious field;
What triumphs have we gain'd? What trophies won?
Say, is the Gallows honourary boon?
Or can it tempt a mortal here to gain
Rewards of infamy, of death, of pain?
I antidate the horrors of that day
When justice arm'd shall snatch my life away!
I hear the grating of the maffy door!
I view the bolts torc'd from the solid floor!
The clanking chains from off our legs are torn!
I fee the eyes of pity round us mourn:
We mount the flags, survey all things around,
We bid adieu to the dark prison's cell,

Much more I'd suffer for my country's good,
Still for her cause I'd weep away my blood;
Yes, could I barter fate, the Gallows wield,
I'd shift my death and seek it in the field.
There wipe away the stigma of my crime,
Nor leave a vestige on the track of time;
But where can I hide myself but in the grave.
The fatal tree now occupies our view,
Where we must bid the joys of life adieu!
There death with grisly dart on one side stands,
Old Time on 'tother counts the feanty sands;
We mount the flags, survey all things around,
Take a last farewell of th' enamel'd ground;

Where faded walks, could they but speak, might tell
The many sorrows and repenting sighs
That flow'd sincerely to th' offended skies!
Could we like lambs unconscious of our fate,
Be led to death, we might support our state,
Nor feel the anguish of departing life,
Till, like the lamb, it feels the wounding knife.
But we alas! are dying while we live,
Nor would our hopes be cherish'd by reprieve.
Dart one floor look to the bright solar rays;
Then shroud our eyes eternal from his blaze!
And now suspence hangs on our quivering souls,
Our eye balls flash like lightning from the poles!
We tread on air, and no support can find,
Unless our Saviour now should prove our friend!
Oh! Now Omnipotent, Omniscient God!
Oh! Hear our prayer, nor crush us with thy rod;
Tho' infamous now our exit, fill we trust
In pardning mercy, we may join the just
In that bright world, where dwells immortal joy,
And bills eestatick cheers without alloy.

Printed and sold at the Printing-Office in Worcester.

THE LAST WORDS

OF WILLIAM HUGGINS AND JOHN MANSFIELD,

Who are to be Executed this Day, June 19th, 1783, at Worcester, in the Commonwealth of Massachusetts, for BURGLARY, committed in October last.

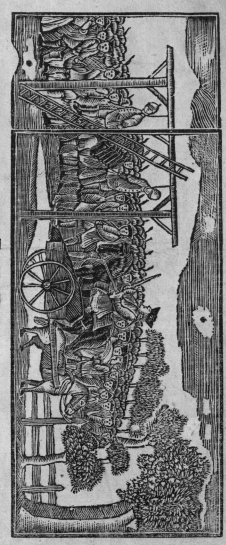

I WILLIAM HUGGINS, was born in *Fish-Kill*, in the State of *New-York*, in the year 1759, of creditable parents, who ufed their utmoft endeavours to bring me up in the light of the Gofpel, by giving me a pious education and good advice. When I was about thirteen years of age, my parents removed from *Fish-Kill*, to another part of the State of *New-York*. At the age of eighteen I inlifted into the army for five months, and at the expiration of that time I returned home, and lived with my parents about two years.

During my fhort ftay in the army, I became acquainted with many vices I had not ran into before. I contracted a love for gaming, playing for money and cheating thofe I played with; took to drinking, and as I grew older thofe fins became more familiar to me, and harder to part with. My parents were grieved at my conduct, and ufed the beft means in their power to reclaim me, but in vain; I again left them and went to *Fish-Kill*, where I went to work at the farming bufinefs, to which I had been bred by my father: Work not agreeing with me I again inlifted for the term of fix months, and after ftaying in the army until the time I had inlifted for was expired, and obtained my difcharge I once more returned to my parents, who were glad to fee me, and received me with open arms.

mentioned offence we were foon after taken up, and having had a fair trial, are now to fuffer Death in the bloom of life!

WILLIAM HUGGINS.

I JOHN MANSFIELD, am now about twenty-two years of age. I was born in the Commonwealth of *Maffachufetts*, in that part of it which is called the *Province of Maine*; my parents were reputable, and perfons of fome note in that part of the country; they have another fon who is older than myfelf, and three daughters, who are all well efteemed by thofe who know them. My parents have been exceeding kind to me; they took all poffible care of my education while I continued with them; I always had their good wifhes, and, when opportunity offered, their beft advice, which had I always followed, I fhould not now have been obliged to tafte the bitter cup of forrow, which has been produced by my late infamous conduct; nor fhould I have been cut off in the flower of my youth, to fatisfy the demands of juftice, which fternly calls for my life as an expiation for my crimes.

When I was about twelve years of age, one of my kinfmen, who was commander of a fhip, took a fan-

night I was without food excepting one fowl which I caught and eat. Being in an enemy's country, I was afraid to go to any houfe, or being feen, left I fhould be taken up and carried back to *Halifax*. With much difficulty, and being greatly fatigued, I arrived at the head of *St. Mary's-Bay*, and there meeting with an old Dutchman, we, with great danger, paffed the *Bay of Fundy*, in a fmall boat. After I had croffed the Bay, I meet with a privateer belonging to *Salem*, on board of which I got a paffage to *Broad-Bay*; there meeting with a coafting floop, I went on board, and arrived at *Beverly*.

Being now without money, and only a few rags on my back, my pride and ambition was fuch that I could not then think of going home to my friends in fuch a naked condition. It was therefore my wifh to take another voyage to fea, but I was unable to fit myfelf out, in the manner I defired. Had I returned to my friends, they had ability and I make not the leaft doubt would have had an inclination to affift me. I could not, however, reconcile myfelf to vifit them until I could make a better appearance; and therefore determined to go into the country, and endeavour to mend my fortune. I fat out with a defign to go to work.

fincerely beg Mr. and Mrs. *Gray's* forgivenefs, and hope as it is not in our power to make them any other recompence, that they will be pleafed to receive this acknowledgement, with our wifhes for their hap-pinefs, as fatisfactory.

From *Pelham* we proceeded to *Harvard*, and went to the houfe of Mr. *Parkhurft*, an innholder, and there called for fome liquor, which we received and paid for. I obferved while there, a watch hanging up againft a window in a bed room; and as Mr. *Parkhurft* had to change a piece of money to pay for the liquor we had received, I faw him take down from an open clofet, near where the watch hung, a box containing money, out of which he gave me the change for the piece of money I gave him. We foon after left the houfe, and agreed that we would return at night, and rob him of the watch and money I had difcovered. We went about two miles from Mr. *Parkhurft's* houfe to another tavern, where we called for dinner, and tarried until towards evening: Between the hours of twelve and one o'clock that night, we returned to the houfe of Mr. *Parkhurft*, which I entered by a window that I fhov-ed up, and went into a room, from that room into

and as with our parents may never know our fhame-ful end, as it might have a great tendency to bring them with forrow to the grave, and would moreover feverely wound the feelings of our other relations and friends; whom by our conduct we have heretofore too much injured.; And as a difcovery could not be of the leaft fervice to the community, we therefore beg ftill to conceal the names of our families from the world, and hope we do not commit fin in fo doing.

We befs God that he hath been pleafed to fpare our lives to this period, and that we have fuch a fenfe of our fins; and that although we are to be punifhed with temporal death for our crimes, yet in various ways has he fhewn us mercy. It is true we have juft endeavoured to make our efcape from prifon, yet we hope it will not be imputed to us as a crime.

We return our fincere thanks to all thofe who by their benevolence have contributed to make our mi-ferable condition lefs wretched, by their tendernefs, good advice, and fupplying us with neceffaries; which benevolence, as we are ftrangers, and our characters unworthy, makes a greater impreffion on our minds. We can make no return, but pray that Almighty God may reward fuch goodnefs.

26. *The Last Words, and Dying Speech of Elisha Thomas.*
[*No place,* 1788.]

As this was the first execution in Strafford County in New Hampshire, many people from surrounding towns flocked to see it. For this reason, the death of Elisha Thomas is well documented in newspapers and history books about Dover, New Hampshire.

The illustration contains the three elements common to woodcut depictions of executions—a crowd, the gallows, and an official on horseback. This particular woodcut combines these traditional elements and succeeds in rendering a specific place. At Elisha Thomas's execution, the gallows stood at the foot of a hill with the townspeople looking down at the spectacle. The place thereafter was called "Gallows Hill."

Evans 45373
13 ⅝ × 17 ¼

THE LAST WORDS, AND DYING SPEECH OF
ELISHA THOMAS,

Who was Executed at DOVER, on the 3d June, 1788,—for the Murder of Captain PETER DROWNE.

I ELISHA THOMAS, now in the Prison, in *Dover*, under sentence of death, upon the charge of murdering Captain *Peter Drowne*, on the fourth of February last ;—willing and desirous to confess to the world, what I recollect of that unhappy event—as a man just launching into the eternal and invisible world, being all I recollect of that unfortunate day.

On the morning of that day being bound to *Portsmouth*, I stopped at the house of Col. *Thomas Tash*, where Capt. *Drowne* lived, and after some conversation, we agreed to go to Mr. *Randall's*, about half a mile distant, in order to procure a dram ; we went and drank as near as I can recollect, one pint and half of Rum, and was about to separate with all that friendship that had subsisted between us for five years, which our acquaintance are convinced was very intimate ; as we were ready to set out we saw a company consisting of Col. *Tash*, *Joshua Davis*, with Col. *Tash's* two sons, coming up to the house ; we had immediately something more to drink ; after a little while we began to pull up from the floor, and unluckily *Davis* and I had some words ; and soon after my heels were knocked up, and I was thrown upon the floor ; I was immediately shoved behind the door, and as Capt. *Drowne* came to speak to me, his heels we're some how or other tripped up ;—the witnesses against me swore, that *Drowne* immediately pulled off his coat, and that I went out of the door and *Drowne* followed ; I solemnly declare, I know not in what manner I got out, nor where I was till nearly one rod from the door, I then turned round and saw Capt. *Drowne* standing in the entry, and saw him stagger ; at the time I turned round and saw Capt. *Drowne*, *Thomas Tash* had taken hold of my shoulder, and I cut his fingers ; I supposed *Drowne's* staggering was owing to liquor ;—I immediately heard somebody call out, " *Drowne is kill*

ed, Thomas has killed him." I should have returned to the door, had not Col. *Tash* exclaimed, " *then I'll kill him ;*" and immediately pursued me with an ax, but was stopt by Mr. *Randall* ; I run to avoid being killed a little way down the road, and then returned and went home ; the next morning I surrendered myself peaceably to justice.

I solemnly declare I had no enmity against Capt. *Drowne*, nor do I know how it happened, unless it was done in the scuffle getting me out of doors ; nor could I have harboured a thought of killing my intimate friend, companion, and benefactor ; and I most sincerely believe, had not the company before-mentioned ever came to the house, that Capt. *Drowne* would still have been living, and that I should not have been under the sentence soon to be executed upon me ; to their violent proceedings I am afraid is to be attributed the loss of both our lives.

The stories that have been propagated round the country, that I had confessed that Mr. *Kenniston* and myself had formerly murdered a man, are void of foundation, and as a dying man I declare, nothing of that kind ever happened. Other stories told about myself alone are equally false.

The Court, Council, and Jury, I firmly believe determined according to the law and evidence given to them, and I lay nothing against them. The witnesses own consciences will best determine, whether from prejudice, they did not in some parts of their testimony injure me ; but I leave them to that God in whose presence I must soon, and they ere long appear.

I solemnly declare that whatever the world may say of me, that I never had any intention of taking the life of any fellow mortal, whatever :—but alas ! I am now called off the stage of existence, at the age of forty-two, for a crime that I should as soon thought of perpetrating up

on my wife and children, as upon Capt. *Drowne*.

I hope most sincerely, that my untimely end, may prove a warning to all, more especially to the rising generation, to avoid bad company, intemperance, and giving way to unruly passions, which I confess have proved my ruin.

I most sincerely thank the Reverend Clergy in the vicinity, for their attention and kindness to me, as well before as since my conviction, for their kind cautions and wholesome instructions, from time to time given me. To the Rev. Mr. *Gray*, in particular, I cannot neglect returning the unfeigned thanks of gratitude, for his pious warnings and admonitions, as well in private as from the desk, the few times I have had the opportunity to hear him, and for his christian consolations from time to time offered.

I cannot forget to return my thanks to the Gentlemen and Ladies of the town of *Dover*, who so humanely petitioned his Excecllency and council, for a short respite of my execution—may they enjoy long and uninterrupted happiness here, and may the best of Heaven's blessings await them hereafter.——Nor must I neglect the same testimonials of gratitude, to Mr Footman and family for the many kindnesses I have received from them during my confinement.

I now recommend my soul to the all-merciful Creator of all Worlds and all Creatures, most ardently imploring the forgiveness, of my manifold transgressions, and that the redeemer would most graciously receive me to the arms of his everlasting mercy, when I leave the world.

ELISHA THOMAS.

Dover Prison, June 3, 1788.
Signed in presence of
JONATHAN RAWSON.

The following Thoughts were taken from Mr. ELISHA THOMAS, not long before his Execution, in conversation with him, when several spectators were present ; and although he never confessed a remembrance of the crime charged upon him, but his general confession as to his past life and conduct was nearly in the idea as hereafter related ; and which is put in the following gloomy measure at the request of some of his friends.

YE gazing crouds that gather round my woe,
  Led by vain custom—or by pity drawn,
To mock my fate, or watch my tears that flow,
  Hear a sad lesson from a wretch forlorn.

Behold a man to infamy consign'd
  A living, dying monitor to all,
These hideous walls must awe the daring mind,
  And chide each hard'ned witness of my fall.

Behold a man from his meridian fair,
  In all the health and vigour nature gave,
Chain'd in this doleful prison of despair,
  Doom'd soon to suffer o'er a shameful grave.

The sons of vice with every artful smile,
  Lur'd me to folly, as they led the way ;
Renew'd temptations, still awoke desire,
  Such friends will always tempt us, and betray.

The snares of youth my treacherous heart beguil'd,
  Unbridl'd passions gnaw'd my canker'd soul ;
The cup (ah fatal poison to the world)
  First caus'd these billows of my grief to roll,

Driven by the impulse of tyrannick lust
  Through the vile stages of my mad career,

The world enchanting was my only trust,
  Nor dream'd a God, a Heav'n, or Hell so near.

In guilt matur'd, nor aw'd by God or man,
  Their laws I broke, and impiously defy'd ;
The blade *was* plung'd, the vital current ran,
  My friend, quick fainting, fault'ring, gasping—died.

My *friend !* ah ! hide the black idea here,
  My twinging heart-strings sever at the sound ;
Ah, let them sever ! for my friend most dear,
  From *rash* confusion caught a deadly wound !

Stern justice ey'd me ; and in thousand forms
  Of awful majesty at once appear'd,
Her voice like thunder, when the howling storm
  By the affrighted traveller is heard.

Where should I fly ? the earth was but a goal,
  Myself the dungeon, and reflection, death,
The world my foes, all shunn'd my haggard soul,
  As if t'escape contagion from my breath.

Confin'd, I lay, the bitter tidings spread,
  My house in flames, my babes alarm'd too late*,
Their better Guardian call'd—to Heav'n they fled,
  Nor knew their Father's infamy or fate.

Trembling I mov'd to that twice awful place,
  The Bar of Justice, and the House of God ;
Unfeeling crouds my every crime relate,
  Unbending justice—then appli'd the rod.

O'erwhelm'd with agony and deep despair,
  I bore the load of my enormous woe,
Till mercy beam'd on patience sincere,
  And grace divine gave tears of joy to flow.

Unheeding youth, O shun the pangs I feel,
  Stem the first current of Heav'n daring sin,
Flee that fell Demon in the cup conceal'd,
  The nurse of vices and the bane of man.

But ah, ill-fated partner of my care !
  Thy bitter cup's repeated ! O remove,
And think not—speak not, of my anguish here,
  Till bless'd, and pardon'd, we may meet above.

Strung by remorse, her keenest shafts I bear ;
  I ask your prayers—I ask your pity too ;
O, grant me one, one sympathetic tear——
  In peace, I bid an injur'd world, *adieu !*

---

* In a very striking manner Mr. *Thomas*, (of New-Durham, in New-Hampshire) and his family have been marked out by fate, as the peculiar objects of destruction : While he was confined in the goal at Dover, for the murder of his benefactor, the worthy Capt. Drowne, his house caught on fire, while his wife was absent from it, on a visit to him in goal, and four of his children perished in the flames.—And as Mrs. Thomas was returning in a sleigh from Dover to New-Durham—probably to view the sad remains of her earthly residence, and to shed a tear over her departed children—the horses took fright, and running against another sleigh, the tongue of which came with such force against the unhappy woman's side, as to break three of her ribs ; and it was with the greatest difficulty she escaped being torn to pieces.

27. *A True Account of a young Lady in Boston.*
Bennington, Vermont: Haswell and Russell, 1790.

In contrast to the frequent stories of lurid crimes and sinister events, there are others whose content is more amusing and intriguing to our ears. The manner in which a young woman managed to marry the man of her own choosing without losing her fortune is the subject of this particular broadside. The methods she used to dupe her avaricious father may not be judged admirable, but they definitely were ingenious.

Evans 46010
10 ½ × 16 ⅜

A true account of a young LADY in

Boston, whose father was resolved she should marry a *rich* FRENCHMAN---shewing how she contrived to marry a *worthy* young LAWYER, of *small fortune*, with her father's *consent*.

COME listen a-while to the tale I shall tell,
Concerning a maid who in Boston did dwell;
Who for beauty and virtue, was fam'd far and near,
And was born to inherit five hundred a-year.

Thus endowed with all things that her heart could desire,
She tho't herself happy, 'till her aged sire,
When she had arrived to the age of fifteen
Told her she must be wed to a man he had seen.

This man was a Frenchman of noble degree,
Whose riches flow'd in like the waves of the sea,
But his person was homely, his graces were few,
To get wealth was the most that he knew how to do.

The maiden was grieved at her father's desire,
But she knew not which way from the match to retire,
For her father was fix'd she should marry his choice,
And he scarce in the motion allowed her a voice.

One evening this lady walked out in the Mall,
To lament that her beauty for riches must fall,
When a handsome young man in the walks she espy'd,
Whose air with attention this pretty maid ey'd.

She thought she perceived in his looks and his mien
Good sense and refinement which seldom is seen,
And while to his graces her heart did attend,
She resolved, if she could she would make him her friend.

She then took occasion to fall in his way,
He bow'd with respect, while his eyes did betray,
That he view'd with delight the bright charms of the fair,
By far the most brilliant of all that were there.

In short he was struck at first blush with surprise,
And scarce from the lady averted his eyes,
'Till good manners at length bid him blush to conceive,
That the lady could scarcely his rudeness forgive.

The lady delighted to view his concern
Beheld him with pleasure, yet blush'd in her turn,
He accosted her sweetly and begged she would please,
To walk with him a-while to enjoy the cool breeze.

She consented, but told him before she could go,
His name and employment she wish'd for to know,
He said he was son to a merchant, and bred,
To the practice of law to gain his daily bread.

They soon got acquainted, and soon got in love,
So deep that no art could their passion remove,
But the Frenchman still ran in this fair lady's mind,
For her heart to the match was by no means inclin'd.

Her lover inform'd her that he would advise,
She should look on the Frenchman with amorous eyes,
Indulge him to hope she would soon be his wife,
In case he would give her this portion for life:—

Three hundred a-year to be spent as she pleas'd
By which his contrivance would surely be eas'd,
And three hundred more to pay servants for her,
Which expence was the least that she meant to incur.

To this he must add for her own private use,
And for treating such friends as her choice should produce
Five hundred pounds more, or she never would wed,
Or consent to partake of the joys of his bed.

And if he could not to these motions agree,
She hop'd that he would in the matter be free,
And resign her to live as she wish'd to remain
A virgin, till she could a worthier obtain.

And as she on his honor tho't fit to reside,
Expecting, 'twas likely, she'd soon be his bride,
He must not let her father the reasons perceive,
Why he chose to resign her, a virgin to live.

The Frenchman amazed by her stating to hear,
She would throw away more than a thousand a-year,
From the love he bore wealth, bid adieu to a wife
Resolv'd he would rather live single for life.

Her father he told he believ'd they must part,
For some how or other he found that his heart,
Had changed of late, and his daughter tho' fair,
And as lovely as ever had no portion there.

Then soon this young lawyer it seems did appear,
And in private proposed to be wed to his dear,
She advised him the whole of his cunning to try,
To make the old man to his wishes comply.

But being convinced as his fortune was low,
And her father loved wealth more than all things below,
She contrived to get a false key to his wealth,
Which for years had been only beheld as by stealth.

'Twas a large iron chest in a garret contain'd
All the treasure his anxious industry had gain'd,
She removed many thousand, and great bars of lead
She contrived for to lay at the bottom instead.

For she knew that her father would never consent,
To her match with the lawyer, on which she was bent,
So she thought it no harm with his chest to make free
Which would make him appear of a noble degree.

A fortune she had of five hundred a-year,
As the reader must doubtless remember to hear,
On this she resolved with her lover to live,
And she wish'd but her father his licence to give.

The wealth she had stol'n to her love she did send,
With directions how he should to matters attend,
Which was that he strait to her father would write,
That his daughter had fill'd him with joy and delight.

And if he would consent he should make her his bride,
The day that the knot of their banns should be tied,
He would thankfully pay him four thousand half joes,
And think it a trifle to gain him his spouse.

The old man was charm'd at the heart for to think,
He was likely to handle four thousand in chink,
So he gave his consent and the money was paid,
And the marriage perform'd with great pomp and parade.

Soon after the marriage the father 'tis said,
Was found in the morning a corpse in his bed,
The son-in-law now in the right of his bride
Enjoys his four thousand---and thousands beside.

His wife is as happy as mortal can be,
From the vice of her father her husband is free,
Distress never pleads unrelieved at their door,
But comfort is ever bestow'd on the poor.

BENNINGTON, (VERMONT) PRINTED AND SOLD BY HASWELL & RUSSELL—1790.

28. *The Grecian Daughter.*
Windsor, Vermont: Printed by the Flying Booksellers, [Alden
Spooner, 1798?]

Although not a contemporary American event, this account about a criminal
from ancient Rome was of apparent interest to Americans since it was published in at least three editions between 1798 and 1811 in Vermont. This
anecdote has a long literary history. Boccaccio, who probably adapted it from
Valerius Maximus, used it in his Latin treatise, *De claris mulieribus*.

The engraving, probably on type metal, is one of the most striking illustrations on any broadside. The artist is unknown, although he signed his initials
R. E. S. below the door frame on the left.

Evans 33815
21 × 16 ⅞

THE GRECIAN DAUGHTER.

Or, an example of a Virtuous WIFE, who fed her father with her own milk---he being condemned to be starved to death by
TIBERIUS CÆSAR, Emperor of Rome; but was afterwards pardoned, and the Daughter highly rewarded.

IN Rome there liv'd a Nobleman
  The Emp'ror did offend,
And for that fault he was adjudg'd
  Unto a cruel end:
That he should be in prison cast
  With irons many a one,
And there be famish'd unto death
  And brought to skin and bone:
And more, if any one were known
  By knight or elke by day
To bring him any kind of food
  His hunger to allay,
The Emp'ror swore a mighty oath,
  Without remorse, quoth he,
They shall sustain the hardest death
  That can devised be.
This cruel sentence thus pronounc'd,
  This nobleman was cast
Into a dungeon deep and dark,
  With irons fetter'd fast,
Where, when he had with hunger great
  Remained ten days' space,
And tasted neither meat nor drink,
  In a most woful case;
The tears along his aged face
  Most piteously did fall,
And grievously he did begin,
  Complaining, thus to call:
O, Lord, quoth he, what shall I do?
  So hungry now am I,
For want of bread, one bit of bread,
  I perish, starve and die.
How precious is one grain of wheat
  Unto a hungry soul?
One crust or crumb, or little piece,
  My hunger to controul.

Had I this dungeon heap'd with gold,
  I now would give it all,
To buy and purchase one small loaf,
  Nay, were it e'er so small.
O that I had but every day
  One bit of bread to eat,
Tho' ne'er so mouldy, black or brown,
  My comfort would be great;
Yes, though oblig'd to take it up
  Trod down in dirt and mire,
It would be pleasing to my taste,
  And sweet to my desire.
O Lord, most happy is the hind
  That labors all the day;
The drudging mule, the peasant poor,
  That at command do stay;
They have their ordinary meals,
  They take no heed at all
Of those small crums & bits that they
  Do carelesly let fall.
How happy is the little chick,
  Who without fear doth go
And pick up many precious crumbs
  Which they away do throw.
O that some pretty little mouse
  So much my friend would be,
To bring some old forsaken crusts
  Into this place to me.
But O, my heart, it is in vain,
  No succour can I have;
No meat, no drink, no water eke,
  My loathed life to save.
O drink some bread, for Jesus sake,
  Some bread, some bread to me;
I die, I die for want of food,
  None but stone walls I see,

Thus night and day he constant cry'd
  In such outrageous sort,
That all the people, far and near,
  Were griev'd at his report.
Though great & many friends he had,
  And daughters in the town,
Yet none durst come to succour him,
  Fearing the Emp'ror's frown,
Yet now behold, one daughter dear,
  He had, as we do find,
Who liv'd in his displeasure great,
  Not wedding to his mind:
Altho' she liv'd in mean estate,
  She was a virtuous wife,
And for to help her father dear,
  She ventured thus her life:
She quickly to her sisters went,
  And of them did entreat,
That by some secret means they woud
  Convey their father meat:
Our Father must both starve, said she,
  The Emp'ro's wrath is such,
He dies, alas, for want of food,
  Whereof we fare too much.
Pray, sisters, therefore, use some means
  His life for to preserve,
And suffer not our father dear
  In prison for to starve.
Alas, said they, what shall we do,
  His hunger to sustain?
You know 'tis death for any one,
  That would his life maintain.
And tho' we wish him well, said they,
  We never will agree
To spoil ourselves; we would as soon
  That he should die as we;

And, sister, if you love yourself,
  Let this attempt alone;
'Tho' you do e'er so secret work,
  In time it will be known.
O hath our father brought us up,
  And nourish'd us, quoth she,
And shall we now forsake him quite
  In his extremity?
No, I will venture life and limb,
  To do my father good;
The worst that is, I can but die,
  For him I'll shed my blood.
With that in haste away she flies,
  And to the prison goes;
But with her dismal Father dear,
  She might not speak, God knows,
Except the Emperor would grant
  Her Father in that case,
The keeper would admit no one,
  To enter in that place.
Then she unto the Emp'ror hies,
  And falling on her knees,
With wringing hands & bitter cries,
  These words pronounced she:
" My hapless Father, sov'reign Sir,
  Offending of your grace;
Judg'd to endure a pining death,
  Within a dismal place;
Which I confess he has deserv'd,
  Yet, mighty Prince, said she,
Vouchsafe in gracious sort to grant
  One simple boon to me:
It chanced so I match'd myself
  Against my father's mind,
Whereby I did procure his wrath,
  As fortune has assigned.

And seeing now the time is come
  He must resign his breath,
Vouchsafe that I may speak to him,
  Before the hour of death;
And reconcile myself to him,
  His favour to obtain,
That when he dies I may not then
  Under his curse remain,"
The Emp'ror granted her request,
  Conditionally that she,
Each day unto her father went,
  Should thoroughly searched be.
No meat nor drink she with her bro't,
  To help him there distrest,
But every day she nourish'd him
  With milk from her own breast.
Thus by her milk he was preserv'd
  A twelve month and a day;
And was so fair and fat to see,
  Yet none could tell what way.
The Emp'ror musing much thereat,
  At length did understand,
How he was fed—and not his laws
  Were broke at any hand.
And much admired at the same,
  And her great virtues shown,
He pardon'd him and honor'd her
  With great preferments known.
Her Father ever after that,
  Lov'd her as his own life,
And blest the day that she was made
  A virtuous loving wife.

WINDSOR,
PRINTED FOR THE FLYING
BOOK-SELLERS.

RELIGION

29. *At a General Court Held at Boston the 16th, of March [1680/1.]*
[*Boston, 1681.*]

This proclamation for a fast to be held on April 21, 1681, is the earliest broadside in the collection of the American Antiquarian Society. After 1660, there were in the Massachusetts Bay Colony thanksgiving days in autumn to celebrate abundant harvests. Less well known are the annual spring fasts. These were generally prefaced with a cry of distress and lamentation. Here we see the "dark, impending clouds" of flood, hurricane ("Blast"), continuing religious persecution in Europe, and loss of life and cargo. The second part of the fast day announcement proclaims the hope that heedful observance of the day will obtain divine favor for the planting of the fields.

The seal on this broadside was cut by John Foster, America's first print maker, and was first used on a broadside dated October 26, 1675. Foster's seal was used until the end of the century and was regarded by his contemporaries as one of his major achievements.

Evans 39216
8 × 12

At a

GENERAL COURT

Held at Boston the 16th. of March 1 6 8 0/1.

THE solemn Consideration of those awful threatnings that are in the face of divine Providence, both toward the world in general, in respect of that fearful Sight and Sign from Heaven, which hath of late been taken notice of; and towards our selves more particularly, for that the Lord hath this last year manifested his holy displeasure against us, having by an unusual Flood, by the Blast, and by worms, which his own own hand (who is able by the most contemptible of his creatures to stain our glory) hath sent among us, diminished the fruits of the earth. Having also dilivered some of our New-England Vessels with those in them, into the hands of such as are enemies to the Christian Name, and more lately frowned upon us by Shipwracks, and considerable losses at Sea; and visited some amongst us by sudden and unexpected Deaths. Being also sensible, that there are in other respects, dark clouds impending over us. And that the present state of the Protestant interest abroad, and more especially in the land of our Fathers Sepulchres, doth call for earnest Prayer before that God unto whom salvation belongeth. The Consideration of all these things calling aloud upon us for more then ordinary seekings of the Face of God in Jesus Christ:

This Court doth therefore appoint the 21 st. day of *April* next to be observed as a Day of Fasting and Prayer, hereby prohibiting all servile labour upon that day, and exhorting all the Ministers, Churches and People throughout this Colony, religiously to observe the same; and to intreat that the favour of God through Jesus Christ may be towards his People in other parts of the world. And that if it may stand with his good pleasure, we may be hid in the day of the Lords anger, our publick Peace, Health, Libertyes stil continued. That Seed time and Harvest may not fail. And that a good success may be to the endeavours of this Court, and particularly for our worthy Agents in their negotiation. And to pray unto him, that he would order a perfect Lot for us, with respect unto those that are in the approaching Election, to be chosen as Rulers over this his People.

By the *COURT,* *Edward Rawson Secr'.*

30. *In Provincial Congress, Cambridge, October 22, 1774.*
[Boston, 1774.]

The circumstances surrounding the publication of this Thanksgiving Day proclamation are quite interesting. Although the Governor of Massachusetts, General Thomas Gage, had the authority to issue proclamations for fast and thanksgiving days, he refused to do so in 1774. The first refusal occurred when the Boston Port Bill was to take effect on June 1, 1774. That date was observed by fasting and prayer, but it was not a public or general observance because General Gage refused to issue a proclamation. His reason: "The request was only to give an opportunity for sedition to flow from the pulpit."

When the time approached for the annual Thanksgiving Day, General Gage again refused to sanction it officially, so the Provincial Congress published its own announcement. Obviously it appears without the customary royal arms and the words "God save the King."

Evans 13415
12 ¼ × 14 ⅞

In Provincial Congress,

Cambridge, *October* 22, 1774.

FROM a Confideration of the Continuance of the Gofpel among us, and the Smiles of Divine Providence upon us with Regard to the Seafons of the Year, and the general Health which has been enjoyed; and in particular, from a Confideration of the Union which fo remarkably prevails not only in this Province, but through the Continent at this alarming Crifis.

IT is *RESOLVED*, as the Senfe of this Congrefs, That it is highly proper that a Day of PUBLIC THANKSGIVING fhould be obferved throughout this Province; and it is accordingly recommended to the feveral Religious Affemblies in the Province, that *Thurfday* the *Fifteenth Day of December* next, be obferved as a Day of THANKSGIVING, to render Thanks to Almighty God for all the Bleffings we enjoy. At the fame Time, we think it incumbent on this People to humble themfelves before God on Account of their Sins, for which he hath been pleafed in his righteous Judgment to fuffer fo great a Calamity to befal us, as the prefent Controverfy between Great-Britain and the Colonies; as alfo to implore the Divine Bleffing upon us, that by the Affiftance of his Grace we may be enabled to reform whatever is amifs among us, that fo God may be pleafed to continue to us the Bleffings we enjoy, and remove the Tokens of his Displeafure, by caufing Harmony and Union to be reftored between Great-Britain and thefe Colonies, that we may again rejoice in the Smiles of our Sovereign and the Poffeffion of thofe Privileges which have been tranfmitted to us, and have the hopeful Profpect that they fhall be handed down intire to Pofterity, under the Proteftant Succeffion in the illuftrious Houfe of Hanover.

By Order of the Provincial Congrefs,

JOHN HANCOCK, Prefident.

31. *Wednesday, January 1. 1701. A little before Break-a-Day, at Boston of the Massachusetts.*
[Boston: Bartholomew Green, 1713?]

This short poem was written by Samuel Sewall, a judge of the Superior Court, who is best known for his involvement in the witchcraft trials. Here we see a strong expression of the missionary zeal of the Puritans. An entry in Sewall's *Diary* includes this poem and mentions that he had it printed: "Just about Break-a-day Jacob Amsden and 3 other Trumpeters gave a Blast with the Trumpets on the common near Mr. Alford's. Then went to the Green Chamber, and sounded there till about sunrise. Bell-man said these verses a little before Break-a-day, which I printed and gave them. [In margin - My verses upon new Century.] The Trumpeters cost me five pieces 8/8."

This copy may not have been printed at that time since it is bound in *Proposals Touching the Accomplishment of Prophesies Humbly Offered* by Samuel Sewall which was printed by Bartholomew Green in Boston in 1713.

6 ¼ × 8 ¼

WEDNESDAY, *January* 1. 1701.

A little before Break-a-Day, at *Boston* of the *Massachusets*.

ONCE more! Our GOD, vouchsafe to Shine:
Tame Thou the Rigour of our Clime.
Make haste with thy Impartial Light,
And terminate this long dark Night.

Let the transplanted **English** Vine
Spread further still : still Call it Thine.
Prune it with Skill : for yield it can
More Fruit to Thee the Husbandman.

Give the poor **Indians** Eyes to see
The Light of Life : and set them free ;
That they Religion may profess,
Denying all Ungodliness.

From hard'ned **Jews** the Vail remove,
Let them their Martyr'd JESUS love ;
And Homage unto Him afford,
Because He is their Rightfull LORD.

So false Religions shall decay,
And Darkness fly before bright Day :
So Men shall GOD in CHRIST adore ;
And worship Idols vain, no more.

So **Asia**, and **Africa**,
Europa, with **America** ;
All Four, in Consort join'd, shall Sing
New Songs of Praise to CHRIST our KING.

32. *Mr. Samuel Gorton's Ghost: Or, the Spirit of Persecution represented in the Similitude of a Dream.*
Newport, Rhode Island: James Franklin, 1728.

Samuel Gorton emigrated to Boston in 1637 and was banished for heresy. From there he went to Plymouth, only to become embroiled in a dispute with Ralph Smith. He left that settlement in 1638 and went to Portsmouth, Rhode Island. After a brief stay, he left for Providence, but Roger Williams would not admit him as an inhabitant. He finally settled at Shawomet, on Narraganset Bay, which he renamed Warwick. Even after his death in 1677, he had a group of followers who called themselves Gortonites. This poem is probably by one of them.

His denial of the Trinity, his idea that each man should be his own priest, his denial of the existence of heaven and hell, and his vigorous opposition towards paying the clergy troubled the authorities exceedingly. It is this last tenet which is the main theme of this poem and which is expressed in such verses as "To sell the Gospel by the Year."

Evans 39894

11 × 15 ⅛

Mr. SAMUEL GORTON's

GHOST:

OR,

The Spirit of PERSECUTION reprefented in the Simili- tude of a DREAM.

AS I lay fleeping on my Bed,
I dream'd of *Gorton* that is dead,
Who perfecuted was of old,
For the Opinion he did hold.

I thought he did rife up and fpeak
Concerning thofe who much do feek
For to come in and fpoil your Peace;
Pray God, *faith he*, they don't increafe;

Or ever Foot-hold get in here,
To fell the Gofpel by the Year,
And fay they Licenfe have from Heaven
To fell to you what Chrift hath given.

Of *Judas* you may think of ole,
Who his bleft Lord and Mafter fold
For Silver Pieces Three Times Ten:
So do thefe blind and filly Men

Think what they do is very well,
When they the holy Gofpel fell.
But which is worft, to fell the SON,
Or the bleft Work which he hath done,

To fave our felves from Hells great Pain,
And make of it their worldly Gain?
Saith he, God will ne'er let them thrive,
Who challenge his Prerogative,

And think to change the Hearts of any
With Perfecutions which are many;
For they may read and plainly fee
The Hearts of Men that turned be,

Like running Rivers of Water fair,
By Gods great Hand they turned are;
While Men have Being or alive,
This is God's great Prerogative:

But Perfecution, ne'er fo fmart,
It never yet could change the Heart,
But if you wifh they may'nt come in,
Then pray to God, and leave your Sin.

For if they once get Foot, that Day,
Your Cattle they muft go to pay,
And pleafant Flocks that fpread the Plains,
For the falfe Notions of their Brains.

For in their Heat and blinded Zeal,
They will pronounce, God did entail
His heavenly Mind unto their Seet;
Therefore they others do reject,

And perfecute them to the Life,
The Hufband parted from the Wife.
And fome affert this Sentence fore,
Saying that God hath given them o'er

Unto the burning Flames of Hell,
E'er fince their Father *Adam* fell:
But yet, fay they, thofe Babes are fafe,
To whom the Father lends his Faith;

Or if their Mother does believe
The Lord will them furely receive.
This dreadful Doctrine who can bear,
Since God the Father he did fwear

By his bleft Self, fince *Adam* fell,
This Proverb fhan't in *Ifrael*
No more for ever ufed be,
Becaufe the Father clim'd the Tree,

And eat the Grapes the Son fhould die;
For fure the Lord doth this defy.
But thofe that fin as Agents free,
And don't repent, fhall damned be.

Let them repent therefore I pray,
Of their great Perfecution,
Before the great High Sheriff of Death
Doth ferve his Execution.

Then will it be too late for them
To cry, yea, or to weep,
Or think for to return again
The Cattle, Horfe or Sheep.

That they from thofe poor Men have took,
While Babes for Food did cry,
Altho' Parents were not of them,
Nor their Society:

Yet would they force them for to buy
The Gofpel by the Year,
Altho' they them did ne'er come nigh,
Nor ne'er a Word did hear.

It's ftrange, faid he, how they mete out
The Gofpel by the Year,
That every Man for what he pays,
Can have his certain Share.

Alas, faid he, you muft not doubt
Their cunning Art and Skill;
They will make you a precious Saint
For Money if you will:

For if that fudden Death fhould fnatch
You fuddenly away,
You muft perhaps half damned in
A gloomy Region lay:

Except fome Friend with his Mony
Doth for your Soul appear,
And with that Money get you pray'd
From that thick gloomy Air,

Unto the brighteft Region
Of Life and perfect Glory:
And th' World it is fo blinded now,
T' have Faith in their falfe Story.

Saith he, I now muft end, left you
With Tedioufnefs fhould urge me,
And pray to God, that by his Grace,
He would purge all their Clergy

From all their foolifh Popifh Stuff,
And their vain glorious Pride,
And that the People they may have
A meek and humble Guide,

That they may teach the Peeple how
The Heavens to inherit;
And how the Lord he has declar'd,
He'll worfhip'd be in Spirit:

And they that will his holy Laws
Obey in Words and Deeds,
Muft more obedience pay to God
Than Mints or Annifeeds.

The Widows Caufe they muft fearch out,
That fhe has Right befure;
No Herd of Cattle muft take from
The Fatherlefs nor poor.

Left God he doth in Anger fwear,
They never fhall be bleft,
For enter in th' Heavens, where
The Righteous they do reft.

Now when he all thofe Words had faid,
Methought he took him Wing and fled,
And vanifh'd from me like a Scroll,
Unto the Father of his Soul.

Some further Talk I did expect
About this *Prefbyterian* Sect,
But found an End unto the Theme;
For when I 'woke 'twas but a Dream.

FINIS.

NEWPORT, *Rhode-Ifland*: Printed by *James Franklin*, at his Printing-Houfe on *Tillinghaft*'s Wharf. 1728.

33. *A Dialogue Between Death and a Lady.*
Boston: Sold at the Heart and Crown in Cornhill, 1731-1775.

"A Dialogue Between Death and a Lady" was printed sometime between 1731 and 1775 and is known in at least six other editions before 1800. This poem was issued even as late as 1835. Although these verses may have been written as an elegy for a particular individual, it is more probable that they were composed as a memento mori for the general public. In particular the custom of giving alms to the poor is stressed. In the words of Death:

> How freely can you let your Silver fly
> To purchase Life, rather than yield to die:
> But while you flourish'd here in all your Store,
> You would not spare one Penny to the Poor.
>
> . . . .
>
> My Lord beheld wherein you did amiss,
> And calls you hence to give Account for this.

In comparison to Europe during the eighteenth century, poverty was less frequent and less severe in the colonies. Nonetheless, giving alms to the poor or helping the distressed in other ways was expected of the wealthy. Perhaps this poem served as a reminder to the uncharitable.

Evans 42033
8 ½ × 12 ½

A DIALOGUE BETWEEN Death and a Lady.

Very suitable for these Times.

Death.

FAIR Lady lay your costly Robes aside,
　No longer may you glory in your Pride;
Take Leave of all your carnal vain Delight,
I'm come to Summon you away this Night.

Lady.

What bold attempt is this, Pray let me know
From whence you came, or whither must I go;
Shall I, who am a Lady yield or bow,
To such a pale fac'd Visage, who art thou?

Death.

Do you not know me? Well, I'll tell you then,
'Tis I that conquer all the Sons of Men;
No Pitch of Honour from my Dart is free,
My Name is *Death*, have you not heard of me?

Lady.

Yes, I have heard of you time after time,
But being in the Glory of my Prime,
I did not think that thou wouldst call so soon,
Why must my Morning Sun go down at Noon?

Death.

Talk not of Noon, you may as well be mute,
This is no time at all for to dispute.
Your richest Jewels, Gold, and Garments brave,
Your Houses, Lands they must new Masters have,
Though thy vain Heart to Riches was inclin'd,
Yet thou, alas! must leave them all behind.

Lady.

My Heart is cold, I tremble at the News,
Here's Bags of Gold if thou wilt me excuse,
And seize on those, thus finish thou the Strife,
With such who are aweary of their Life.
Are there not many bound in Prison strong,
In bitter grief of Soul have languish'd long.
From all would find a Grave a Place of Rest,
From all their Grief in which they are opprest?
Besides there's many with their Hoary Head,
And Palsie Joynts, by which their Joys are fled,
Release thou them whose Grief and Sorrow's great,
And spare my Life to have a longer Date.

Death.

Tho' they with Age are full of Grief and Pain,
While their appointed Time they must remain,
I come to none before my Warrant's seal'd,
And when it is they must submit and yield:
I take no Bribes, believe me, it is true,
Prepare your self to go, I come for you.

Lady.

Death, be not so severe, let me obtain,
A little longer Time to live and Reign;
Fain would I stay, if thou my Life wilt spare,
I have a Daughter Beautiful and Fair,
I'd live to see her Wed, whom I adore;
Grant me but this and then I'll ask no more.

Death.

This is a slender frivolous Excuse,
I have you fast, and will not let you loose;
Leave her to Providence, for you must go
Along with me whether you will or no.
I *Death* command great Kings to leave their Crown,
And at my Feet to lay their Scepter down;
If unto Kings this Favour I'll not give,
But cut them down, can you expect to live
Beyond the Limits of your time and space?
No, I must send you to another Place.

Lady.

You learned Doctors now express your Skill;
And let not Death of me obtain his Will;
Prepare your Cordials, let me Comfort find,
My Gold shall fly like Chaff before the Wind.

Death.

Forbear to call, their Skill will never do,
They are but Mortals here as well as you.
I give the fatal Wound, my Dart is sure,
'Tis far beyond a Doctor's Skill or cure.
How freely can you let your Silver fly
To purchase Life, rather than yield to die:
But while you flourish'd here in all your Store,
You would not spare one Penny to the Poor.
In all your Pomp the Poor you then did hate,
And like rich *Dives*, scourg'd them from thy Gate:
But tho' you did those whom thus you did scorn,
They like to you into this World were born;
Tho' for your Alms they did both cringe and bow,
They bore GOD's Image here as well as you.
Tho' in his Name their Suit to you they make,
You would not give one Penny for his sake;
My Lord beheld wherein you did amiss,
And calls you hence to give Account for this.

Lady.

O heavy News! Must I no longer stay?
How shall I stand good God, in thy great Day?
Down from her Eyes the dying Tears did flow
And said, there's none knows what I undergo
Upon a Bed of Sorrow here I lie,
My carnal Life makes me afraid to die;
My Sins, alas! are many great and foul,
Which have deformed my immortal Soul;
And tho' I do deserve the righteous Frown,
Yet Pardon, Lord and pour a Blessing down;
Then with a dying Sigh her Heart did break,
And did the Pleasures of the World forsake.

Here we may see the High and Mighty fall,
For *Death* he sheweth no Respect at all,
To any one of high or low Degree,
Great Men submit to *Death* as well as we;
Tho' they are gay, their Lives are but a Span,
A Lump of Clay, so poor a Creature's MAN.

Sold at the Heart and Crown in Cornhill, Boston.

34. *A Dialogue Between Death, the Soul, Body, World and Jesus Christ. Composed by Edmond Weld.*
Boston: E. Russell, [1787].

Very little is known about the author of this poem. Edmund Weld was graduated from Harvard College in 1650 and went to Ireland to be a minister at Inniskean where he died on March 2, 1668. This was a popular broadside: there were at least nine editions published before 1800, the earliest of which was published around 1720.

Perhaps the popularity of this poem was due to its tone—optimistic and faintly humorous. The notion of the body complaining to the soul about the coming separation of the two ("But ah! poor I/ Must rotting lye/ As one forgot amongst the dead") is quite amusing. It is possible that Edmund Weld was influenced by the current of English literature during the mid-seventeenth century led by Milton which included satiric and humorous elegies.

Evans 45203
12 ¾ × 12 ½

A DIALOGUE

Between DEATH, the SOUL, BODY, WORLD and JESUS CHRIST.

Composed by *EDMOND WELD*, formerly of HARVARD-COLLEGE, who removing from hence to *Ireland*, became a Preacher of the Gospel there, who upon the Meditation of his Death, (which was so finished the 2d of March, 1668) made this following POEM, which was sent hither by his Wife, to his Relations here. *Ætatis Suæ.* 39.

DEATH.

HO, Ho, prepare to go with me,
  For I am sent to summon thee,
See my commission seal'd with blood:
Who sent me He will make it good.
    The life of man
    Is like a span,
Whose slender thread I must divide.
    My Name is DEATH,
    I'll stop thy breath;
From my arrests thou canst not hide.

SOUL.

O Death, triumph not over me,
My SAVIOUR's death hath conquer'd thee,
Man's sin at first did give thee breath,
Whose *Exit* now must be thy death.
    But yet thro' grace,
    (So stands the case)
Harm thou canst not, but only fright.
    Ah death thou'rt dead,
    Broke is thy head,
Thy sting and strength removed quite.

But what dost think to scare me so?
Me to assault so like a foe?
Nay Death, thy power and all that's thine
The second cov'nant made it mine.
    Come let's shake hands,
    I'll kiss thy bands;
'Tis happy news for me to die.

    What dost thou think
    That I will shrink?
I'll go to immortality.
    Transported is my ravish'd heart
To think now hence I must depart;
Long waited I for such a day,
Thrice welcome summons come away,
    Come strike the blow,
    That I may go,
Why stay thy chariot wheels so long?
    To stay 'tis pain,
    To die 'tis gain;
Delay me not, you do me wrong.

    This is my FATHER's Messenger,
My King and Bridegroom's Harbinger;
See here his chariot driving fast,
Home to conduct me in all haste.
    I'm sick of love
    For HIM above.
I grow impatient to be gone,
    Him for to see
    Who loved me,
That precious, loving, lovely ONE.

    Hadst thou but knock'd the other day
I had been forced then to say,
O spare a little, give me space
Until I see thy pleasant face.
    Because my light
    Was turn'd to night,
Hid was his face, eclips'd his love;
    Then inward fears
    Caus'd many tears;
Few visits had I from above.

    His name forever blessed is,
To send at such a time as this;
Nought have I now to do but die,
And sleep in JESUS quietly:
    For lately He
    Refreshed me
With sweet embraces from above.
    I beg'd a smile,
    And he mean while
Caus'd me to understand his love.

BODY.

    And must we part, my dearest Mate,
So many years consociate:
What makes thee long uncas'd to lie?
What means this great disparity?
    Thou tak'st thy flight
    To Heavens' height
To be conjoin'd with CHRIST thy Head;
    But ah I poor I
    Must rotting lye
As one forgot amongst the dead.

SOUL.

Companion mine, why blam'st thou me
Longing to leave mortality;
My choicest acts have spoiled been,
By such a mass of death and sin;
    My joys were small
    Disturbed all
In thy cold, dark and leaky tent,
    My duties were
    Put out of square
With thine unhandy instrument.
But CHRIST shall change thy sinful dust,
The grave shall rot out all thy rust;
That body of thine shall fashion'd be,
Like to His own in its degree:
    Yea tho' they rot,
    Yet not one jot
Of all thy dust shall perish aye:
    He in thy sleep
    Safe will thee keep
'Till *trumpet's sound* shall call away,

    Whose sound shall cause thee to awake
Omnipotency shall thee take
Then to receive, so we shall meet,
And one another kindly greet;
    Made one again,
    So to remain
Embosom'd friends, in lasting bliss,
    And never more,
    As heretofore,
Act any thing that is amiss.

WORLD.

What's this I hear? Guest so unkind,
To thrust me so quite out of mind!
Have I so hard a Landlord been
As not to value me a pin?
    To kick at me
    Who nourish'd thee,
And so to change old friends for new.
    Men so unkind
    I seldom find;
I'll care as little now for you.

SOUL.

We're well agreed, vain World farewel,
Thy flattering smiles begin to smell;
They never did deserve my love,
Nor do thy frowns at all me move;
    Because my heart
    Is set apart
For things that are of best account:
    The husk and shell,
    With thee did dwell,
My better part did higher mount.

'Twas yonder, yonder, up above,
Where I did live, converse and love;
A stranger here, and strangely us'd,
By thee and thine I was abus'd;
    I'm not thine own,
    Nor am I known
By those of thy ungodly race;
    And therefore I
    So cruelly
Was hated in that weary place.

    But as for you, my weeping Friends,
My God will make you all amends,
Your care and kindness shewn to me
Shall all by him rewarded be:
    Yourselves have seen
    How GOD hath been
Most sweetly gracious unto me;
    Live holily,
    Then when you die
The same to you this GOD may be.

JESUS CHRIST.

Welcome to me, my lovely Bride,
For whom I liv'd for whom I dy'd;
Nor do I count my heart's blood dear
To purchase a possession here.
    Come satisfy
    Both heart and I,
With purest joys up to the brim;
    Here's endless store,
    What can be more
Than in love's ocean aye to swim?

    Make haste, bring forth the nuptial vest
And let the fatted calf be dress'd;
Angels and Seraphims come sing,
And with your shout make Heaven ring.
    Come thou possess
    That blessedness
Prepar'd before the world was made,
    And wear the crown
    With great renown.
'Tis honour that shall never fade.

SOUL.

Blest be thy glorious Majesty
That looks on such a worm as I;
Thou didst me from the dungeon raise,
That I might here advance thy praise.
    When I did dwell
    In lowest Hell,
Love everlasting fetch'd me thence,
    Else I had been
    Through Satan's spleen
For evermore excluded hence.

    When I was dead grace quickned me,
When I was lost fought out by thee,
Thou didst me pardon, call and save;
Bou't with thy blood whate'er I have.
    Now blessed be
    The LAMB so free
To die that I might life obtain;
    For this therefore
    For evermore
Blest be the LAMB forever slain.

BOSTON: Printed by E. RUSSELL, next Liberty-Pole, for JOHN HOWE, of *Ringe*, (*New-Hampshire.*) [Pr. 5 Cop.]

Also, just published, a curious and remarkable Account of the Life, Death and Burial of a most wonderful and surprising HERMIT, lately discovered in a Cave in *Virginia.*—Likewise, Mrs. *Olney's* remarkable DREAM. (☞ Very cheap to *Travelling Traders.*) BICKERSTAFF's *genuine* BOSTON ALMANACK for 1788, is in the press.

ELEGIES

35. *Tears Dropt at the Funeral of . . . Mrs. Elizabeth Hatch.*
By J[oseph] M[etcalf].
[Boston? 1710.]

Probably written by the Reverend Joseph Metcalf of Falmouth, this elegy
has several distinct parts. There are sections addressed to the husband of
Elizabeth Hatch, to her father, to her other relatives, and to the town of
Falmouth. Together with a severe drought and an infestation of insects, Mrs.
Hatch's death, closely following three others, inspired the Reverend Metcalf
to exhort the town to repent of its sins.

Metcalf was the minister in Falmouth from 1707 to his death in 1723. This
is the only poem he wrote that is still extant. Part of the ire which he vents
against the town may be due to the fact that his salary was a year in arrears.

Evans 39514
13 ¼ × 17 ⅛

TEARS Dropt at the Funeral of that Eminently Pious Christian,

Mrs. Elizabeth Hatch,

The late Vertuous Wife of Ensign *Moses Hatch*, of *Falmouth*, and Daughter of the Honourable *JOHN THACHER* Esq. of *Yarmouth*, Who Exchanged Earth for Heaven, *May 18th. Anno* 1710. in the 33*d.* Year of her Age.

The Memory of the Just is blessed, Prov. X. 7.

NEws, News, they say, alas! Bad News, I fear!
A Shining *Star* has left our *Hemi-sphere*!
A precious Saint is newly gone to Rest,
Whom we have lost; and therefore are distrest.
Our grief renew'd, by this most awful Stroke,
To Weep and Mourn afresh, doth us provoke.
Before we could have time to wipe our eyes
From brinish Tears, or cease from dismal Cryes
For those most heavy strokes, which late were sent
In sore Bereavements for our punishment;
Wherein we all sustain most grievous loss:
Some more are fallen, to augment the Cross.
An Aged Man was yesterday intomb'd:
And now this Sister Dear is hither doom'd.
Our dear *Elizabeth*, that gracious Saint;
She's gone! She's gone! alas, our hearts do faint!
What shall we do! alas! where shall we find
Her Match in Grace, amongst us, left behind?
Many, yea most, be sure, She did excel,
Especially in Things which I shall tell.
She labour'd much to live in holy Fear
Of GOD, to whom she daily did draw near.
She striv'd, with all her might, to do God's Will:
And took the greatest pains her Sin to kill.
An holy Walk with God she did Endeavour:
And now she's gone to be with Him for ever.
The Sacred Scriptures were her daily Food;
More sweet to her than any worldly good.
God's holy Sabbaths were her hearts delight, }
Wherein she Serv'd the Lord with all her Might; }
And labour'd much to hear the Word aright. }
The Word and Ordinances of the Lord
Did precious Comforts to her Soul afford:
She priz'd the same above the finest Gold;
Her Heart therein would burn, and not be cold.
Her Soul did long and pant for Heav'nly cheer,
And leap for Joy, when Sacraments drew near:
She oft would speak as if she could not live
Without those Things, which there she did receive.
Christ and her Soul did very often meet:
And her Communion with Him very sweet.
Tho' Doubts and Fears, and holy Jealousies
Did oft perplex her Heart, and swell her eyes;
Yet still, when she did come God's Word to hear,
Her doubts and fears would quickly disappear.
God found her oft alone, on bended knees.
Her Faith and Love increased by degrees:
Especially of late, her Graces grew
Aspiring for the *Mark*, she had in view.
She Soar'd aloft in Heav'nly Meditation:
And did not shun strict Self-Examination.
A singular Affection she did bare
To all that gracious and religious were;
Especially to holy *Men of God*,
Whose feet, with Gospel-News of Peace, were shod.
The choicest Saints she made her chief delight:
In Christian Conversation most upright.
Experiences choice she had in store:
And in Good Works abounding more, and more.
Most low and humble, in her own esteem:
Clad with that Robe that doth the Saints beseem.
Others she did extol and magnify;
While Self was much abased in her eye.
'Mongst pious Christians in her Element;
Most forward for to have the Time well spent:
And if 'twere not, while she did sit with Such;
She wanted Ease, and did the time begrutch.
Her Heart and Tongue together ever went;
And both were Heaven-ward and Christ-ward bent.
Those who the most acquainted with her were,
To speak her Praises now they cant forbare.
Her choice discourse so oft reviv'd their hearts,
That they are stung with Grief, when she departs.
When Such were dead and dull, and out of frame,
And in her sweet company then came.
They who had their hearts touch'd by her gracious Tongue,
And into Heav'nly Places led along.
For me; while I this *Lamentation* frame,
Rather with Tears than Ink I pen the same.
When I remember how I've often felt,
While in discourse with her my heart did melt;
And how Divine Affections rais'd have bin
Into a Flame, my sluggish Heart within.
Lord, Why am I bereav'd of such a Friend!
Why hast thou brought her to such sudden End?
If I an Opportunity had had
Of some Discourse, 'twould not have been so sad.
I had a Call, just to step out of Town;
And e're returned home, this Star was down:
And, if I had been here, 'twere much the same;
Her Death and Sickness in such manner came,
So hasty, and with so much Violence,
As to prevent her Much from speaking sense.
Stop, Stop, my Pen, why should I thus complain?
As if my own dear Consort here were slain: }
Should I not rather on Another Strain }
Thank God that 'tis no worse? and then, again, }
Labour to Comfort him, who doth sustain }
The greatest loss, and feel the sharpest Pain: }
Since my own Loss is but a little Part
Of his, who stands by with a bleeding heart:
Whose lovely *Mate* is snatch't away so soon;
Which into Midnight turns his brightest Noon:
His House and Children dear, much ill betiding,
For want of Mother's Prudence, Love and Guiding.
My *Brother* dear, I therefore turn to you;
Assure your self my *Sympathy* is true:
And for your Comfort, This I have to say,
Your Wife took Wing for Heaven yesterday.
You've lost her, true; yet she's not lost; but gone
To reap the wages of the Work she's done.
Take Comfort then, since you may well believe
That Jesus Christ did her dear Soul receive,
As soon as it took flight from sinful earth;
To live with Him, in endless Blissful Mirth:
Where you likewise, if you hold on your way
Shall live with her in perfect State for aye.
You know she liv'd amidst much trouble here, }
Surrounded many times with Grief and Fear: }
And now's but mounted to an higher Sphere. }
Why should you grieve that she is got above,
Incircled in her Saviour's Arms of Love.
She's got the start of you; her Work is done:
And therefore 'tis her Intrest to be gone
God calls her home: and Him you will provoke,
Unless you bless the Hand, that gives the Stroke:
Then say Amen. And had you her so long?
And prov'd she such a Blessing us among?
Was you so long, so happy in a Wife?
Beyond what Most experience all their Life:
So Pious, and so very Prudent too;
And brought she such a Blessing upon you?
Thank God for That: His Sov'raignty adore:
GOD did it: then be dumb, and say no more.
And now, dear Mourning *Father*, whence she sprung;
A Song of Comfort, Pray *Sir*, let be Sung.
I know that, *Abra'm*-like, you've done a Deal
Instruction-wise; for your dear Children's Weal:
And good Success God granted to the same,
Whereby you've gain'd an everlasting Name:
I've seen the Lines, which you did write and weep,
When this blest Daughters *Mother* fell asleep:
How our *Elizabeth*, among the rest, }
When but a little Child, therein was blest, }
In one short Verse; which you have well exprest. }
You said, *Elizabeth is next in Count*:
You pray'd, *God grant her Faith aloft may Mount*.
And I observ'd, when first I saw the same,
A Prophets Guess, in blessing her by name:
And did adore Gods Grace, who did fulfil
That Prophecy, according to his Will.
O happy Father! Such a Child to own;
So Rich in Grace, so Tall in vertue grown:
Who tho' grim Death too soon hath clos'd her eyes;
Yet liveth still, above the Starry skies:
With her translated Mother, and the rest
Of your's; Who are in Robes of Glory drest.
Part of your self wing'd upwards long before }
And now Another *Part* is past the Door, }
And happily got all the danger o're; }
And safely landed on the Upper Shoar: }
And who can either hope or wish for more? }
Sure these are Pledges, that it won't be long
E're you, their *Head* shall meet them in the Throng,
At Christ's Right hand, in Resurrection Day,
And there, with ravisht heart, stand forth and say,
Lord, here am I, and here are all of Mine, }
Who thro' Free Grace for ever shall be Thine: }
And in thy Glorious Kingdom ever shine. }
Hold out: 'tis but a little while at most,
And you shall joyn with all the Heav'nly Host.
Mean while, Remember an unworthy *Son*:
Your Blessing let me have, and I'll have done.
Brothers and *Sisters* dear, and each *Relation*,
Of whatsoever Name, or Occupation;
A Word to you under your present Pain,
For such a loss, as herein you sustain.
Grieve not for her, whom Death hath thus cut down?
For, look; She's now inthron'd, and wears the Crown:
Yet for your selves with moderation mourn,
In Godly Sort, so as from Sin to turn.
The Warning take, which God to you doth give:
Let her Example, in your Practice, live.
And still stand ready for your own Decease;
That when Death comes, you may depart in Peace.
Keep clear Accompts, and daily watch and pray;
Still looking out for your appointed day;
And then you'll meet with her again at last;
For aye refresht, feasting on sweet Repast.
And now, Poor *Falmouth*, I'll conclude with you,
By adding to the former lines a Few,
Wherein some of my Fears I shall express;
And then bespeak you, in a brief Address.
A *Mourning-Weed* to you I lately sent
When divers Saints from hence together went;
Wherein our case was mention'd, and bewail'd,
In brine and gall, until I almost fail'd:
And yet, I fear, we do not lay to heart
Those heavy Judgments, under which we smart.
I fear, we are too stupid, void of Sense;
And that we ha'nt reform'd our great Offence.
God still goes on against us many wayes;
And yet, I fear, we hear not what He says.
His Judgments still increase and multiply:
It seems as if we all were like to dye.
What Scarcity do we already see?
And yet have cause to fear, much worse 'twill be.
Such Awful Time for want of former Rain
We never knew; nor ever felt such Pain.
The Grass begins in Spots to die apace,
And other fruits, upon Earth's parched face,
Do languish much, and likely are to fail;
Both by the Drought, and infinite long Trayl
Of swarming Insects which do All devour:
Destroying to the utmost of their Pow'r.
Lord, what's a-coming on us? Troubles near:
Thy Warning-pieces, loud discharg'd, we hear:
Thy choicest Ones, we see, Thou callest home
Lest they should see those fearful Evils come.
Such as have greatest intrest in God's Grace,
And do by Righteousness defend the Place;
Such choice Ones, as our chief Protection are;
Who tie God's hands, by Faith and fervent Pray'r;
He doth remove? and break our Hedges down;
That so He may more freely on us frown.
Such Deaths are *Ominous* unto a Place;
Symptomes of Judgments coming on apace.
O miserable *Falmouth*! wilt thou see?
Consider well, and lay to heart with me
God's Judgments threatned, and our Fall fore-told;
As once it was with *Nineveh* of old:
And let's repent of Sin, and turn to God;
Lest otherwise we feel his Iron Rod.
All you, that fear the Lord, and wish for Weal;
Let's pray with one consent that God would heal
Our awful Breach, and grievous loss repair;
By giving to those that Survivers are
A double Portion of that Pious Spirit;
Which the Deceased did so much inherit.
For otherwise, should God go on to glean
His brightest Jewels, and his Wheat so clean,
And sow no more; the rubbish, chaff and dross
Would quickly be expos'd to utter loss:
And this is like to be our case; unless
We timely hearken unto such Address:
And by our fervent Prayers do obtain
The Spirit from on high, for to remain
With us, upon us, yea, and in us too;
Prompting us for to Think and Speak and Do
The Will of God, by keeping his Commands;
Resigning up our All into his Hands.
And therefore for to do accordingly
Let's ever labour, till we come to dye.
And let us not give out, nor weary be,
Until an Answer of our Suit we see.
And if we shall be thus in Duty found,
We shall at last with Glory bright be crown'd:
But if our Duty we do not attend,
We must expect a bitter Latter-end.
Oh, let us then be striving to excel
In Piety, like her, who lately fell.
This shining Saints Example let us mind
If Heaven we at last would hope to find.
For sure we may, if we her Foot-steps trace,
Arrive at God's most holy dwelling-place;
Where we, with her, shall live, rejoyce and sing
Eternal Praises unto Christ, our King;
In joynt Consort with all that went before,
Triumphing in God's Grace for ever-more.

J. M.

Fear Thacher

36. *An Elegy Occasioned by the sudden and awful Death of Mr. Nathanael Baker of Dedham.*
[*Boston?* 1733.]

In contrast to the very brief newspaper accounts on incidents such as this, the broadside elegy is an outlet for emotions. This poem was probably written by Margaret Fisher, the fiancée of Mr. Baker. The brief account in the *New England Weekly Journal* for May 14, 1733, reads as follows: "On Monday last a Young Man (who was to have been married the Thursday following), as he was riding home fell from off his Horse, and as 'tis tho't crack'd his Skull; he was soon after taken up, and died the next Night, not being able to speak one word after his Fall."

Evans 40017
8 ½ × 13 ¼

Memento Mori   Remember DEATH.

AN
ELEGY
Occasioned by the sudden and awful Death
OF
Mr. *Nathanael Baker*
of *Dedham* :

A Young Man just upon the point of Marriage.
And Son to Lieuten't *JOHN BAKER.*

He fell from his Horse on Monday Night the 7th of **May,** 1733; and Died
the Wednesday following. Ætat. 27.

Come *Melpomene*, sing thou Tragic Muse,
But I your mournful Subject now will chose;
In doleful ! doleful Lays ! tune up your Ly
And raise in us a melancholy Fire:
Say mourning Muse, how dreadful does it seem ?
That youthful, lovely, *Baker* is your Theme.
Assist ye N I N E, or else I cant relate,
In Strains of Woe, that shall be adequate ;
To the surprizing awful Accident.
Oh ! boundless Grief, Oh ! Tears that cant be pen
I tremble tho' I only mourn a Friend,
That came to a most unexpected End ;
It seems to me, my Song would give relief,
If I could imitate his Parents Grief.
But that I know is far beyond the Pen,
Or Rhet'ric of the Sons of mortal Men ;
We can't express by Words, they can't reveal,
The Floods of Grief, the Agonies they feel.
O this our Son, in all his Strength and Prime
When Youth and Beauty in their Lustre shine,
Is hurl'd away to Shades of Death, and Gloom;
How melancholy is the mournful Room ?
How broken is the House, and desolate the Bed,
And all the Places, where he frequented.
The Fields shall miss him, & the Herds that low
The Grass seems humble where he us'd to mow ;
But chiefly all his Friends with Anguish mourn,
And have their Hearts with Grief and Sorrow torn,
All his acquaintance bathe his Urn with Tears,
A sprightly Youth, in midst of blooming Years ;
A winning Aier, a manly Innocence,
A Conversation void of all Offence ;
Nay comely too, and decent in his Mein,
A thousand winning Graces in him seen.
Where are they now ? where is he gone ? ah where ?
He feeds the Worms that can't be brib'd to spare ;

O ye his Brethren and Sister say,
How kind a Brother now is mov'd away,
Into the Grave, from whence he came again;
His Face shall bless no more your longing Eyes,
I fail ! I fail ! or else I would relate,
The boundless Grief of (the unfortunate)
Young *Marg'ret Fisher* his designed Mate.
In doleful Strains the mourning Damsel Crys,
But Death is deaf to all her Agonies ;
This Night he left me, but I little thought,
To see him die, I should so soon be brought
Oh ! cruel Death your conquer'd Victim spare,
And let him once but beat the yielding Air,
To speak one Word to me before he go,
And tell me something that I want to know.
But Oh farewel ! He's dying now I find,
His Life and Breath is scatter'd in the Wind ;
Farewell my Friend, my kind Associate,
I thought that Heaven design'd you for my Mate,
My Heart is yours, only my backward Hand,
Was not stretch'd forth to tye the Nuptial Band.
You can't return, but I shall go to you,
Farewell sweet Soul, Adieu, Adieu, Adieu.
But cease to Mourn, your boundless Passions sway,
God says be mute, therefore you must obey ;
He governs all in Wisdom by his Power,
And orders out your Lot from Hour to Hour.
And though by you, his Ways ben't Understood,
They always end in the Eternal Good,
Of those that have an int'rest in his Love,
I wish you all this Blessing from above.
Dry up your Tears, and now like Christians say,
Blessed be God, who gives and takes away.

F I N I S.

37. *Phillis' Poem on the Death of Mr. Whitefield.*
[*No place*, 1770.]

Phillis Wheatley, America's first black poetess, was brought from Africa at the age of eight and sold as a slave to the Wheatley family of Boston in 1761. She received an excellent education and was encouraged in her literary efforts by the Wheatley family who treated her as one of them. This elegy on George Whitefield was her first published work. In 1773, she traveled to England where she was introduced to various members of society by the Countess of Huntingdon, to whom Phillis had addressed this broadside elegy. The Countess was undoubtedly instrumental in the publication of a volume of the poetess' work in London in 1773 under the title *Poems on Various Subjects, Religious and Moral.*

   George Whitefield, born in England in 1714, was ordained in 1739. Among the several positions he held was that of domestic chaplain to the Countess of Huntingdon. His career in America spanned several decades during which he founded orphanages and schools. His preaching stimulated the religious revival in this country and thousands were converted by his evangelical zeal.

Evans 42198

9 ¾ × 13 ¾

Phillis's POEM

ON THE

DEATH of Mr. WHITEFIELD.

HAIL happy Saint on thy immortal throne!
  To thee complaints of grievance are unknown;
We hear no more the music of thy tongue,
Thy wonted auditories cease to throng.
Thy lessons in unequal'd accents flow'd!
While emulation in each bosom glow'd;
Thou didst, in strains of eloquence refin'd,
Inflame the soul and captivate the mind,
Unhappy we, the setting Sun deplore!
Which once was splendid, but it shines no more;
He leaves this earth for Heaven's unmeasur'd height,
And worlds unknown recieve him from our sight;
There WHITEFIELD wings with rapid course his way,
And sails to Zion, through vast seas of day.
When his AMERICANS were burden'd sore,
When streets were crimson'd with their guiltless gore!
Unrival'd friendship in his breast now strove:
The fruit thereof was charity and love
Towards America-----couldst thou do more
Than leave thy native home, the British shore,
To cross the great Atlantic's watr'y road,
To see America distress'd abode?
Thy prayers, great Saint, and thy incessant cries,
Have pierc'd the bosom of thy native skies!
Thou moon hast seen, and ye bright stars of light
Have witness been of his requests by night!
He pray'd that grace in every heart might dwell:
He long'd to see America excell;
He charg'd its youth to let the grace divine
Arise, and in their future actions shine;
He offer'd THAT he did himself receive,
A greater gift not GOD himself can give:

He urg'd the need of HIM to every one;
It was no less than GOD's co-equal SON!
Take HIM ye wretched for your only good;
Take HIM ye starving souls to be your food.
Ye thirsty, come to this life giving stream:
Ye Preachers, take him for your joyful theme:
Take HIM, " my dear AMERICANS," he said,
Be your complaints in his kind bosom laid:
Take HIM ye Africans, he longs for you;
Impartial SAVIOUR, is his title due;
If you will chuse to walk in grace's road,
You shall be sons, and kings, and priests to God.
  Great COUNTESS! we Americans revere
Thy name, and thus condole thy grief sincere:
We mourn with thee, that Tomb obscurely plac'd,
In which thy Chaplain undisturb'd doth rest
New-England sure, doth feel the Orphan's smart;
Reveals the true sensations of his heart:
Since this fair Sun, withdraws his golden rays,
No more to brighten these distressful days!
His lonely Tabernacle, sees no more
A WHITEFIELD landing on the British shore:
Then let us view him on yon azure skies:
Let every mind with this lov'd object rise.
No more can he exert his lab'ring breath,
Seiz'd by the cruel messenger of death.
What can his dear AMERICA return?
But drop a tear upon his happy urn,
Thou tomb, shalt safe retain thy sacred trust,
Till life divine re-animate his dust.

38. *An Elegiac Poem. Composed by F[reema]n H[earse]y.* *[Boston: Ezekiel Russell, 1791?]*

In 1791, Congress passed the Northwest Ordinance which encouraged expansion westward to the Mississippi. Despite treaties with the Indians, clashes between them and the settlers were inevitable. The culmination of the troubles was the efforts of General Arthur St. Clair, Governor of the Northwest Territory, to force the Indians to abide by the provisions of the Treaty of Fort Harmar. On November 4, 1791, near Fort Wayne, Indiana, General St. Clair and his United States troops were overwhelmed by the confederated Indians led by Little Turtle. Six hundred soldiers were killed or wounded including sixty-one staff officers. A disaster of this magnitude caused the publication of several different elegies and accounts of the battle.

Freeman Hearsey later included this poem in a small pamphlet of his verse which was published about 1805. In the preface he wrote: "Dear reader, in order that you may more readily wink at imperfections, I will inform you how some of these pieces were written. In the year 1791, I trust my goings were established on the Rock of Ages by that grace wherein we stand; and being then a bound apprentice to the carpenter's business, and my mind being thus led, I took my pencil and shingle, and while labouring with my body, my mind formed the verse, and I wrote them on the shingle, and at night carried it home and wrote them on paper. . . . Another thing I would observe; I never had any education of any kind. What learning I have seemed to come to me naturally, without the tuition of any."

Evans 46186

10 ¾ × 17

The BLOODY BATTLE, fought in *Nov.* 1790, by GEN. *HARMAR.*

AN ELEGIAC POEM.

Bloody INDIAN BATTLE at *Miami,* 1791.

Composed by F----N H----Y,
A Citizen of BOSTON, and published by the earnest Request of many FRIENDS, as a sacred Testimony of GRATITUDE and REGARD to the IMMORTAL ME-MORY of those BRAVE and GAL-LANT HEROES, who fell GLORIOUS-LY fighting for their COUNTRY in the BLOODY INDIAN BATTLE at MIAMI, near FORT-WASHINGTON, in the *Ohio-Country*, Nov. 4, 1791; in which shocking and desperate Fight *Thirty-nine* STAFF-OFFICERS were KILLED and *Twenty-two Wounded, viz.* Maj. Gen. RICHARD BUTLER.—Col. Oldham.—Majors Ferguson, Clark, Hart.—Capts. Bradford, P. Phelon, Kirkwood, Price, V. Swearingin, Tip-ton, Smith, Purdy, Pratt, Guthrie, Cribbs, Newman—Lts Spear, War-ren, Boyd, M'Math, Burgess, Kelso, Read, Little, Hopper and Lickins—

Ensi. Balch, Cobb, Chase, Turner, Wilson, Brooks, Beatty, Purdy.—*Quar. Mst.* Reynolds, Ward.—*Ass* Anderson.—39. Dr. Grasson.

WOUNDED *Adj.* Gen. Sargent.—*Lt. Col.* Gibson, Dart. *Maj.* Butler.— *Capts* Doyle, Truman, Ford, Buchanan, Dark, Slough.—*Lts.* Greaton Davidson, DeButts, Price, Morgan, M'Crea, Lysle and Thompson.—*Adjs.* Whistler and Crawford.—*Ensi.* Bines.—*Visc.* Malertie.

The gallant and intrepid MAJOR *BUTLER*, (Brother to the unfortunate GENERAL) who fought *three Hours* at the Head of his Battalion, after his Leg was shattered by a Ball.

MISSASAGO Or CHIEF WAR-RIOR, who was Commander of the INDIAN ARMY at the late Bloody and desperate BATTLE.

AN *ELEGIAC POEM*, &c.

"MAN *knoweth not his Time*; he is caught
"*in an* EVIL HOUR."

HARK! while the Thunders roar aloud,
The Field of Battle's lin'd with Blood,
Hundreds have fell by the fierce Sword,
Of those who long and thirst for Blood.

2. A dismal Tale for to relate,
Of those that were unfortunate:
They left their native Shores to go,
Up to the distant OHIO.

3. The *Savage-Tribes* for to destroy,
They all engag'd in this Employ,
But lo the *Mighty Hand* of GOD!
Their Garments now are roll'd in Blood.

4. Hark! while the Cannons loudly roar!
The Fields are drest in purple Gore,
The *Savage-Tribes* both fierce and bold,
The Battle win, as we are told.

5. AMERICA the Loss sustain
Of those *brave Men* who thus were slain,
On the OHIO *Fields*, where they
Expected for to win the Day.

6. A gloomy Scene for to behold,
Almost a *Thousand* Men so bold;
Alass! they all are swept away,
The *Savages* they win the Day.

7. Many *brave Youth* that left their Home,
Have fell, they never will return;
Their Parents do the Loss sustain,
In this brave Battle they were slain.

8. Many that dwelt on BOSTON's Shore,
Are swept away, they are no more;
The *brave* and *bold* they Victims fell,
As we may long remember well.

9. But now behold the Battle's o'er,
The Field is left in purple Gore,
That dismal Day is past and gone,
And never will again return.

10. But still the noise of War we hear,
Thousands are waiting in the Rear,
But if the *LORD* is on their Side,
He'll be their sure Defence and Guide.

11. His mighty Hand will lead them thro'
And they shall win the Victory too,
No mortal can his Power controul,
His undisturb'd Decrees he'll roll.

12. Lo! how they shine in Armor bright,
When *GOD* prepares them for the Fight,
Undaunted they will stand the Field,
And make the *Savage-Tribes* to yield.

13. But soon we hope this War will cease,
And these two Nations be at Peace,
Then human Blood will cease to flow
Upon the distant OHIO.

14. Perhaps this *War* will soon be o'er,
Then Cannons they will cease to roar;
The Trump of Peace will sound abroad,
And no more Garments roll'd in Blood.

39. *The Awful Malignant Fever of Newburyport, in the Year 1796. By Jonathan Plummer.*
[*Newburyport: Jonathan Plummer, 1796.*]

Jonathan Plummer wrote and printed many poems on events which occurred in his native town, Newburyport, Massachusetts. More than thirty poems, issued as broadsides, are still extant. Others are to be found in Newburyport newspapers. Plummer led a strange life and followed a variety of careers. He was pawnbroker, bottle buyer, writer of love letters, traveling teacher, itinerant preacher, even peddlar of halibut. His last claim to fame was as poet-laureate to Lord Timothy Dexter of Newburyport, one of the great eccentrics of late eighteenth century New England.

Epidemics of yellow fever were common from colonial times until the mid-nineteenth century. Second only to smallpox in its virulence, this disease entered the colonies by the slave ships from the West Indies and Africa.

Evans 31018

22 × 17

Prepar'd for our destiny:
Prepar'd to go at any hour,
That he who reigns with matchless pow'r
Thinks fit to call us to the skies,
By his connivance g—d and wife.
Some think they long grim death can shun,
Until their race is nearly run,
They eat and drink, and work and play,
Quite *debonair*, alert and gay,
And rarely think at all of death
Till he's prepar'd to stop their breath.
Others borne down with dismal sorrow,
Expecting they must die to-morrow.
All these are wrong in the extreme,
Though to themselves they right may seem—
We oft should think about the grave,
And from above protection crave.
We well our courses ought to run,
And sin and folly ought to shun;
But never baneful grief should chuse,
Nor blessings of the world refuse.
We should not now our friends are gone
Too much their dreadful fates bemoan;
Nor give to grief too great a scope;
We mourn; but yet we've blessed hope.—
Hopes that the Sovereign Lord of all,
Who has of late thought fit to call
So many of our comrades hence,
From all the joys of time and sense,
Has greater joys prepar'd for them;
Joys too sublime for us to name.
This thought should moderate our grief,
This ought to give our souls relief.
Great is our loss we must confess,
And great our sorrow and distress.
The wife, the learn'd, the good and gay,—
Quite suddenly were snatch'd away.
The skillful Swett, we see no more!
Good Madam Boardman we deplore !!
No art the Doctor's life could save,
And ah! the Lady's in her grave!
Her goodness could not death disarm,
Her lovely beauty could not charm
The ruthless monster-in-the-leaf;
He plung'd his dagger in her breast,
Up to the hilt, without remorse,
Nor did the deed obstruct his course.
Long did the days of darkness last!
Dull were the nights of grief we pass'd.
No sooner had we heard with dread
That a companion good was dead,
Than we had news of others seiz'd,
With pains that were not often eas'd,
Till conquering death had with his dart
Pierc'd the poor patients to the heart—

A short account of the ravages of the Yellow Fever; at Newburyport, in the year 1796.

ALTHOUGH the execution done by this disorder in that town is, through the kindness of God, extremely small compared to its baneful effects in some of our southern cities, it yet seems by no means improper to publish a brief and impartial account of the matter. Every circumstance relating to this disease ought to be recorded and remembered on account of its being very likely that all the experience gained in it, will be wanting to enable us to withstand future attacks from this moral foe.

Many of our country brethren, who have heard alarming news of 30, 40 or 50 persons dying of the yellow fever in a night in Newburyport, will be surprized, when they read here that less than 40 have died there with it in the whole; but they must rest assured that 'tis a fact; and one I hope that will make them more cautious for the future about believing falsehoods. They ought to remember that people in the neighbouring seaports were interested in deceiving them about this matter, and that some of them have actually much misrepresented the affair. We must however acknowledge that many others have done us the justice to propagate true accounts from time to time of the sickness, and our thanks are due to most or all the editors of newspapers in the States for publishing the authentic reports of our committee of health.

Whenever a malignant disorder has established itself in a populous place, the people will find it to their advantage immediately to organize a committee of health, and to make it the duty of the committee to publish authentic accounts of the distemper. By this mode of conduct, men of sense in the country, who read the public news learn the truth, deal it out to their neighbors, and are enabled to contradict the extravagant and exaggerated stories of their more ignorant and superstitious townsmen—'Tis ten times as well to have the truth told in such cases, by Tom Wiseman, Esq: or Doctor Knowall, as it is to have the alarming reports of Deacon Longface or Dick Kickflaw spread abroad. The Papers in Newburyport were too long silent about the fever, and the town was too long without a Committee of Health.

This Fever in Newburyport was attended by symptoms nearly similar to those which attended it in Philadelphia: it was however more acute here than there in general. There the sick commonly lived from 5 to 8 days, but here their career was often finished sooner. The disease was new to all our Physicians, and at first their endeavours were crowned with small success; nor were they at any time very able to beat the enemy, especially when not sent for at the beginning of the battle. Dr. Swett who fell a victim, was seized with vomiting, and immediately pronounced his fate. "I (said he to his amiable consort) am seized now with a disorder that I have been trying to check in others—I can do

---

...house in Newbury, died there soon after.

On the 3d of July Mr. Davis Lambert, who lived in the same house that Miss Flood was seized in, died of the same disorder; and on the 5th Miss Silley in the same house also died. The disorder now began to be considered as a little alarming, and Miss Silley was prudently buried without the customary ceremonies; the same morning she died.

The scourge thus got footing in a place rendered by several circumstances very capable of supporting it. That part of Water-street of which I am speaking is situated low, by the Merrimack, while a very considerable part of the town is built on higher ground, all a-

long at the S. W. of it, which is the point from which the Summer breezes generally come. Thus situated, it must be expected that the air in that part of the town will sometimes in the hottest part of the year, stagnate and become extremely unwholesome; the effluvia from all the filth in the city, S. W. of this spot is naturally wafted over and hovers there. But besides these natural disadvantages, the people in Water-street laboured under a very formidable one, hatched by an inhabitant who paid his life for his inattention. A very considerable quantity of the heads and entrails of a kind of fish were suffered to lie and putrify on a wharf. So insupportable was the stench arising from this nuisance that when an officer of Police was appointed, he was not able for love nor money to hire any man to remove it; and was actually obliged to cover it over with earth where ever he found it.

It was yet early in July; full four months longer the fever might naturally be expected to rage with encrease of fury! Considering this that 30 or 40 persons have died with it is not the wonder; but that at least four times as many have not died.

About a week after the death of Miss Silley, master Arnold died in the same house.

On the 16th of July, Mr. Jonathan Gage was seized —he recovered; but his wife and a daughter died soon after; and his parents from Bradford having visited him during his illness were infected and died at home, one on the 28th and the other on the 29th of July. On the 19th Mr. Z. Atwood died.

The town now began to be a little more alarmed, and appointed an officer of Police; Many groundless fears were entertained by many, while others did not take the necessary precautions.

A girl at Mrs. Atwoods, and another at Mr. Gages were the next victims. It seemed now to be time for the surviving part of these bereaved families to fly from their infected abodes; but they had the hardihood to stay: and what is more surprizing, the lovely Miss Long now, or a little before, flew right to the jaws of death, by going to keep Mr. Gages house. The lovely Miss Long died, and on the 16th Dr. Swett took his departure.

On the 20th of August four persons died of the fever.

---

the first week of September, it then began to decrease. Five persons, of whom we had but little hopes, recovered. There were few new cases, and on the 5th of October not one person in the town remained sick with it.

The narrow circle in which the adversary moved, and its very seasonable end are pretty evident marks of the friendly interposition of him who lives forever. During nearly the whole interposition of the friendly weather. In July he sent us two showers, in which the rain fell very plentifully, and twice as fast perhaps as the oldest person living ever saw it come before. These were probably the oldest person living in the town of the Yellow Fever in New-York. On the 25th of Aug. he sent us a great shower, attended with a very uncommon quantity of lightning; and on the 29th it being to amazing warm, that the thermometer flood at 96, he caused such an alteration in the weather that the thermometer from about 90 ... tered to 64. In the course of four days it grew so much colder that it actually froze, and no further north than Portsmouth, ice of a considerable thickness was seen.

From this we ought to take encouragement still to strive, by leading virtuous lives, to secure the kindly aid of indulgent heaven: or if we believe we cannot do this by any of our own works, let us take care not to draw his vindictive vengeance of an Almighty arm down on our guilty heads, by vicious practices.

INVITATION to the Inhabitants of Newburyport, who have fled to the Country, on account of the Malignant Fever.

I.
THE dreadful Fever is no more;
It now no longer can distress us;
Our frightful troubles now are o'er,
And rosy health has come to bless us.
Then blithful swains and lasses gay,
Come from the country, come away.

II.
The trade and commerce of the town
Quite slowly moves with body stooping;
We have not yet deserv'd renown,
And all the sciences are drooping.
Ahoi! ye merchants, do not stay,
Ye men of science come away.

III.
No fever now but that of love,
In all the town remains to harm us;
And that the Ladies can remove,
Though they will never cease to charm us:
Then lovely nymphs without delay
Quick from the country come away.

IV.
Again our smiling streets parade—
Bless me how winning God has made you!
Trip in fine sattins or brocade,
And have the homage proper paid you;
Regard my amorous nymphs I pray,
Quick to the city come away.

Newburyport, October 6, 1796.

Printed for and sold by the Author—Price 4½ d.

THE AWFUL MALIGNANT FEVER AT NEWBURYPORT, IN THE YEAR 1796.

AN ELEGIAC EPISTLE to the Mourners; on the Death of FORTY FOUR Persons, who died of a Malignant Fever in *Newburyport* and the adjacent towns, in the Summer and Autumn of the Year 1796---Together with a short account of that alarming disorder---BY *Jonathan Plummer*, jun.

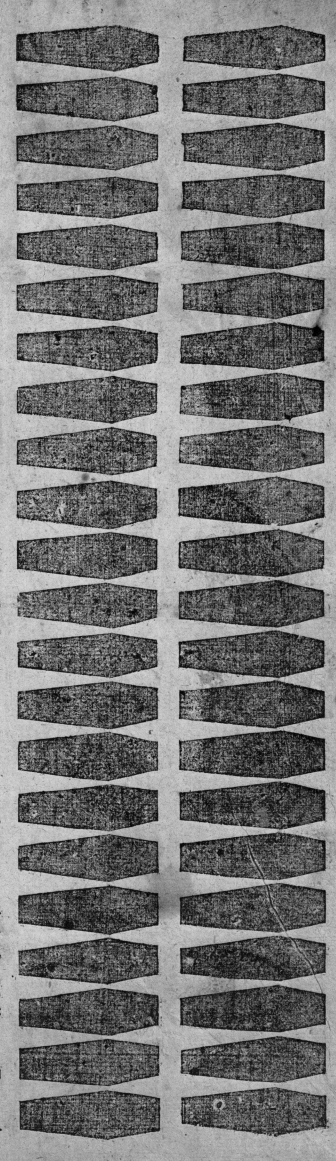

LIST of those who died.

MISS Flood, Mr. Davis Lambert, Miss Hannah Cilley; Mr. Zachariah Atwood, aged 48, Mr. Joseph Jewett, aged 44, Major Benjamin Gage, Priscilla Gage, his consort, Mrs. Susanna Gage, Mrs. 36, Miss Sally Gage aged 11, Master Arnold, aged 11, Miss Nancy Stone, aged 21, Miss Phebe Boynton, aged 12, Mrs. Hill, widow, the consort of Mr. Enoch Toppan, aged 63, Dr. John B. Swett, aged 45, Mr. Jacob Boardman, Miss Susanna Moody, Miss Polly Long, Atwood, Miss Polly Long, the consort of Mr. Enoch Somerby, Mrs. Sarah Woodroute, Mr. Jacob Pearson, Mrs. Sarah Boardman, Miss Polly Patten, Mr. James Lord, Mr. Jeremiah Tyler, aged 34, Mr. John Stone, Mr. Ebenezer Greenleaf, his consort Mrs. Hannah Greenleaf, Miss Betsey Keazer, Mr. Moses Todd, Master Benjamin Ely, Mr. Silas Noyes, aged 43, Miss Mary Novel, aged 53, Master John Carnes, the consort of Doctor Charles Coffin, Miss Mary Smith, Mr. David Moody, jun. aged 24, Mr. John Wood Brown, Miss Eleanor Ford, Miss Elizabeth Timmons, Ebenezer Pike, Mr. Moses Rogers, jun. and Mrs. Mary Brazier.

The lovely blooming Polly Long
Is worthy of a deathless song:
And many others we have lost,
In whom our hopes are sadly crost;
Are worthy of the fame renown,
And are lamented by the town.
Long will our streaming eyes confess
Our sorrow and our deep distress,
While we reflect with silent dread
Upon the virtues of the dead,
Who by this fever have been kill'd;
Which has with grief our lodgings fill'd.
But let us not forget to praise
The multiplier of our days,
Who yet bestows upon us life
So free from sickness, grief and strife,

You're welcome to the blissful shore,
Where racking death can kill no more!
Where not a single ill can harm you,
And where ten thousand raptures charm you.
You're welcome from the painful strife,
And all the ills of mortal life.

nothing for it: nobody in this place can, and I must fall by it! The Doctor's mind at this time must have been awfully agitated! An hour before perhaps in perfect health, with a shining prospect of thirty happy, uncommonly happy years, and now as certain of dying in a few days, as if his neck had been under a French guillotine! No language could express his feelings! No pen is adequate to the task of doing justice to the affecting, the melancholy subject! Drop, courteous reader, drop with me a tear to his memory, and let us endeavour to be ready to travel after him, through the dark and awful valley, and to hail him triumphantly in the realms of light, by the assistance of him who is able to save. Oh! may 'tis first address to us, when we quit this transitory world, be as follows, viz.

It is uncertain whether the fever was imported or took its origin in the town; but 'tis certain that it was

er, one of which was Miss Long and another Mr. P. Atwood, who had been only two or three days out of his deceased brother's house. I was surprised at the inhardiness of those people who still continued at the infected houses in Water-street, and thought it high time to try to alarm them; fearing among the rest that the lovely Mrs. Atwood would lose her life 40 or 50 years too soon, and hoping that what I said to her might have some effect on others who were in danger, I immediately hove the following note into her house, viz.

Newburyport, Aug. 20, '96

DEAR MADAM,

"For Heaven's sake, if you prize your life, fly immediately from your present abode—Fly lovely nymph to the country, some western higher part of the town, or any where else—Your life where you now are will probably, and almost beyond doubt, be very short—stay not to the funeral of Mr. Atwood—get home negro to take care of your house or shut it up—I am, &c.

Mrs. PEGGY ATWOOD.

This lady having took considerable pains to cleanse her house, thought herself pretty secure; but about a week after another of her family, Mr. Stone, was seized by the iron hand of the fever, and the wretch fled

ADVERTISEMENTS

40. *By His Excellency Jonathan Belcher, Esq; . . . A Proclamation.*
[*Boston: John Draper,* 1740.]

One of the chronic currency shortages experienced by the colonists is referred to in this proclamation. Around 1710, there was a currency shortage in Massachusetts since the colonists were forbidden to issue their own currency. John Colman, a Boston merchant, was among those who attempted a reform. His plan to form a private bank which would issue bills on the strength of real estate mortgages was not adopted. In late 1720, he published a pamphlet encouraging the formation of a land bank open to all landowners in the province. This project was not adopted either and lay dormant until 1739, when he revived it. This time the bank was organized and notes were issued and in circulation, but the bank was suppressed by the English government. This broadside warns individuals against accepting these notes, which were considered worthless by the merchants whose names appear after the proclamation.

Evans 40203
7 ⅞ × 12

By His EXCELLENCY
JONATHAN BELCHER, Esq;

Captain General and Governour in Chief, in and over His Majesty's Province of the Massachusetts Bay in New England.

A PROCLAMATION.

HEREAS a Scheme for emitting Bills or Notes by John Colman, Esq; and others, was laid before the Great and General Court or Assembly of this His Majesty's Province, in their Session held at Boston, the Fifth Day of December 1 7 3 9, and by the Report of a Committee appointed by said Court was represented, if carried on, to have a great Tendency to endamage His Majesty's good Subjects as to their Properties ;

And whereas Application has been very lately made to Me and His Majesty's Council, by a great Number of Men of the most considerable Estates and Business, praying that some proper Method may be taken to prevent the Inhabitants of this Province being imposed upon by the said Scheme ; and it being very apparent that these Bills or Notes promise nothing of any determinate Value, and cannot have any general, certain or established Credit ;

Wherefore,

I Have thought fit, by and with the Advice of His Majesty's Council, to issue this Proclamation, hereby giving Notice and Warning to all His Majesty's good Subjects of the Danger they are in, and cautioning them against receiving or passing the said Notes, as tending to defraud Men of their Substance, and to disturb the Peace and good Order of the People, and to give just Interruption, and bring much Confusion into their Trade and Business.

Given at the Council Chamber in *Boston*, the Seventeenth Day of *July* 1740. In the Fourteenth Year of the Reign of Our Sovereign Lord GEORGE the Second by the Grace of GOD of *Great Britain*, *France* and *Ireland*, KING Defender of the Faith, &c.

J. BELCHER.

By Order of His Excellency the Governour, with the Advice of the Council, *J. Willard*, Secr.

GOD save the KING.

WHereas the Committee of the Great and General Court or Assembly at their Sessions begun and held at Boston Dec. 5th 1739, Reported that the Bills proposed to be emitted by John Colman, Esq; and others, would tend to endamage the Properties of His Majesty's good Subjects of this Province; and whereas a large Number of the principal Men of Estates and Business have petitioned His Excellency the Governour and Council to take such Measures as they in their Wisdom should think proper to prevent People's being imposed upon by the said Scheme commonly called the Land Scheme or Bank ; whereupon the Governour & Council have issued a Proclamation warning and cautioning People against the said Bills : And we the Subscribers being abundantly perswaded that the said Scheme, if carried on, will be of pernicious Consequence ; and being willing and desirous to do what in us lies to prevent the said Imposition, hereby Agree, Declare and Promise, that we will not, directly or indirectly by our selves or any for us, receive or take any Bills emitted on the said Scheme, commonly called the Land Bank. And we hereby caution and advise all Persons whatsoever who are indebted to us, or deal with us, that they refuse the said Bills, and do not take any of them in Expectation of our receiving them at their Hands, we being determined not to take the said Bills for any Debts due, nor for any Goods, or on any Consideration whatever.

John Osborne	Thomas Green	Habijah Savage
Edward Hutchinson	John Spooner	Jonathan Armitage
John Alford	Joseph Dowse	James Allen
Samuel Welles	Robert Temple	William Bolean
Benjamin Lynde	Joseph Brandon	Nathanael Vial
Joshua Winslow	Rufus Green	John Winslow
James Bowdoin	Samuel Demming	John Gibbins
Peter Fanueil	Thomas Palmer	John Tyler
James Smith	Stephen Bouteneau	Nathanael Balston
Charles Apthorp	John Green	William Douglas
John Erving	Benjamin Green	Thomas Austin
Hugh Hall	Byfield Lyde	William Wyer
John Jekyl	Nath Shower	Andrew Hall
Benjamin Fanueil	Benjamin Hallowell	Benjamin Pollard
James Boutenea	Peter Kenwood	John Trail
John Gooch	Thomas Childs	John Hill
Henry Caswell	Thomas Perkins	Joseph Fitch
Edward Tyng	Charles Paxton	Francis Johonnet
Nath. Cunningham	Samuel Wentwort	Thomas Lambert
William Spikeman	Robert Lightfoot	Joseph Gooch
William Lambert	James Gould	David Le Galley
Andrew Oliver	Ralph Inman	Jeremiah Green
Thomas Oxnard	John Homans	Isaac Gridley
Samuel Sewall	Thomas Lechmere	Benjamin Bagnall
Thomas Gunter	William Winslow	William Lance
Edmund Quincy	Joseph Lee	Josh. Henshaw, jun.
Josiah Quincy	Benjamin Bourn	David Wyar
Joseph Gerrish	Jacob Griggs	James Russell
John Barrel	Richard Clark	Andrew Newell
William Bowdoin	Henry Laughton	Robert Lewis
Francis Boreland	John Cutler	John Minot
John Fayerweather	John Dennie	Samuel Cary
Thomas Hutchinson	John Simpson	John Austin
Thomas Hubbard	Jonathan Simpson	Richard Sutton
Thomas Hancock	James Pitts	John Jones
John Wendell	Stephen Greenlease	Cornelius Waldo
William Coffin	Joshua Cheever	James Day
Harrison Gray	Thomas Jackson	Thomas Hawden
Timothy Emerson	Samuel Gardner	Henry Withered
Isaac Winslow	Thomas Gardner	John Barret
Joseph Green	Thomas Lee	Norton Quincy
Isaac Walker	Benjamin Clark	Zech. Johonnet
Edward Jackson	Joseph Green	Hopestill Foster
Ebenezer Holmes	John Turner, jun.	John Grant
William Clark	William Tyler	Charles Deming.
William Sheaffe	Samuel Bridgham	

It is hoped, That Masters and Mistresses of Family's will caution their Servants from taking in exchange or otherwise, any of said Bills if offered them, as such a thing may serve to give 'em an entrance into Credit, which would prove of dangerous consequence.

41. *Advertisement. Twenty Pounds Reward.*
[*Charleston, South Carolina: Robert Wells, 1767.*]

Advertisement. South-Carolina, October 1768.
[*Charleston, South Carolina: Robert Wells, 1768.*]

These two advertisements are typical of those so numerous in eighteenth century newspapers. However, an advertisement issued separately had its own advantages. It could be widely and cheaply circulated and its larger size made it more conspicuous. This type of advertisement was probably posted in taverns, stores, and other public gathering places. In areas without newspapers, the broadside advertisement was the best means of calling attention to lost or stolen property.

    These two broadsides were probably by the same printer, since the elements of the decorative borders are identical, although they are turned at different angles. The same elements appear on another broadside which is known to have been printed by Robert Wells, the publisher of the *South-Carolina & American General Gazette* in Charleston.

Evans 41683
6¼ × 7⅝
Evans 41837
7½ × 12½

42. *Just published, . . . The Massachusetts Calendar, or an Almanack for . . . 1772.*
Boston: Isaiah Thomas [1771].

The handsome cut of Jonathan Weatherwise on this broadside also appears on the cover of *The Massachusetts Almanack* for 1772 and was executed by Isaiah Thomas some years earlier. The contents listed on the broadside are typical of almanacs of the period.

Almanacs played a very important role in colonial life. As Nathaniel Low writes in his *Astronomical Diary or Almanack* for 1786, "No books or pamphlets are so much the objects of ridicule and contempt as Almanacks; and it is easy to prove that no book we read (except the Bible) is so much valued, and so serviceable to the community. Almanacks serve as clocks and watches for nine-tenths of mankind; and in fair weather are far more sure and regular than the best time-piece manufactur'd here or in London. . . ." Almanacs also provided a sure income for the printer. They were published in large editions (several thousand copies or more) and were always best sellers. The most famous of the almanac printers, Benjamin Franklin, issued as many as ten thousand copies of *Poor Richard's Almanack* each year.

As the colonies grew and began to feel oppressed, the tone of almanacs often became very serious. Hence, in *The Massachusetts Calendar* for 1772, Isaiah Thomas included an essay on Liberty and Government as well as "Thoughts on Government" by William Penn. Often newspapers were under government control so that almanacs served as an outlet for political thought.

Evans 42285

9 ⅞ × 15 ⅜

Just publiſhed,

Embelliſhed with four Plates, neatly engraved, viz. The Boſton Maſſacre, The four Seaſons, with the Twelve Signs of the Zodiack.---The King of Denmark.---Jonathan Weatherwiſe.

Price 22s. 6d. Old Tenor the Dozen, and ſeven Coppers ſingle.

Printed on much larger Paper than Almanacks commonly are,

The Maſſachuſetts Calendar,

OR AN

ALMANACK

FOR

The Year of our LORD 1772,

From the CREATION, according to Prophane Hiſtory,   5722,
According to the Sacred Scriptures,   5674,

Being BISSEXTILE or LEAP-YEAR:

CALCULATED FOR

The Meridian of BOSTON, New-England, Lat. 42 Deg. 25 Min. North.

By PHILOMATHES.

CONTAINING,

The Lunations,
Eclipſes,
Planets Places,
Aſpects,
Judgment of the Weather,
Feaſts and Faſts of the Church,
Courts,
The riſing, ſouthing, and ſetting of the Seven Stars,
Sun and Moon's riſing and ſetting.
Time of High Water,
Moon's Place,
Clock's Equation,
Ephemeris, &c.
Vulgar Notes for 1772,
Names and Characters of the Twelve Signs, Seven Planets, and Five Aſpects,
The Parts of the Body that are governed by the Twelve Signs,
Roads, &c.

ALSO,
Several ſelect Pieces, viz.
On Liberty and Government,
Thoughts on Government,
On the Culture of Silk,
Man of Pleaſure,
Woman of Pleaſure,
Jonathan Weatherwiſe's Prognoſticks,
A Table of Intereſt on an entire new Conſtruction; reviſed and corrected by Mr. JOHN LEACH, Teacher of the Mathematicks in Boſton,
POETRY, viz.
The Difference between To-Day and To-Morrow,
Of Time. Of Pride. Of Vice.
Reflections on Time, &c.
On the Boſton Maſſacre,
On the King of Denmark,
On the Twelve Signs,

BOSTON,

Printed and ſold by ISAIAH THOMAS, in Union-ſtreet, near the Market.

43. *In the House of Representatives, February 16, 1776.*
Salem: Ezekiel Russell [1776].

Although the first printing press in North America was established in Cambridge, Massachusetts, in 1638, the first paper mill was not operating until the 1690's in Pennsylvania. Throughout the colonial period, printers and publishers felt the shortage of paper and much was imported from Europe. Indeed, a common watermark of the eighteenth century was "Save Rags." After Lexington and Concord, it was apparent that the colonies would have to become more self-sustaining. Hence this resolve of the Massachusetts Council and the advertisement of Hugh McLean appealing to the colonists' frugality and patriotism to save and sell their cotton and linen rags to make paper.

Evans 43056
10 × 15 ½

In the HOUSE OF REPRESENTATIVES, *February* 16, 1776.

WHEREAS *this Colony cannot be supplied with a sufficient Quantity of* PAPER *for its own Consumption, without the particular Care of its In-habitants in saving* RAGS *for the Paper-Mills :* Therefore,

RESOLVED, That the Committees of Correspondence, Inspection, and Safety in the several Towns in this Colony be, and they hereby are required *immediately* to appoint some suitable Person in their respective Towns (where it is not already done) to receive RAGS for the Paper-Mills : And the Inhabitants of this Colony are hereby desired to be very careful in saving even the smallest Quantity of Rags proper for making Paper, which will be a further Evidence of their Disposition to promote the Public Good.

Sent up for Concurrence.   WILLIAM COOPER, Speak. Pro. Tem.
In Council, Feb. 16, 1776.   Read and Concurred,
                 PEREZ MORTON, Dep'y. Sec'y.

Consented to, by the Major Part of the Council.
A true Copy,   Attest. PEREZ MORTON, Dep'y. Sec'y.

PAPER-MILLS,

At the SLITTING-MILL, in MILTON.

In Compliance with the foregoing RESOLVE,

and to *Encourage* the

PAPER-MANUFACTURE,

WE now propose to give *Three Coppers* per Pound for all white *Linnen,* and *Cotton* and *Linnen* RAGS, suitable for making WRITING-PAPER ; which is Three Pence O. T. per Pound more than has been given :----Also, One Copper and an Half per Pound is now given for Check and course Rags, and Two Coppers for Canvass, that is either made of Hemp or Flax ; and Half a Copper a Pound for old Ropes and Junk.----Ropes and Junk that are too bad for Oakum will make good Paper.

☞ It is therefore hoped, that more Attention will be paid to this Affair in future, both from a Principle of *Patriotism* and *Frugality.* The present alarming Situation of the *Colonies,* renders it entirely needless to point out the Utility of establishing this, and every Kind of *Manufacture* among us ; and if each Family will but lend their Aid, to encourage this Business, by saving their *Rags,* there may be a Sufficiency of Paper made here, and entirely prevent the Importation of that Article into this Country.

** Any Gentlemen, Traders, or others throughout this Country, that will so far promote the Interest of AMERICA, by receiving *Rags* for the aforesaid Purpose, shall be paid Ten per Cent. Commissions, and necessary Charges of Transportation, either by Land or Water to said Mills : And the smallest Favors gratefully acknowledged by their very Humble Servants,

HUGH McLEAN AND C°.

TO BE SOLD at said MILL, all Sorts of PRINTING

PAPER,

Writing ditto, *London* Brown, Whitish Brown, Bonnet Paper : Likewise Press Paper for Clothiers, for glazing and goodness superior to any made in *America,* and not inferior to the best made in *England.*

CASH given for RAGS by

SALEM : Printed by E. RUSSELL, Upper End of Main-street : Who gives CASH for all Kinds of Cotton and Linnen and Check RAGS, for the Use of the above PAPER-MILLS.

44. *Now fitting for a Privateer, . . . The Brigantine Washington.*
[*No place*, 1776.]

The brigantine *Washington* was the second privateer to be commissioned from Beverly, Massachusetts. She had a crew of eighty and carried twelve guns. Her career was short, but within a year she had captured eight prizes before being captured herself by an English ship, the *Levant*, in 1777.

Privateering had always been important in warfare. It was only natural for American colonists to engage in this practice whenever England was at war with other nations. American privateers were particularly active during the Seven Years War.

At the outbreak of the Revolution, shipowners and seamen were well practiced in this form of harassment and quick profit. The owners of the vessels usually received one half of the value of a prize ship and its cargo, with the officers and seamen receiving the rest. Wages were also higher than in the Continental Navy, whose weakness was the impetus for the extensive use of privateers.

Evans 43020

7 ⅛ × 9 ¾

Now fitting for a

Privateer,

In the Harbour of *BEVERLY*,

The BRIGANTINE

Wafhington,

A ftrong, good veffel for that purpofe and a prime failer.

Any Seamen or Landmen that have an inclination to

Make their Fortunes in a few Months,

May have an Opportunity, by applying to

JOHN DYSON.

Beverly, September 17th, 1776.

45. *Broke open last night, (13th October) The City Coffee-House, . . .*
[*New London, Connecticut, 1787.*]

This advertisement was very effective, probably since it was published immediately after the robbery. Had the owner of the City Coffee-House waited to insert this notice in the newspaper, it would have appeared several days after the robbery, possibly too late to be effective. As it happened, the thief, James Hambleton, was captured in Stonington, Connecticut, with many of the stolen articles. The notice of his capture in the *Connecticut Gazette* also mentions that he had broken into a slaughter house on the night of October 13.

From a typographical point of view, the printer's ornament is cunningly contrived to include the skull and crossed bones motif.

Evans 20188
8 ¼ × 13

Broke open laft Night, (the 13th October)

The CITY COFFEE-HOUSE,

And ftolen thereout, fundry ARTICLES, viz.

A.

2 Silver Pepper Cafters, marked M. A. N. D.----12 Silver Tea Spoons marked M. A. L. S.---2 Silver Salt Cellars.----2 Silver Salt Spoons.---1 pair Silver bow Sugar Tongs, marked G. R. in a cypher.----1 Silver Punch Ladle with a mahogany handle.---9 Half Johannes from 48 to 49s.---5 Englifh Guineas.---7 or 9 Dollars---Some fmall Silver.----2 Cafe Bottles of Arrack.---1 double flint white two-quart eight fquare Bottle, full of Brandy.---4 or 5lb. Loaf Sugar, broke up for punch.--3lb. Coffee burnt.

Alfo, a pair Saddle-Bags, containing three or four Shirts, two boy's ditto, fome Stockings, pair cloth-coloured Breeches, a pair Silver Spurs, a number of Maffachufetts State Notes, amounting to £. 301 10s.----Alfo, a number of private Gentlemen's Notes of Hand, in favour of *Samuel Gragg*, of *Peterfborough Slip*, State of *New-Hampfhire*, amounting to about £. 700. The Saddle-Bags, and the contents therein contained, were the property of faid *Samuel Gragg*, of *Peterfborough-Slip*.

Whoever apprehends the Thief or Thieves, fo that they may be brought to juftice, and the property recovered, fhall receive FORTY DOLLARS Reward, paid by

T. ALLEN, (59)

New-London, October 14, 1787.

Notes contained in a leather Book, in Saddle-Bags.
Maffachufetts confolidated State Notes, payable to Mr. *Wallace Little.*

1 for the fum of £.106	
1 do.	100
1 do.	74
1 do to fome other perfon	19
Certificate for intereft thereon about	22
————£.321	

1 Order on Mr. ——— *Robins* of *Bofton*, drawn by Mr. *Thomas Penniman* of *Wafhington*, for the fum of £.111 10s. L. Money.

1 Note Hand againft *David Quinton* of *Walpole*, payable to *Chrifto. Thayer*, indorfed to *Samuel Gragg*, for £.60 L. Money.

1 Note againft *Wm. Swan* of *Peterfborough*, payable to *Lewis Wheelock*, indorfed to *Samuel Gragg*, for £.52 10s. L. Money.

1 Note by *Hugh Gragg*, of *Colerain*, payable to *Samuel Gragg*, for £. 89 odd fhillings, lawful money.

2 or 3 Notes figned by *William Gragg*, payable to *Samuel Gragg*, for £. 52 11s. lawful money.

A Receipt for a Note of Hand in favour of faid *Samuel Gragg*, fent to *Nova-Scotia*, for £. 34 10s. 10d.

Alfo, an Account with Mr. *Samuel Mather*, of *Lyme*, for Horfes fold him. With a number of other Writings, and other Demands in favour of faid *Gragg*. The whole amounting to about £. 700 L. Money.

46. *Valuable Medicines, Just received from Lee and Co's.*
Patent and Family Medicine Store, Baltimore, and for Sale By
Charles Pierce.
[Portsmouth, New Hampshire: Nutting P. Whitelock, 1800.]

One of many broadsides used to advertise various products, this notice for patent medicines is notable for several reasons. First, we are accustomed to drugstores selling all manner of products, but these medicines were sold in a bookstore. The availability of patent medicines after the Revolution supplanted many home remedies. They were easier to obtain than the home variety, which often required such items as dried toads, spider webs, cow dung, snails, bees, liquor, animal grease, spices, and herbs. The descriptions of the many ailments together with the knowledge that the medicine was probably of little or no use make one wonder how anyone survived.

Evans 38310

12 ¼ × 20 ⅝

a most extraordinary thickness, (supposed from half an inch to an inch in diameter) was opened and found to contain a quantity of young ones. The above is communicated by Mr. Wiley, believing its perusal may be useful to many, by extending the knowledge of a medicine which merits universal attention.

MICHAEL DUFFY, residing at No. 47, Wilke's-street, Fell's point, in the city of Baltimore, voluntarily maketh oath, that the following statement is just and true.

In the beginning of May last my three children, a boy of seven, and two girls, the one five, and the other three years of age, were taken very ill, nearly at the same time, of a common fever, as I then supposed; but was soon convinced the disorder was caused by worms; they were frequently troubled with convulsion fits, and violent startings in their sleep, and with almost continual vomiting and purging, particularly the youngest. I made immediate application to a physician of the first reputation, and his medicines were administered with a confidence of success which only increased our disappointment. The children grew daily worse, and I was absolutely without hopes

HAMILTON's Genuine ESSENCE and
EXTRACT of MUSTARD.

A safe and effectual remedy for acute and chronic rheumatism, gout, rheumatic gout, palsy, lumbago, numbness, white swellings, chilblains, sprains, bruises, pains in the face and neck, &c.

A great number of well authenticated cases of cure, from almost every part of the union, might here be cited, did the limits of this advertisement permit. The following must serve by way of specimen.

JOHN HOOVER, Ropemaker, South Second-street, between Mary & Christian streets, Philadelphia, voluntarily maketh oath as follows, viz: that his wife Mary Hoover, was so severely afflicted with violent rheumatism, very dangerously situated, the consequence of a cold after lying in, as to be confined to her bed for several weeks, and was at length reduced to the most melancholy apprehension of remaining a cripple for life; notwithstanding the most respectable medical advice was followed, and every probable remedy attempted: When seeing several cases of cures performed by Hamilton's Essence & Extract of Mustard, they were procured from

---

Sprains, &c.

lips, and every blemish and inconvenience occasioned by colds, fevers, &c. the usual remedy made use of, but being a very nauseous medicine, and seldom taken in a sufficient quantity, it very often fails; and children and those who have weak stomachs are frequently loth for want of a more easy and pleasant remedy.

Dr. Hahn's Genuine
Eye Water,

A sovereign remedy for all diseases of the eyes, whether the effect of natural weakness, or of accident, speedily removing inflamations, defluxions of the rheum, dullness, itching and films on the eyes; never failing to cure those maladies which frequently succeed the small pox, measles and fevers, and wonderfully strengthening a weak sight: Hundreds have experienced its excellent virtues when nearly deprived of sight.

Teeth and Gums.
Restorative Powder for the TEETH
and GUMS.

This excellent preparation comforts and strengthens the gums, preserves the enamel from decay, and cleanses and whitens the teeth, absorbing all

---

upon trial have been found either dangerous or useless. The bark is the usual remedy made use of, but being a very nauseous medicine, and speedily restoring a beautiful rosy color, and delicate softness to the lips.

Toothache Drops
The only remedy yet discovered, which gives immediate and lasting relief in the most severe cases.

Certain cure for
the ITCH.
Sovereign & safe OINTMENT for the
ITCH.

Which is warranted an infallible remedy at one application, and may be used with the most perfect safety by pregnant women, or on infants a week old, not containing a particle of mercury or any dangerous ingredient whatever, and is not accompanied with that tormenting smart which attends the exhibition of other remedies.

---

of the 4th volumes may be had separate;—Blackstone's commentaries in 4 volumes well printed bound and lettered; Park on Insurance; Kyd on bills of exchange, Laws of New-Hampshire; Freeman's American Clerk's Magazine; Town Officer, and Probate Auxiliary; Vattel's law of Nations; Burlamaqui's principles of natural and political law; Law of Bailments, &c.

Hopkins' System of Divinity; Blair's excellent Sermons; Whitfield's do; Butler's analogy; *Edward's*, History of Redemption, do. on the affections; Watts' Glory of Christ; Newton on the Prophecies; Hunter's Sacred Biography; Hervey's Meditations & contemplations among the tombs, on a flower-garden, on the night, on the Starry Heaven, on creation, a written piece, all in 1 book, at the low priced of 5/3. Carver's Travels; Jenks' Devotion; Morse's Universal Geography, Abridgement, and Elements; Belknap's Biography, and History of New-Hampshire; History of the French Revolution; Hutchinson's History of Massachusetts.

Account Books of various sizes
A variety of ivory, fine teeth Combs; Spectacles suited to almost every sight.

☞ All the above articles will be sold at the lowest Boston prices, by C. Peirce No. 5 Daniel-street Portsmouth, N. H.

are diſagreeable breath, eſpecially in the morning; hard and corrupted gums;—itching in the noſe and about the feet;—convulſions and epileptic fits, and ſome-times privation of ſpeech; ſtarting and grinding of the teeth in ſleep; irregular appetite, ſometimes loathing food, and ſometimes voracious; purging, with ſlimy and fœtid ſtools; vomiting; large and hard belly; pains and ſickneſs at the ſtomach; pains in the head and thighs, with lowneſs of ſpirits; a dry cough; ſmall and irregular pulſe; flow fever with healthy countenance, and ſometimes the face bloated and fluſhed.

☞ Perſons afflicted with any of the above ſymptoms ſhould have immediate recourſe to Hamilton's Worm-deſtroying Lozenges, which have been conſtantly attended with ſucceſs in all complaints incident to thoſe above deſcribed.

*** Recent cures, ſelected from ſeve-ral hundreds, the authenticity of which any perſon may aſcertain by letter or perſonal application, not being perform-ed in Europe, no body knows where—but at home.

A daughter of Mr. Ewing Wiley, No. 109, Cedar-ſtreet, Philadelphia, was dreadfully afflicted; with worms, inſomuch that her life was with great reaſon de-ſpaired of; her complexion faded and grew pale and ſallow; her eyes ſunken; her appetite was loſt, and ſucceeded by a painful and conſtant ſickneſs at the ſto-mach; which general waſting and debil-ity, was accompanied with every appear-ance of a dangerous fever. From this ſhe was relieved, and reſtored to a ſtate of perfect health and ſtrength in a few days, by the uſe of Hamilton's Worm-deſtroying Lozenges; which expelled a great number of large pointed worms, from ſix to nine or 12

DANGEROUS COLD.

DAVID GILBERT, Toyman, No. 46, South-Fourth-ſtreet, Philadelphia, vo-luntarily maketh oath, as follows, viz:—That about eight months ago, he caught a ſevere cold, which reſiſted every reme-dy he could think of, and produced the moſt alarming effects; he could procure no reſt for inceſſant coughing, nor breathe without great pain and difficulty, and was finally ſo exhauſted, as to be ſcarcely able to walk about, which left his friends little hopes of his recovery, though the preſcriptions of a reſpectable phyſician were conſtantly attended to. In this ſi-tuation hearing of the efficacy of Hamil-ton's Elixir, a bottle was procured from Mr. Birch, No. 17, South-Second-ſtreet, the firſt doſe of which afforded the moſt ſurpriſing relief, and gave him more eaſe than he had enjoyed during the whole of the above period, and before the contents of one bottle were taken, he was perfect-ly cured, his ſtrength and appetite recov-ered, and not a ſymptom of his former diſtreſſing complaints remained.

The above particulars the ſaid David Gilbert wiſhes to be made public, as a teſtimony of his gratitude, and for the benefit of mankind.

DAVID GILBERT.

Sworn and ſubſcribed before me the 24th day of March, 1802.

JOHN JENNINGS, Alderman.

A ſovereign remedy for coughs, Catarrhs, Aſthmas, ſore throats, and approaching conſumptions.

☞ To parents who may have children afflicted with the Hooping Cough,

This diſcovery is of the firſt magnitude, as it affords, immediate relief, checks the progreſs, and in a ſhort time entirely re-moves the moſt cruel diſorder to which children are liable. The Elixir is ſo per-fectly agreeable, and the doſe ſo ſmall, that no difficulty ariſes in taking it.

Excellent Corn Plaiſter

Dr. Hahn's true and genuine German CORN PLAISTER.

An infallible remedy for corns, ſpeedily removing them root and branch, without giving pain.

Pimples, Freckles,

Ringworms, &c.

Genuine PERSIAN LOTION.

So celebrated among the faſhiona-ble throughout Europe, as an inval-uable coſmetic, perfectly innocent in preventing and removing blemiſh-es of the face and ſkin of every kind, particularly freckles, pimples, pits af-ter ſmall pox, inflammatory redneſs, ſcurfs, tetters, ringworms, ſunburns, prickly heat, premature wrinkles, &c. The Perſian lotion operates mildly, without impeding that natural inſen-ſible perſpiration, which is eſſential to health; yet its effects are ſpeedy and permanent, rendering the ſkin deli-cately ſoft and clear, improving the complexion and reſtoring the bloom of youth. Never failing to render an ordinary countenance beautiful, and an handſome one more ſo.

Damaſk Lip Salve

Is recommended (particularly to the Ladies) as an elegant and pleaſ-

---

cures.

The Grand Reſtorative is prepar-ed in pills as well as in fluid form, which aſſiſts conſiderably in produc-ing a gradual & laſting effect. Their virtues remain unimpaired for many years in any climate.

carry off ſuperfluous bile, and prevent its morbid ſecretion—to produce a free perſpiration, and hereby prevent colds, which are often of mortal con-ſequences—A doſe never fails to re-move a cold, if taken on its firſt ap-pearance.

They are entirely ve-getable, and ought to be taken by all perſons on change of climate.

They have been found remarkably efficacious, in preventing and curing diſorders attendant on long voyages, and ſhould be procured, and careful-ly preſerved for uſe by every ſeaman.

Anodyne Elixir.

For the cure of every kind of Head-ache.

Infallible Ague &

FEVER DROPS,

For the cure of Agues, remittent and intermittent Fevers.

Thouſands can teſtify of their be-ing cured by theſe drops, after the bark and every other medicine has proved ineffectual; and not one in a hundred has had occaſion, to take more than one, and numbers not half a bottle.

Theſe drops are particularly re-commended to the inhabitants of low marſhy countries, where the worſt ſort of agues generally prevail, which unleſs early attended to and ſpeedily removed, injure the conſtitution ex-ceedingly, and bring on dropſies, pu-trid fevers, and a variety of com-plaints, of the moſt dangerous and a-larming nature. Many other medi-cines are daily offered to the public

---

HAS lately received per late arrivals from London, and from the firſt Book-ſtores in Boſton, a very extenſive aſſortment of Books, Stationary, &c.— Among which are the following :—

Pocket Books, from

An elegant aſſortment of ladies faſhionable

4/6 to 3/6/ each; Gentlemen's morocco purſes and pocket books; Memorandum books from 2/3 to 2/ each

An extenſive aſſortment of Penknives from 6 cents to 6/each; Razors from 1/6 to 6/each; and excellent Razor ſtraps.

Glaſs, cheſt, braſs, pewter, japanned and paper inkſtands; Wafers of all colours and different qualities; red and black ſealing wax; Pounce and pounce boxes; Dutch quills from 1/3 to 9/per hundred; Slates; ſlate and lead pencils; beſt Britiſh Ink Powder by the groſs, dozen or ſingle paper; Demi, poſt, foolſcap, pot & quarto paper per ream or quire; leg book do.

An elegant and cheap aſſortment of

BIBLES

of the following prices, 6/ 7/6 9/9 10/6 11/3 12/ 13/6 14/3 15/9 19/6 24/ 25/6 33/6 36/ 37/6 38/ 45/ 45/ 48/ 54/ 13 dols. 50 cents, 15 dols. 20 dollars and 25 dols. each.

Dr. Brown's Dictionary to the Bi-ble; Butterworth's Concordance; Burkits Ex-poſition of the New Teſtament;

The late Rev. and pious Mr. Henry's Explanation of the whole ſacred ſcriptures, from the beginning of Geneſis to the end of Revelations; contained in 6 large quarto vol-umes, price 32 dollars.

Teſtaments of various ſizes and pri-ces, from 2/3 to 6/ each.

An extenſive aſſortment of Claſſical and School Books.

Almoſt all kinds of Seamens' books; fcales, dividers &c. &c.

Marſhal's excellent treatiſe on Gar-dening; Valuable ſecrets concerning arts and trades; Dean's Georgical Dictionary and New-England Farmer; Beauties of St. Pierre; Adams' defence of the American Conſtitution; Laws of the United States con-

VALUABLE MEDICINES,

JUST received from LEE and CO's; Patent and Family Medicine Store, Baltimore;

AND FOR SALE

BY CHARLES PEIRCE,

At the COLUMBIAN Book-store, No. 5, Daniel-street, Portsmouth, New-Hampshire.

Eighty thousand Persons,

Of all ages, have, within 2 years past, found relief from

HAMILTON's

Worm-destroying Lozenges,

IN various dangerous complaints arifing from worms, and from foulnefs or obftruction in the ftomach and bowels.

This medicine, bears no analogy whatever to others of fimilar title, fo commonly complained of as operating with a degree of violence, fufficient not only to kill worms, but fometimes to endanger the patient's life ; on the contrary, a peculiar excellence of this remedy is its being fuited to every age and conftitution ;—contains nothing but what is perfectly innocent, and is fo mild in its operation, that it cannot injure the moft delicate health, which they ftill enjoy, though five months have nearly elapfed, fince they were on the borders of the grave, and the death of the whole appeared to be inevitable.

Sworn before me this 26th day of September, 1799.

J. SMITH.

Letter from Mr. John Abercromby, Soap and Candle Manufacturer, No. 28, Bridge-street, Baltimore, to the Proprietor of Hamilton's Worm-deftroying Lozenges.

Sir,

I think it my duty to inform you that I have experienced the happieft effects from your Lozenges, having been much affected for four years paft with various complaints carried by a cold, particularly a conftant pain in my ftomach and bowels, frequent and fevere head ache, with a general laffitude and weaknefs, during which time I had the beft medical advice that could be obtained from the moft fkilful phyficians I could hear of, both American and European, but without any alleviation

---

DESCRIPTION OF WORMS,

And the fymptoms by which they are known.

Worms which infeft the human body are chiefly of four kinds, viz.—The teres or large round worm, the afcarides, or fmall maw-worm, the cucurbitina, or fhort,

of their recovery. The youngeft one appeared almoft devoid of animation, and fcarcely an inhabitant of this world. In this diftreffing moment I was told that Hamilton's Worm-deftroying Lozenges had performed many cures, in cafes equally defperate. I immediately purchafed a box, and gave each of them a dofe, which in a few hours produced the moft defirable effects ; the eldeft vomited a great number of very large worms, and the fecond thoufands of fmall ones, many of them not a quarter of an inch long ;—in the youngeft they feemed to be confumed, and had the appearance of fkins of a flimy matter. I repeated the dofe agreeably to the paper of directions, and they all fpeedily recovered a good ftate of health.

Children generally take this medicine with eagernefs ; having a pleafant appearance and an agreeable tafte.

South-Second-ftreet. The firft application enabled her to walk acrofs the room, and the ufe of one bottle reftored her to her ufual ftate of health and ftrength. John Hoover.

Sworn &, fubfcribed the 25th day of March, 1800, before Ebenezer Ferguson, Efq; one of the Juftices of the Peace, for Philadelphia County.

Dr. HAMILTON's

Grand Reftorative

Is recommended as an invaluable medicine, for the fpeedy relief and permanent cure of the various complaints which refult from diffipated pleafures, juvenile indiscretions, refidence in climates unfavorable to the conftitution ; the immoderate ufe of tea, frequent intoxication, or any other deftructive intemperance ; the unfkilful or exceffive ufe of mercury; the difeafes peculiar to females, at a certain period of life ; bad lyings in, &c.

And is proved by long and extenfive experience to be abfolutely unparalleled in the cure of nervous diforders—Confumptions—lownefs of fpirits—Lofs of appetite—Impurity of the blood—Hyfterical affections—Inward weakneffes—Violent cramps in the ftomach and back—Indigeftion—Melancholy—Gout in the ftomach—Pains in the limbs—Relaxations—Involuntary emiffions—Seminal weakneffes—Obftinate gleets—Fluor albus or whites—Impotency—Barrennefs, &c. &c.

In cafes of extremity where the long prevalence and obftinacy of difeafe has brought on a general impo-

---

that acrimonious flime and foulnefs, which fuffered to accumulate, never fails to injure, and finally to ruin them.

For the prevention and cure of Bilious & Malignant Fevers, is recommended,

Dr. HAHN's

Anti-billious Pills,

Which have been attended with a degree of fuccefs highly grateful to the inventor's feelings, in feveral parts of the Weft-Indies, and the Southern parts of the United States, particularly in Baltimore, Peterfburg, Richmond, Norfolk, Edenton, Wilmington, Charlefton and Savannah. The teftimony of a number of perfons in each of the above places can be adduced, who have reafon to believe that a timely ufe of this falutary remedy has, under Providence, preferved their lives when in the moft alarming circumftances.

Facts of this conclufive nature, fpeak more in favor of a medicine than columns of pompous eulogy founded on mere affertion, could do. It is not indeed prefumptuoufly propofed as an infallible cure, but the inventor has every poffible reafon that can refult, from extenfive experience, for believing that a dofe of thefe Pills, taken once every two weeks, during the prevalence of our billious fevers, will prove an infallible preventative—and further ; that in the earlier ftages of thofe difeafes, their ufe will very generally fucceed in reftoring health, and frequently in cafes efteem-

---

CURE OF

Venereal Complaints.

Prepared by Dr. Leroux,

The Patent Indian Vegetable Specific.

The experience of feveral thoufands who have been cured by this medicine, (a great proportion of them after the fkill of eminent phyficians had proved ineffectual) demonftrate its efficacy in expelling the Venereal poifon, however deeply rooted in the Conftitution, and in counteracting thefe dreadful effects which often refult from the improper ufe of mercury.

The mildnefs of the Vegetable Specific is equal to its furprifing efficacy, its operation is fo gentle that it is given to Venereal patients in a ftate of pregnancy, with the utmoft fafety, and performs a cure without difturbing the fyftem, or producing any of thofe difagreeable effects infeparable from the common remedies.

With the medicine is given, a defcription of the fymptoms which obtain in every ftage of the difeafe, with copious directions for their treatment, fo as to accomplifh a perfect cure in the fhorteft time, and with the leaft inconvenience poffible.

AMUSEMENTS

47. Boston, May 13, 1756. To be seen . . . The Microcosm,
Or, The World in Miniature.
[Boston: J. Draper, 1756.]

Since theater was banned in Boston from 1750 to 1792, the inhabitants resorted to other forms of amusement. Despite the Puritan clergy, dancing and dicing, chess and billiards, and like games were popular in New England towns. In the country, colonists enjoyed fairs, corn husking, horse racing, and wrestling matches.

The exhibition of "that elaborate and matchless pile of art, the Microcosm," must have been an amusing and wondrous spectacle for the townspeople, particularly at a time when Boston was still fairly rustic.

This advertisement was published in the *Boston Weekly News-Letter* on May 13, 1756, using the same format. Printing such advertisements was a good and steady income for the printers of newspapers.

Evans 40825
6 ⅞ × 10 ¼

BOSTON, *May* 13, 1756.

To be seen (for a short Time) at the House of Mr. *William Fletcher*, Merchant, *New-Boston*;

That ELABORATE and MATCHLESS PILE of A R T, called, The

MICROCOSM,

Or, The WORLD in MINIATURE.

BUILT in the Form of a Roman *Temple*, after *Twenty-two Years close Study and Application*, by the late ingenious Mr. HENRY BRIDGES, of London; who, having received the Approbation and Applause of the Royal Society, &c. afterwards made considerable Additions and Improvements; so that the Whole, being now compleatly finished, is humbly offered to the Curious of this City, as a Performance which has been the Admiration of every Spectator, and proved itself by its singular Perfections the most instructive as well as entertaining Piece of Work in Europe.

A PIECE of such complicated Workmanship, and that affords such a Variety of Representations (tho' all upon the most simple Principles) can but very imperfectly be described in Words the best chosen; therefore 'tis desired, what little is said in this Advertisement may not pass for an Account of the MICROCOSM, but only what is thought meerly necessary in the Title of such an Account, &c.

ITS outward Structure is a most beautiful Composition of Architecture, Sculpture and Painting. The inward Contents are as judiciously adapted to gratify the Ear, the Eye, and the Understanding; for it plays with great Exactness several fine Pieces of Musick, and exhibits, by an amazing Variety of moving Figures, Scenes diversified with natural Beauties, Operations of Art, of human Employments and Diversions, all passing as in real Life, &c.

1. SHEWS all the celestial Phænomena, with just Regard to the proportionable Magnitudes of their Bodies, the Figures of their Orbits, and the Periods of their Revolutions, with the Doctrine of JUPITER's Satellites, of Eclipses, and of the Earth's annual and diurnal Motions, which are all rendered familiarly intelligible. In Particular will be seen the Trajectory and Type of a Comet, predicted by Sir ISAAC NEWTON, to appear the Beginning of 1758; likewise a Transit of VENUS over the Sun's Disk, the Sixth of *June* 1761; also a large and visible Eclipse of the Sun, the First of *April* 1764, &c.

2. ARE the nine Muses playing in Concert on divers musical Instruments, as the Harp, Hautboy, Bass Viol, &c.

3. IS ORPHEUS in the Forest, playing on his Lyre, and beating exact Time to each Tune; who, by his exquisite Harmony, charms even the wild Beasts.

4. IS a Carpenter's Yard, wherein the various Branches of that Trade are most naturally represented, &c.

5. IS a delightful Grove, wherein are Birds flying, and in many other Motions warbling forth their melodious Notes, &c.

6. IS a fine Landskip, with a Prospect of the Sea, where Ships are sailing with a proportionable Motion according to their Distance. On the Land are Coaches, Carts and Chaises passing along, with their Wheels turning round as if on the Road, and altering their Positions as they ascend or descend a steep Hill; and nearer, on a River, is a Gunpowder-Mill at Work. On the same River are Swans swimming, fishing, and bending their Necks backwards to feather themselves; as also the Sporting of the Dog and Duck, &c.

7. AND lastly, Is shewn the whole Machine in Motion, when upwards of twelve Hundred Wheels and Pinnions are in Motion at once: And during the whole Performance it plays several fine Pieces of Musick on the Organ and other Instruments, both single and in Concert, in a very elegant Manner, &c.

It will be shewn every Day, exactly at Eleven o'Clock in the Morning, and again at Three and Five in the Afternoon, at Four Shillings and Six Pence each, and Children under Twelve Years of Age, at Three Shillings (*Lawful Money*) though Prices quite inferior to the Expences and Merits of this Machine.

N. B. Any Person subscribing *Thirteen Shillings and Six Pence*, will be entitled to see the MICROCOSM at the above Hours, during it's Stay in *Boston*.

☞ TICKETS to be had of Edes & Gill in Queen-Street, and at the above Mr. Fletcher's.

48. *A Catalogue of Books, Lately imported from Britain; And to be Sold by A. Barclay.*
[*Boston, ca.* 1765.]

One gauge of the colonists' interests is the books they are known to have purchased. There are, for example, catalogues for the Harvard and Yale libraries going back to 1723 and 1743, respectively. Many of the books imported by Andrew Barclay, early Boston bookseller and binder, were either religious or historical in subject matter. Of great interest to us are the books of a less solemn nature such as *Hocus Pocus*—a book of magic, *Joe Miller's Jest, Laugh and be Fat*, and several children's books—*Robin Red Breast, Goose's Tales*, and *Robinson Crusoe*. Works of a practical nature also had an appeal but not to the exclusion of *belles lettres*. Like their European counterparts, the colonists read Congreve, Thompson, Milton, Young, Fénelon, and Cervantes.

Evans 41516
8 5/8 × 13 7/8

A Catalogue of BOOKS,

Lately imported from Britain;

And to be Sold by *A. BARCLAY.*

Second Door North of the three King's

Corn-hill *BOSTON.*

Addinson's Evidence.
Ambrose's looking to Jesus.
ditto Primæ Media et ultima.
Allen's Works 2 Vol.
Afflicted Man's Companion.
Allen's Allarm,
Adventures of a black Coat.
Arabian Night's Entertainment.
Argalus & Parthema.
Bowman's principals of Christianity.
British Letter Writer.
Bells Travels 2 Vol.
Boston's four fold State.
Boston on the Covenant.
Boston's crook of the Lot.
Boston's Catechism.
Balm of Gilead.
Boyle's Voyages.
Bruces Life.
Brook's Remedies.
Buckanniers of America.
Barren fig Tree.
Congreave's Poems.
Cloud of Witnesses.
Calvin's Institutions, 4o
Crook-shank's History 2 Vol.
Cole on God's Sovereignty.
Crawford's dying Thoughts.
Cromwell's Life.
Charles 12th.
Companion for the Altar.
Cocker's Arethmetick.
Col Jack
Cyrus's Travels.
Countryman's Jewell.
Cynthiæ.
Crawford's Catechism.
Craighead on the Sacrament.
Clark on Baptism.
12 Cæsers.
Confession of Faith, large.
ditto Small.
Doddridge's Rise and Progress.
Death of Abel.
Durham on Death, ditto Isaiah.
Durham on the unsearchable riches
of Christ. Dyer's Works.
Don Quixot.

Drake's Voyages.
Devil on two Sticks.
Doddridge on Regeneration.
Erskin's Sermons 4 Vol.
Eæsops Fables.
Flavel's Works, Folio.
ditto on Reformation.
ditto Navigation spiritualiz'd.
ditto on Providence.
ditto Saint indeed.
Fisher's English Grammer.
Foucault's Maxims.
French Convert.
Francis Spira.
Fortunate Viliager.
Fisher's Arethmatick.
Firmin's real Christian.
Fenlon on Eloquence.
Gospel Sonnets.
Gaudentia di Lucca.
Gray on Prayer.
ditto precious Promises.
Gulliver's Travels. Guardian,
Guthry's Tryal.
Grace abounding.
Gray's Sermons.
Goose's Tales.
Hervey's Dialogues, 2 Vol.
Hervey's Meditations
Hales Contemplations, 2 Vol.
Hill's Arethmatick.
Heaven's Glory.
Heavenly Footman.
History of Scotland.
Hocus, Pocus.
Heaven upon Earth.
Joe Miller's Jest.
Knoxe's History.
Laugh and be Fat.
Lark.
Lennet.
London Jests.
Mason on Self-Knowledge.
Marshal on Sanctificatian.
Mystery of Faith.
Montague's Letters.
Mair's Book-keeping.
Mair's Geography.

New Book of Knowledge.
Owen on Communion.
Œconomy of human Life.
Papers concerning the Rebellion.
Pocket Dictionary.
Parish Girl.
Pennetential Cries.
Pilgrim's Progress.
Present for an Apprentice
ditto a Servant Maid
Ralph Erskin's Works 2 Vol Folio
Row's Letters.
Row's devout Exercises.
Ramsey's Songs.
Ramsay's Poems.
Review of America.
Reynard the Fox.
Reading made Easy.
Russell's Seven Sermons.
Robin Red Breast.
Robinson Cruso.
Sherlock on Death.
Sherlock on Judgment
Spiritual Warfare
Scougal's Life of God
Secretary's Guide.
Seven wise masters,
Seven wise mistresses,
Telemachus 2 Vol.
Tell tale
Triumphs of Love.
Truth, Victory over Error
Thomson's Seasons
Tansurs's royal Melody.
Universal Dictionary.
Whole duty of Man
Watt's Lyrick Poems
Willison's Catechisms
Willison's Example
Willison's Sacramental Meditations
Watson's Body of Divinity
Week's Preperation
Warden on the Lord's Supper
Wifes Companion
Webster's Book-keeping.
Vincents Catechism
Young's Night Thoughts.

At the said Shop may be had, Bibles Gilt or Plain, Testaments, Prayer-Books, Tate & Brady's Psalms, gilt or plain, Watts' Psalms & Hymns, with or without Tunes, Accidenees, Dilworth's and other Spelling Books, Primers Psalters Singing-Books, Account-Books, Receipt Books, Morocco letter Cases Plays, Pamphlets, Paper, Pens, Ink, Ink Powder, Wax, Wafers, &c. &c.

N. B. All Sorts of Books bound, gilt or plain, in the neatest Manner by said *Barclay.* Gentlemen in Town and Country, who please to favour him with their Custom, may depend upon being served with Fidelity and Dispatch.
☞ Cash given for Sheep-skins fit for Book-binding, at the same Place.

49. *The Amorous Sailor's Letter To His Sweetheart. And the*
Jolly Orange Woman.
Worcester: [Isaiah Thomas], 1781.

The two songs on this broadside ballad are probably both English in origin. "The Orange Woman" refers, of course, not to the songstress's complexion but to what she is selling. The ditty was published as a piece of sheet music in London in 1770 after being sung by a Miss Brown at Sadler's Wells. "The Amorous Sailor's Letter" probably dates from the Seven Years War since the lovelorn sailor says "tho' I go,/ To fight 'gainst France and Spain,/ My heart I leave along with you." The juxtaposition of these two songs shows that levity was not entirely foreign to the colonial mind. To the sweetheart's rather saccharine fidelity, the orange vendor offers her carefree desire to "kiss where'er I find 'em."

Although separately printed music had long been published in Europe, sheet music published in the United States was practically unknown until 1789. Popular songs such as this were issued as broadsides. The tunes for the ballads were well known so that printed music was unnecessary.

Evans 19397
8 ⅝ × 13 ⅜

THE AMOROUS
SAILOR's LETTER
To his SWEETHEART.
AND THE
JOLLY ORANGE WOMAN.

BRIGHT was the morning, cool the air,
　Serene was all the sky,
When on the waves I left my Fair,
　The centre of my joys ;
Heaven and nature smiling were,
　Nothing was sad but I ;
My Breast was fill'd with anxious care,
　Strange thoughts did me annoy.
Each rosy field sweet ardour spread,
　All fragrant was the shore ;
Each River-God rose from his bed,
　And fighting own'd his power ;
The curling waves they deck'd their head,
　Being proud of what they bore ;
But my poor heart she carried,
　With her unto the shore.
Glide on ye waters bear these lines,
　Tell her I am distress'd ;
Bear all my sighs ye gentle winds,
　Waft them to her sweet breast ;
Should Polly to others incline,
　My woes would be increas'd
Tell her if e'er she proves unkind.
　I never can have rest.
Sweet lovely charmer tho' I go,
　To fight 'gainst France and Spain,
My heart I leave along with you,
　'Till I return again ;
And since my foes have forc'd me hence,
　From my sweet lovely dear ;
Their cruelty I'll recompence,
　When them I do come near.
May Heaven foreend my sweetest love,
　From sorrow, grief and care :
May guardian Angels still preserve
　My charming Polly dear,
What through from you I am apart,
　I faithful will remain,
So fare you well my pretty heart,
　Until we meet again.

THE ANSWER.

MY dearest Johnny, since I find,
　You are faithful, just and true ;
I vow forever I'll prove kind
　And constant unto you ;

No rivals will I entertain,
　My Jewel to perplex ;
I faithful will to you remain,
　And never will you vex.
May heavens preserve that gallant ship,
　Wherein my love does sail :
And while she roles upon the deep,
　May you have gentle gales,
To waft you to the British shore,
　Unto your own true love,
And I forever shall adore,
　The heavenly powers above.

THE ORANGE WOMAN.

A HEARTY buxom Girl am I,
　I came from Dublin city,
I never heard a Man, not I,
　Though some say more's the pity ;
Well, let them say so once again,
　I've got no cause to mind 'em,
I always fancy pretty Men,
　Whenever I can find 'em.
I'll never marry, no indeed,
　For marriage causes trouble :
And after all the priest has said,
　'Tis merely hubble bubble.
The Rakes will still be counted Rakes,
　Not Hymen's chains can bind 'em,
And so preventing all mistakes,
　I'll kiss where'er I find 'em.
The game of Wedlock's all a chance,
　Cry over or cry under,
Yet many folks to Church will dance,
　At which I often wonder.
Some fancy this, some fancy that,
　All hope the joy design'd 'em ;
I'll have my whim, that's tit for tat,
　Where'er I can find 'em.
But a silly Jade am I,
　Thus idly to be singing,
There's not one here my fruit to buy ;
　Nor any to be flinging ;
In pretty Men all pleasure dwells,
　All hope the joy design'd 'em,
So now I'll wheel to Saddler's Wells,
　And there I'm sure to find 'em.

Printed at WORCESTER, 1781.

50. *To the Curious . . . Two Camels . . . from Arabia.*
[Salem, Massachusetts? 1789?]

The strange and the exotic, even if only a beast of burden from the East, lent a certain relief to the tedium of hard work in early America. Similar notices exist for an elephant, a leopard, and a bull moose, as well as for deformed domesticated animals. One of the earliest advertisements for an exhibition of a wild animal appeared in the *Boston News-Letter* for November 26, 1716, announcing a lion on display to the public.

These particular camels evidently toured from town to town since a notice for their exhibition in New Haven appeared in the *Connecticut Journal* for June 30 and July 7, 1790.

Exhibitions of single animals evolved into the formation of menageries, so that by 1820 there were very few individual animals being exhibited. Also during this period itinerant acrobats and equestrian acts toured from town to town. In New York and Philadelphia, however, there were resident circuses with acrobats, equestrian acts and clowns (but no wild animals) as early as 1792.

Evans 45607
6⅜ × 8⅛

To the CURIOUS.

To be seen at Major Leavenworth's Stable, opposite Mr. Lothrop's, State-Street,

Two CAMELS,

Male and Female, lately imported from

A R A B I A.

THESE stupendous Animals are most deserving the Attention of the Curious, being the greatest natural Curiosity ever exhibited to the Public on this Continent. They are Nineteen Hands high; have Necks near Four Feet long; have a large high Bunch on their Backs, and another under their Breasts, in the Form of a Pedestal, on which they support themselves when lying down; they have Four Joints in their hind Legs, and will travel Twelve or Fourteen Days without drinking, and carry a Burden of Fifteen Hundred Weight; they are remarkably harmless and docile, and will lie down and rise at Command.

Price of Admittance for a Gentleman or Lady, NINE-PENCE *each.*

- - - - - - - - - - - - - -

[*Abraham was old and well stricken in Age: And the Lord had blessed Abraham in all Things. And Abraham said unto his eldest Servant of his House, that ruled over all that he had, Thou shalt go unto my Country, and to my Kindred, and take a Wife unto my Son Isaac. And the Servant took Ten Camels, of the Camels of his Master, and departed; and went to Mesopotamia, unto the City Nahor. And he made his Camels to kneel down without the City, by a Well of Water, at the Time of the Evening, even the Time that Women go out to draw Water. Pure Wisdom directed the Servant, and succeeded him in obtaining the Consent of the Parents, Brethren and Kindred of* REBECCAH, *that she should go to the Land of Canaan, and become the Wife of* ISAAC. *And they sent away Rebeccah, their Sister, with her Damsels, and her Nurse, and Abraham's Servant, and his Men, and they rode upon the Camels.* GEN. XXIV.]

51. *Theatre, Frederick-Town.*
Fredericktown, Maryland: John Winter [1791].

Many claims have been made about *The Contrast*. This comedy, composed by Royall Tyler, a jurist and prolific writer, had four performances in New York in 1787 and was the first American comedy to be professionally produced. More importantly, through the characters of Brother Jonathan and Dimple, opposing characteristics of the young republic were epitomized. One theme—the European versus the American—is stated in the Prologue:

> Our author pictures not from foreign climes
> The fashions or the follies of the times;
> But has confin'd the subject of his work
> To the gay scenes—the circles of New York.
> But modern youths, with imitative sense,
> Deem taste in dress the proof of excellence;
> And spurn the meanness of your homespun arts,
> Since homespun habits would obscure their parts;
> Whilst all, which aims at splendour and parade,
> Must come from Europe, and be ready made.
> Strange! we should thus our native worth disclaim,
> And check the progress of our rising fame.
> Yet one, whilst imitation bears the sway,
> Aspires to nobler heights, and points the way.

Evans 46169
10 ⅝ × 17

THEATRE,

Frederick-Town.

❋×✕×✕×✕×✕×✕×✕×✕×❋

By Mr. M'GRATH's COMPANY of COMEDIANS.

━━━━━━━━━━━━━━━━━━━━

Mr. FITZ-GERALD and Miſs KITELY's NIGHT.

━━━━━━━━━━━━━━━━━

On *THURSDAY EVENING*, *March* the 10th, *will be preſented,*

The Celebrated COMEDY of---

THE CONTRAST.

(*Written by a* CITIZEN *of the* UNITED STATES)
Performed with Univerſal Applauſe *at the Theatres, Philadelphia, New-York,*
Baltimore, Alexandria, &ʒ George-Town.

" EXULT each Patriot heart! this night is ſhewn
" A Piece, which we may, fairly, call our own.

The Original PROLOGUE to be ſpoken by *Mr.* M'GRATH.

Colonel Manly,	Mr. M'GRATH.
Van-Rough,	Mr. BALENTINE.
Jeſſamy,	Mr. SMITH.
Dimple,	by an Aſſiſtant.
And Jonathan, (with the comic ſong of " Yankey Doodle")	Mr. FITZ-GERALD.
Maria, & Letitia,	Miſs KITELY.
Jenny	Mrs. PARSONS.
And Charlotte,	Mrs. M'GRATH.

Between the Play and Farce, " Belles have at ye All," *by Mrs.* M'Grath.

To which will be added, *a Farce,* (*written by the Author of the Poor Soldier*)
Called---The

AGREEABLE SURPRISE.

Sir Felix Friendly,	Mr. SMITH.
Eugene,	Mr. FITZ-GERALD.
Compton,	Mr. BALENTINE.
Chicane,	Mr. FITZ-GERALD.
John,	by an Aſſiſtant.
And Lingo,	Mr. M'GRATH.
Mrs. Cheſhire,	Mrs. PARSONS.
Laura,	Miſs KITELY.
And Cowſlip,	Mrs. M'GRATH,

The whole to conclude with A MORAL DEFENCE OF THE STAGE, by MR. FITZ-GERALD.

Mr. Fitz-Gerald, &ʒ Miſs Kitely, at the ſame time that they ſolicit the Patronage of the *Ladies,* and *Gentlemen* of Frederick-Town, and its Vicinage, on this *Intereſting Night,* moſt reſpectfully aſſure them, that the Entertainments ſhall be as faithfully performed *On the Stage,* as temptingly held out *In the Bill.*

☞ The Curtain to riſe *preciſely* at the appointed time. (Twenty Minutes paſt SIX o'Clock.)

☞ Tickets of Admiſſion, at *Half a Dollar* each, to be had at Mrs. *Kimboll's* Tavern, and of Mr. *Fitz-Gerald,* and *Miſs* Kitely, at the THEATRE.

Mr. and Mrs. M'GRATH return their beſt acknowledgements to their Friends, and the Public, who Honoured their *propoſed* Benefit with their preſence---reſpectfully announce, that in conſequence of the *Weather,* and *other circumſtances* militating againſt their Intereſt, they have thrown up the Receipts of that Night's Exhibition among the Company, on the hope of being advantaged by a *real Benefit* at a future evening, for which occaſion, a well ſelected Play and Farce will be prepared, and *duly Notified.* (*Floreat Reſpublica!*)

❋×✕×✕×✕×✕×✕×✕×✕×✕×✕×❋

FREDERICK-TOWN:

Printed by *JOHN WINTER,* at the Printing-Office in *Patrick-ſtreet.*

FITZGERALD's   FITZGERALD's   FITZGERALD's   FITZGERALD's

HUMOR

52. *Father Ab--y's Will.*
[*No place, ca.* 1731.]

At least ten other editions of "Father Abbey's Will" printed before 1800 have survived. Its popularity can probably be explained by noting the scarcity of humorous verses in the early eighteenth century. Matthew Abdy was the sweeper and bedmaker at Harvard College. On Abdy's death, John Seccomb, a graduate of Harvard in 1728, wrote this poem. The response from New Haven was written by John Hubbard, apparently the first of a long series of rival clashes between Harvard and Yale! Jonathan Belcher, governor of Massachusetts at the time, sent both sets of verses to London, where they were reprinted in the *Gentlemen's Magazine.* The first set was published in May of 1732, the New Haven response in June. These verses were popular in England and were reprinted many times. Indeed, as late as 1782, a copy in the Society's collection was purchased in London.

Evans 3475
8 ½ × 12 ¼

Father Ab--y's Will.

To which is now addded, A Letter of Courtship to his Virtuous and Amiable Widow.

Cambridge, December 1731.

Some Time since died here Mr. *Matthew Ab--y,* in a very advanced Age :—He had for a great Number of Years served the College in Quality of Bed-maker and Sweeper :—Having no Child, his Wife inherits his whole Estate, which he bequeathed to her by his last Will and Testament, as follows, *viz.*

1
TO my dear Wife
My Joy and Life,
I freely now do give her,
My whole Estate,
With all my Plate,
Being just about to leave her.

2
My Tub of Soap,
A long Cart Rope,
A Frying Pan and Kettle,
An Ashes Pail,
A threshing Flail,
An Iron Wedge and Beetle.

3
Two painted Chairs,
Nine Warden Pears,
A large old dripping Platter,
This Bed of Hay
On which I lay,
An old Sauce-Pan for Butter.

4
A little Mug,
A Two Quart Jugg,
A Bottle full of Brandy,
A Looking Glass,
To see your Face,
You'll find it very handy.

5
A Musket true,
As ever flew,
A Pound of Shot and Wallet,
A Leather Sash,
My Calabash,
My Powder Horn and Bullet.

6
An old Sword Blade,
A Garden Spade,
A Hoe, a Rake, a Ladder,
A Wooden Can,
A Close-Stool Pan,
A Clyster-Pipe and Bladder.

7
A greasy Hat,
My old Ram Cat,
A Yard and half of Linen,
A Pot of Grease,
My Woollen Fleece,
In order for your Spinning.

8
A small Tooth Comb,
An Ashen Broom,
A Candlestick and Hatchet,
A Coverlid
Strip'd down with Red,
A Bag of Rags to patch it.

9
A ragged Mat,
A Tub of Fat,
A Book put out by *Bunyan,*
Another Book
By *Robin Rook,*
A Skain or two of Spunyarn.

10
An old black Muff,
Some Garden Stuff,
A Quantity of Burridge.
Some Devil's Weed
And Burdock Seed,
To season well your Porridge.

11
A Chafing Dish,
With one Salt Fish,
If I am not mistaken,
A Leg of Pork,
A broken Fork,
And half a Flitch of Bacon.

12
A Spinning Wheel,
One Peck of Meal,
A Knife without a Handle,
A rusty Lamp,
Two Quarts of Samp,
And half a Tallow Candle.

13
My Pouch and Pipes,
Two Oxen Tripes,
An Oaken Dish well carved,
My little Dog,
And spotted Hog,
With two young Pigs just starved.

14
This is my Store,
I have no more,
I heartily do give it,
My Years are spun,
My Days are done,
And so I think to leave it.

***

New-Haven, January 1731-2.

Our Sweeper having lately buried his Spouse, and accidentally hearing of the Death and Will of his deceas'd *Cambridge* Brother, has conceived a violent Passion for his Relict. And, as Love softens the Mind and disposes to Poetry, he has eas'd himself in the following Strains, which he transmits to the charming Widow, as the first Essay of his Courtship.

1
Mistress *Ab——y,*
To you I fly,
You only can relieve me,
To you I turn, for you I burn,
If you will but believe me.

2
Then gentle Dame,
Admit my Flame,
And grant me my Petition,
If you deny,
Alas ! I die
In pitiful Condition.

3
Before the News
Of your poor Spouse
Had reach'd us at *New-Haven,*
My dear Wife dy'd
Who was my Bride
In *Anno* Eighty seven.

4
Thus being free,
Let's both agree
To join our Hands, for I do
Boldly aver
A Widower
Is fittest for a Widow.

5
You may be sure
'Tis not your Dower
I make this flowing Verse on;
In these smooth Lays
I only praise
The Glories of your Person.

6
For the whole that
Was left by *Mat,*
Fortune to me has granted
In equal Store,
I've one Thing more,
Which *Matthew* long had wanted.

7
No Teeth, 'tis true,
You have to shew,
The Young think Teeth inviting,
But silly Youths !
I love those Mouths
Where there's no fear of biting.

8
A leaky Eye,
That's never dry
These woful Times is fitting,
A wrinkled Face
Adds solemn Grace
To Folk devout at Meeting.

9
Thus to go on,
I would pen down
Your Charms from Head to Foot,
Set all your Glory
In Verse before ye,
But I've no Mind to do't.

10
Then haste away
And make no Stay,
For soon as you come hither,
We'll eat and sleep,
Make Beds and sweep,
And smoke and talk together.

11
But if, my Dear,
I must move there.
Tow'rds *Cambridge* strait I'll set me,
To touze the Hay
On which you lay,
If *Age* and *You* will let me.

Thus Father Ab--y left his Spouse,
As rich as Church or College *Mouse;*

Which is sufficient Invitation
To serve the College in his Station.

53. Job Weeden, Salem News-Boy, . . . Jan. 1, 1772.
[Salem, 1772.]

Carrier's addresses first appeared in the *American Weekly Mercury*, a Philadelphia newspaper in 1720. Composed by the apprentice to the printer or by the carrier of the newspaper, these poems are generally amusing in their frank appeal for cash. Other addresses summarize past events or make predictions for the future. Nor was it unusual for these poems to be political in nature.

The *Essex Gazette* was established in Salem, Massachusetts, by Samuel Hall in 1768, the first newspaper in that town. In 1775, shortly after Lexington and Concord, the newspaper was moved to Cambridge.

Evans 42389
6 × 6 ⅛

Job Weeden, Salem News-Boy,

Begs Leave to prefent the following Lines to the GENTLEMEN *and* LADIES *to whom he carries the* Effex Gazette.

Jan. 1, 1772.

NOW happily dawns the Year --- *Seventy-two*.--

Accept my Regards--they're chearful and true.

Pray grant me a Smile---*a little Cafh too*.

No Heat nor no Cold my Courfe does retard:

Your Servise is all I ever regard.

Shall I not meet with an ample Reward?

To pleafe and amufe you---ftill I will go,

As patient as *Job*---blow high or blow low.

Tho' drenched with Rain, or fmother'd in Snow.

Your Goodnefs is great---my Boldnefs excufe,

'Tis not for Beggars to have what they chufe;

But pray remember, *'tis Job brings the News*.

54. *Verses for the Year* 1790.
[*New York: Harrisson and Purdy*, 1790.]

The printer's devil of the *New-York Weekly Museum* must have amused himself by composing this poem with its description of the whirlwind journey to gather news. This carrier's address closes with the customary pleas for a tip.

The *New-York Weekly Museum* was the continuation of *The Impartial Gazetteer and Saturday Evening's Post*, established in May of 1788 by John Harrisson and Stephen Purdy. In September of 1788 the title changed to the *New-York Weekly Museum*. This newspaper continued to be published until after 1820.

This is one of the most handsomely printed carrier's addresses. Undoubtedly, most printers enjoyed the opportunity to experiment with their ornaments and woodcuts. Unhappily, many of these addresses were discarded, so that few have survived.

Evans 46085

9 × 10 ½

VERSES *for the* YEAR 1790.

Addreſſed to the *Generous Subſcribers* of the

NEW-YORK WEEKLY MUSEUM,

Wiſhing them a Happy New Year.

ONCE more awake the ſtrain of grateful praiſe,
    Accept your votary's humble annual lays;
To you my Patrons—I'm in duty bound,
To ſerve while life runs its continual round,
Collecting every ſubject worth a ſingle line,
Apollo's notes—ſung by the ſacred nine.
What's done in foreign climes freſh come to hand,
Array'd in order—in the MUSEUM ſtand.
From Heſper's ſilver flood-gates (from the ſtar,
That ſhoots its pale and glimmering rays afar)
To old Oceanus off I ſend the muſe,
To bring the cream—the beſt of all the news;
Swift-footed Hermes, trips acroſs the main,
Viſits the cabinets of France and Spain;
From thence to China, where he leaps the wall,
That's fifty cubits high, nor dreads the fall.
He viſits Pekin—peeps into their ſchemes,
And finds ſome more abſurd than madmen's dreams.
With twiſted rod he cleaves the nether ſkies,
And ſwift to London and St. James's flies;
Next to the Houſe of Commons—reads the bill,
Where ſullen Juſtice ſat with ſtumpy quill—
Inebriate Faction, hoodwink'd reel'd along,
And leering Folly ſang Deception's ſong.
Hermes returns, and brings the pond'rous mail,
And bids fair Freedom's preſs the truth reveal.

No doubt you've wonder'd whence we had our news,
While you our WEEKLY MUSEUM did peruſe;
Therefore to ſatisfy my Patron's anxious thought,
I aroſe this morning—and the muſe I ſought,
Long e'er the ſun awoke the new born day,
I ſtood prepar'd to ſtrike th' accuſtom'd lay.
I rang'd the types, ſtraightway to work I went,
To pleaſe my Patrons—was my chief intent;
And now preſent the offering of my muſe,
Though ſmall the gift—pray don't the ſame refuſe.
With it I wiſh you all an *Happy Year*,
Content of *mind*, with plenty of *good cheer*;
And as the year rolls on its annual round,
May *Health* and *Peace* within your doors be found.
May ſmiling *Fortune* all your ſteps attend—
May *Heaven* all your wiſhes ſtill befriend—
May conſcious *Virtue* in your boſom blaze,
And ſweet *Contentment* crown your *happy days*.

    With due ſubmiſſion now I take my leave,
Soon as your GENEROUS BOUNTY I receive,
For which with grateful heart I'll thank moſt fervent,
And am with due reſpect—
                                your humble ſervant.

                    The PRINTER's DEVIL.

55. *By his High and Mighty Laziness Ephraim Eager.*
[No place, 1799.]

There were numerous organizations and societies for the improvement of agriculture, the encouragement of manufactures, the prevention of fires, the study of history, and for the lending of books before 1800. This society must be a reaction against all the others. The Idle Society lasted at least six years, since the American Antiquarian Society has another certificate dated 1804.

Clark Chandler, newly appointed captain of the Worcester chapter, was a member of one of the important Massachusetts families.

Evans 48892

12 ⅝ × 15 ½

By his High and Mighty LAZINESS

EPHRAIM EAGER,

Captain General and *Commander in chief*, of the *Idle* SOCIETY
throughout the *United States of America.*
To *Clark Chandler* Gentleman, Greeting.

YOU being appointed *Captain* of an *Idle Society* in the
town of *Worcester* in the county of *Worcester* By virtue of the
Power vested in me, I do by these presents (Confiding in your *everlasting Idleness* and *Laziness,)* Commission you accordingly. You
are constantly to refrain from all necessary labor, never rise before
the sun ; nor take off your boots when going to bed ; never stand
without leaning, nor walk without some person to loll upon ; never to run in the most extreme and urgent cases, such as fire, for a
Doctor, nor when powerfully agitated by a dose of Jallap ; you are
to be constant in doing nothing, unwearied in drowsiness, and ever pursuing the *works* of *Idleness* : to observe such *signs* and *gestures*
as shall from time to time *escape* your superior officers.

Ephraim Eager

Given under my Hand and the seal of the Society, at LEOMINSTER, the
First Day of Nov 1799 First year of the Idle Society.

By his High and Mighty Laziness :
Secretary.

Oliver Nox

C

STRANGE AND WONDROUS EVENTS

56. An Account of the remarkable recovery of Mrs. Mary Read.
[Providence? 1769?]

Although this miraculous cure occurred in Rehoboth, Massachusetts, it is likely that this account was printed in Providence, Rhode Island, the closest town with a printing press. Several women by the name of Mary Read lived in Rehoboth during the eighteenth century, but no mention of this astonishing incident occurs in contemporary newspapers or in later histories of the town.

Evans 41904

6 ½ × 8 ⅞

An Account of the remarkable Recovery of Mrs. MARY READ, of *Rehoboth*, to the Ufe of her Limbs, of which fhe had been deprived Three Years.

MARY READ having been confined to her Bed Three Years fuc-ceffively, namely, from June, 1766, to June, 1769, and never walked a Step; on the 24th Day of July, 1769, as fhe lay medi-tating, thefe Words came to her like a Voice audibly fpoken, "Daughter be of good Cheer, thy Sins are forgiven thee, arife and walk:" They were repeated Three Times over, which caufed her to think it was the Voice of God fpeaking to her by his Word and Spirit. But this Queftion was put in her Mind, How do you know it is the Voice of God? With this Suggeftion, It is not the Voice of God. Then fhe doubted whether it was God's Voice or not; upon which thefe Words came unto her,---"It is I the Lord that fpeaketh unto thee,---fear not." She ftill hefitating about the Matter, faid, I truft that God fpoke to me by Way of Command. The Words were repeated the Second Time,---"It is I, the Lord of Hofts, that fpeaketh unto thee, arife and walk, fear not."---As fhe was greatly folicitous to know whether it was the Voice of God or not, the Words were repeated over the Third Time,---"It is the Lord of Hofts, the God of Ifrael that commandeth thee,---Arife and walk, fear not." This was backed with the Words of Samuel, "Behold, to obey is better than Sacrifice, and to hearken than the Fat of Rams." This confirmed her that it was the Voice of God, and his almighty Power. Now fee the Power of God! For while the Words were repeating, the Ufe of her Limbs were reftored to her again; the Cords and Sinews on one Side of her, which had been fhrunk up fix or feven Inches, for fo long a Time, were then ftretched out, and fhe became ftraight, and received Strength, and immediately rofe up from her Bed and walked! And now fhe defires that all People would praife GOD for this mi-raculous and glorious Deliverance vouchfafed unto her. Afterward the 55th Hymn of Doctor Watts's, in the firft Book, was brought fweetly to her Mind.

57. On the Dark Day, May Nineteenth, 1780.
[Boston? 1780.]

Eclipses, earthquakes, comets, hurricanes, and other natural phenomena always elicited a good number of pamphlets, broadside ballads, and newspaper accounts, as well as sermons. These events were considered omens of evil and evidence of God's wrath. Even as late as 1780, such a reaction to naturally occurring phenomena was the rule. The *Boston Gazette* for May 22, 1780, contains an account of this event. "The Printers acknowledge their Incapacity of describing the Phaenomenon which appeared in this Town on Friday last, and shall therefore leave it to Astronomers, whose more particular Business it is. They however, would inform those who were not in the Contents of it, that on Friday last About Ten o'clock, there came over this Town a dark Cloud, which continued increasing darker and darker 'till near One o'Clock, when it became so dark that the Inhabitants were obliged to quit their Business. . . . W have already heard of its Extent as far as Greenwich, in the State of Rhode Island, and as far as Portsmouth, in the State of New-Hampshire, which is about 120 miles." A week later in the same newspaper, an explanation was offered for the strange occurrence—rain had brought down smoke from burning leaves.

Evans 43859
7 ½ × 11 ¼

ON THE
DARK DAY,

MAY Nineteenth, 1780.

LET us adore, and bow before
   The sovereign Lord of might,
Who turns away the shining day,
   Into the shades of night.

All nature stands, when he commands,
   Or changes in its course ;
His mighty hand rules sea and land—
   He is the LORD of Host.

Nineteenth of May, a gloomy day,
   When darkness veil'd the sky ;
The sun's decline may be a sign
   Some great event is nigh.

Let us remark, how black and dark,
   Was the ensuing night ;
And for a time the moon's decline,
   And did not give her light.

Can mortal man this wonder scan ?
   Or tell a second cause ?
Did not our GOD then shake his rod,
   And alter nature's laws ?

What great event, next will be sent
   Upon this guilty land ?
He only knows, who can dispose
   All things at his command.

Our wickedness, we must confess,
   Is terrible and great ;
Sin is the thing that we should shun,
   The thing GOD s soul doth hate.

Our mighty sins, GOD's judgment brings
   But still we hard'ned grow ;
Then judgments great may not abate,
   Until our overthrow.

How sin abounds in all our towns,
   Now in these gospel days ;
How vice prevails and virtue fails,
   And godliness decays.

If we reflect, can we expect,
   According to our doing—
But that we are, as we may fear,
   Just on the brink of ruin.

Awake, awake, your sins forsake,
   And that immediately ;
If we don't turn, his wrath will burn,
   To all eternity.

This is the day, that sinners may
   Repent, and turn to God !
If they delay and won't obey,
   Then they must feel his rod.

How good and kind, would sinners find
   Their great Redeemer now ;
If they'd awake, their sins forsake,
   And to His sceptre bow.

The gospel's call, is unto all—
   Repent ! why will you die ?
Why will you go to endless woe,
   And pass my mercy by ?

Come unto me ! JESUS doth say !
   All ye that weary are ;
Ye shall find rest ! ye shall be blest !
   For so his words declare !

If after all, this gracious call,
   You utterly refuse ;
And stop your ear, and will not hear,
   But your own ruin choose.

Mercy abuse, and grace refuse,
   Justice then takes the throne ;
And in some hour Almighty Power,
   Will make his vengeance known.

O dreadful state, when 'tis too late,
   For sinners to return ;
When life and breath is lost in death,
   The soul in hell must burn.

What mortal tongue, what human pen,
   The terror can declare,
That sinners all in hell who shall
   That dreadful torments bear ?

Eternity ! Eternity !
   Behold there is no end ;
Where sinners lie, and wish to die,
   Who into hell descend.

And now let all, who hear this call,
   And saw the day so dark !
Make haste away without delay,
   And get into the ARK !

Then safe shall he, forever be,
   That doth to JESUS come,
He need not fear though death be near,
   Since heaven is his home.

58. *The Vision of John Mills, In Bedford County, at Virginia, in the year 1785.*
[*No place, 1785.*]

A substantial body of literature has made varied use of visions from the lengthy medieval allegorical treatises such as the *Roman de la Rose* to expressions of religious fervor like Joseph Smith's record of the revelation of the Golden Tablets of Mormon in 1827. In fact, intense visionary experiences of a religious nature were prerequisites for membership in some colonial churches. John Mills' description of hell is very vivid. The sins of many of the damned were joking and jesting. Or, as one soul says, "Jesting and joking brought more souls to that place of torment, than willful sin, though it was called innocent mirth in the world."

Evans 44727
8 ⅞ × 13 ⅜

THE
VISION
OF
JOHN MILLS,

In Bedford County, at Virginia, in the year 1785.

IT pleased Almighty God to let me see wonderful things in a Vision as follows :——I being conducted by a light shining guide, saw the glory of heaven and souls singing praises to God and the Lamb in a wonderful and inexpressible manner. My guide asked me if I knew any which I saw? I said I did. I saw souls fetching to judgment. I had knowledge of them that were for happiness, they being drest in bright shining robes. I also had knowledge of them that were for destruction, they being naked, with a sorrowful countenance, looking ghastly and trembling; I saw the devil taking them in a fearful manner, and dragging them down to torment, which kept continually raining, foaming, and stinking with brimstone. I saw streams pouring down into it as the wrath of God which increased the flames : I was afraid, but my guide told me that nothing should hurt me. He then asked me if I knew any that were there? I told him I did. The damned souls in hell would cry and say, that it was just in God to condemn and punish them; continually reflecting on themselves, and saying, that jesting and joking brought them to that place of torment: I saw a cord stretched over that place of torment, and many that were living in the world, standing thereon, going on in all kinds of sin: some swearing, lying, jesting, gaming, drinking, and all kinds of iniquity. I saw many living in the world standing on the brink of eternity; going on in the same course of sin, I saw a man that had been pressed last war, who was shot in the forehead; the blood seemed to run down as fresh as if it had been done that moment : He blamed the pressmaster for bringing him to such an untimely end, but I immediately heard a voice, saying, do not blame the pressmaster for I have him here as I have you. I saw my oldest sister in that place of torment; she came shrieking and crying to me, and saying, that her miseries were inexpressible, and disobedience to her parents brought her to that place of torment.

I saw a man who had been dead ten years; he came shrieking and crying to me, and told me that his miseries were greater than he could express, and told me that jesting and joking brought him to that place of torment; and that jesting and joking brought more souls to that place of torment, than willful sin, though it was called innocent mirth in the world.

I saw an old acquaintance of mine who had been dead four years; he came shrieking and crying to me, and saying, that his miseries were very great, and that swearing, lying, jesting, and drinking brought him to that place of torment : And further added, that he had a brother yet living in the world, going on in the same kind of sin; he desired me to inform him of his distruction, and request him to return from his evil ways.

I saw men and their wives against each other, and cursing each other. I saw the Devil stand before them, agravating them, saying, where is the God which you pretended to serve while you was in the world.

Now my guide told me that I must return to the world, and tell the people of the world what I had heard and seen. And this I do declare in the presence of Almighty God, to be the truth, and nothing but the truth, I being three days and three nights in a trance.

59. *An Account of the Wonderful Old Hermit's Death, and Burial.*
[Boston: E. Russell, 1787.]

In 1785 two Virginia gentlemen, Captain James Buckland and John Fielding, while traveling across the Allegheny Mountains chanced to meet a hermit who claimed to be two hundred and twenty-seven years old. This discovery was soon recorded in several broadsides and pamphlets giving the life story of the hermit.

After publication of these accounts, Dr. Samuel Brake, a curiosity seeker, went in search of the hermit. In the company of some servants, he succeeded in finding him again and this broadside relates the recluse's demise. Particularly curious is the moral stance of this account. The doctor at length convinces the hermit to drink of his rum, which effectively transforms the noble, learned recluse and ultimately kills him. The doctor feels "no remorse of conscience"; the blame is placed on cursed drink.

This broadside is quite unusual for its clarity of presentation, both of the story in the text and the story in the illustration.

Evans 43740
11 ⅝ × 18 ¼

An Account of the Wonderful *Old Hermit's Death,* and Burial.

SOMETIME in June, 1786, Doctor SAMUEL BRAKE, a gentleman eminent both for Physic and Surgery, and a man indefatigable in the search of Curiosities, hearing of the wonderful Account of the HERMIT, set out with a full determination to go and find him. The Doctor furnished himself with the best intelligence Capt. *Buckland* could possibly give him, and took with him two Attendants well armed, and as much Provisions as was necessary for such a Journey, and being favoured with good weather they soon came to the Allegany Mountains.——Here the Doctor discovered a certain Root never known nor heard of before, which proves a remedy for all diseases.——After a great deal of trouble they found the Hermit, but it was entirely by accident that they happened at last to discover him; for the Country was very wild, covered with shrubs as thick as possible, and the trees grew large beyond description.——One day the Doctor discovered with his Spy-Glass, a very high Hill, at a considerable distance; and thought he would go and take an Observation from the top of that Hill;——when he arrived there he soon found the Old Hermits path, just as Capt. Buckland had directed.——They followed the path down the valley, and soon came to the Hermit's Cave;——nothing was seen of the Hermit for some time, and they supposed that he was asleep in his Cave, and not one soul durst venture into his old Habitation, at length, whilst they were listening at the mouth of the Cave, they discovered the Hermit at a little distance, coming with a handful of Roots which he had been gathering for food;——he walked in a slow and grave manner, and when he saw them he came and embraced them;——but did not seem to be so much surprised to see them as when he was first discovered by Capt. Buckland, &c.——He invited them in a very friendly manner into his Cave, and was overjoyed to see them. The Cave was very curious, which appeared to be dug out of a solid white flint rock; but as particular description has been given of it before, it will be needless to say any thing farther concerning it.——The Hermit made

particular enquiry after Capt. *Buckland* and Mr. *Fielding,* and said that he received great satisfaction from a visit which they had made him, and added, that they were the first human beings that he had seen from the time he first landed on this shore, which was about 200 years.——Doctor Brake tarried there several days, and in that time became very intimate with the Hermit, and found several things which were not discovered before :——Two Books in particular, which he brought with him from England, one in Poetry the other in Prose.——The Hermit appeared to have had a good education, when he was young, and discovered a surprising greatness of mind.——His eyes were good, but his teeth were very poor, he had but little hair on his head, but his beard was very long.——He could not articulate his words very distinctly, but his language was better than any spoken in England at the time he left it, which makes it appear evident that he was an extraordinary genius when he was young :——He shewed Doctor Brake his Books, Writings, &c. he had a large Pile of them in one corner of his Cave, some were done on barks of trees, and some on skins made into a kind of Parchment.——The Doctor obtained liberty to take a copy of the Hermit's Composition.——One contained principally Moral Sentiments, and the following Sentences were found written in one of them " *Young Men and young Women beware of seducing appearances which may surround you, and recollect what others have suffered from the power of headstrong desire.——This world is but a wilderness.——Eager passions and violent desires were not made for Man.——Pitch upon that course of life which is best, and habit will render it the most delightful.*" —

After a while the Doctor determined to try the old fellow with a little rum, and see what the effect would be; but it was with great difficulty that he could persuade him to drink : The Doctor told him that it was an excellent cordial that tended to strengthen the constitution, 'till at last the poor innocent Hermit was persuaded to drink a little of that acrid bane, which hath sent thousands out of the world.——He

drank about three quarters of a gill of that poison liquour, and in a quarter of an hour there was a sensible alteration in his looks and conduct ;——and in half an hour he appeared wild and almost mad, and attempted to tell a kind of a love story,——and in about an hour he was entirely senseless, and remained in that shocking situation until twelve o'clock at night, and then died.

Poor Old Man ! he lived about 200 years in his Cave, enjoying all the happiness of a retired life ! and might have lived 200 years more, had he not drank that horrid draught ! Cursed liquor ! Thousands have fell a sacrifice to its bewitching power !

Among the Hermit's writings was found his WILL, which appeared to have been made soon after he was first discovered.—— He had given his Cave to Capt. Buckland and Mr. Fielding, as also all his Writings : His curious Cane he willed to one of Capt. Buckland's Servants, which was all the Hermit was possessed of, excepting a few old Skins which had served to cloath him, those he gave to the other Servant, as a reward for his kindness in singing a love-song to him before they departed.

Doctor Brake was much affected at the sudden death of the Hermit, more especially the manner in which he was brought to his *untimely* death ;——but the Doctor said that he felt no remorse of conscience, as he really supposed that a little of that cordial would serve to raise his spirits and make him more cheerful with his new visitors.

The next day the Doctor and his Attendants employed themselves about burying the Old Gentleman in as decent a manner as possible in his Cave, which was done with great solemnity and good order.——The Doctor ordered one of his Attendants to shave the Hermit, and his Beard is carefully preserved as a very great curiosity, it being at least twelve inches long.

N. B. Doctor Brake mentions that this good Old Man made it his constant custom to devote himself to Prayer every Day, and there is no doubt of his final and everlasting happiness.

☞ Those who do not credit the above may apply to Dr. Brake for better information.

60. *The following is copied from the Journal kept by Mr. Jacob M. Berriman, during his tour to the Westward of Fort Recovery.*
Suffield, Connecticut: Edward Gray [1799].

Unhappily, attempts to verify this capture of a thirty-six foot long snake have been fruitless. It is possible that Jacob Berriman was an inhabitant of Connecticut who set out to explore parts of "New Connecticut" which in another broadside is described as "that part of the Connecticut Reserve, . . . lying West of Pennsylvania, and South of Lake Erie." Fort Recovery is to the west of this area, almost on the Indiana–Ohio border.

The last line, which mentions "Mr. Peck's Museum in Philadelphia," is of particular interest. The museum which would have been the likely repository for such a snake was Charles Willson Peale's Museum in Philadelphia, which opened in April of 1786. This was the first important museum in North America. Although animals, rocks, shells, bones, fishes, birds, and all other natural subjects were included in this collection, snakes were favored by Peale.

Evans 35187
10 ⅝ × 18

The following is copied from the Journal kept by Mr. Jacob M. Berriman, during his tour to the Weſtward of FORT RECOVERY.

May 27, 1794: THIS morning about an hour after ſun-riſe, as we proceeded on our rout about a mile weſt from the place where we had lodged the preceding night, we were alarmed by a terrible barking of our dogs a-head, and all eagerly puſhed forward to take poſſeſſion of the game thus pointed out by our faithful dogs. About a quarter of a mile a-head we diſcovered the moſt terrible Monſter which human eyes ever beheld to which our dogs dare not approach; but only ſtood barking at a conſiderable diſtance. At the ſight of ſo monſtrous a creature, every hair on our heads ſeemed to ſtand on end with fear: Though we had no reaſon to apprehend ourſelves in danger, for he was buſily employed in deſtroying a large Panter, which ſeemed as incapable of reſiſtance, as a common ſquirrel would have been in competition with one of our dogs.

We halted, and placed ourſelves to the beſt advantage in order to view his manner of diſpatching the panter, which he did by winding his tail around him, & drawing to ſuch a degree as to cruſh and break his bones, which we could frequently hear ſounding like the ſnapping of a whip accompanied by the moſt hideous howls of the agonizing animal. A conſultation was next held in order to choſe the moſt effectual method of attacking ſo formidable an enemy. It was finally determined, that one of the company ſhould go back to the houſe and procure a horſe, on which one of us, being mounted and armed with a muſket, ſhould approach within a convenient diſtance of the ſnake, and giving him a well aimed ſhot, ſhould retreat precipitately in caſe he was attacked. Accordingly the perſon appointed, proceeded back to the houſe, and in leſs than an hour returned mounted on a horſe well calculated for the purpoſe. It was then concluded to ſuſpend our attack, till he ſhould have devoured his game; which he did in the following manner—After having broken all his bones as above, he licked him with his mouth till he appeared all over wet and ſlippery, and then ſwallowed him without much difficulty. The large animal which he had now gorged appeared to have greatly abated the agility of his motion, which we thought a cir-

cumſtance much in our favor; but on the other hand, we were not without great apprehenſions of his ſcales being ſo hard that a ball could not penetrate them—However, having mounted the horſe myſelf, I attacked him in the manner above deſcribed, & after giving him three ſhots, he was ſo far diſabled, that we all approached him with long gads and diſpatched him without much further difficulty—It was not till about two o'clock in the afternoon that we accompliſhed a part of our buſineſs ſo ſatisfactory, both to our fears and curioſity—We had now an opportunity to view him leiſurely, and ſuch a mixture of horror and beauty, I believe was never before ſeen blended in one object. After we had drawn him out ſtraight, we proceeded to meaſure his dimentions which we did exactly, and found him to be no leſs than 36 feet, 2 inches in length, and the largeſt part of his body to be 3 feet, 1 inch in diamater—His eyes were indeſcribably large and piercing. His head was of a moſt beautiful changeable green, toward the top inclining to a yellow, but darker towards his neck and round his jaws—upon the top of his head was a large oval black ſpot—His neck was incircled with three rows of ſpots, of the moſt beautiful crimſon. His back, from his neck nearly to the end of his tail, was covered with ſcales of the beautifuleſt green I ever beheld, on each ſide was a row of large black ſcales, between two ſmall red ſtripes. His belly was perfectly white along the middle. but bearing upon a yellow toward each ſide. The next part of our buſineſs was to determine upon the beſt manner to diſpoſe of the ſkin, which we looked upon as the moſt valuable part of our game.

As the day was ſo far ſpent that we could not complete the ſkinning of it before dark, and as we could not poſſibly carry it away whole, we concluded to leave it until morning—Accordingly we went back to the above mentioned hut, & in the morning returned with knives, and in about three hours, we completed the buſineſs to our ſatisfaction. The ſkin we carefully waſhed, and ſtuffed it with hay until it was dry, when we opened it and rolled up for the convenience of carrying.

As many perſons, perhaps, will doubt the truth of the above account, they may ſatisfy themſelves by calling at Mr. Peck's Muſeum in Philadelphia, where the ſkin was preſented.

Suffield: Printed by EDWARD GRAY.

LIST OF PLATES

32. Mr. Samuel Gorton's Ghost. Newport, 1728.
33. A Dialogue between Death and Lady. Boston, 1731-1775.
34. A Dialogue between Death, the Soul, Body, World and Jesus Christ. Boston, 1787.

ELEGIES

35. Tears Dropt at the Funeral of that Eminently Pious Christian, Mrs. Elizabeth Hatch. [Boston?, 1710.]
36. An Elegy Occasioned by the sudden and Awful Death of Mr. Nathaneal Baker of Dedham. [Boston, 1733.]
37. Phillis' Poem on the Death of Mr. Whitefield. [No place, 1770.]
38. An Elegiac Poem. [Boston, 1791.]
39. The Awful Malignant Fever at Newburyport, in the Year 1796. Newburyport, 1796.

ADVERTISEMENTS

40. By His Excellency Jonathan Belcher, Esq. Boston, 1740.
41. Advertisement. Twenty Pounds Reward. 1767. [Charleston, 1767.] Advertisement. Seventy Dollars Reward. 1768. [Charleston, 1768.]
42. Just Published, . . . The Massachusetts Calendar. Boston, 1771.
43. In the House of Representatives, Feburary 16, 1776. Salem, 1776.
44. Now fitting for a Privateer. [No place, 1776.]
45. Broke Open last Night, (13th October) the City Coffee House. [New London, 1787.]
46. Valuable Medicines. [Portsmouth, 1800.]

AMUSEMENTS

47. Boston, May 13, 1756. To be seen . . . The Microcosm. [Boston, 1756.]
48. A Catalogue of Books. A Barclay. [Boston, 1765?]
49. The Amorous Sailor's Letter to his Sweetheart. Worcester, 1781.
50. To the Curious. To be seen . . . Two Camels. [Salem, 1789?]
51. Theatre, Frederick-Town. . . . The Contrast. Frederick-Town, 1791.

HUMOR

52. Father Ab--y's Will. [No place, ca. 1731.]
53. Job Weeden, Salem News-Boy. [Salem, 1772.]
54. Verses for the Year 1790. [New York, 1790.]
55. By his High and Mighty Laziness Ephraim Eager. [No place, 1799.]

STRANGE AND WONDROUS EVENTS

56. An Account of the remarkable Recovery of Mrs. Mary Read. [Providence, 1769?]
57. On the Dark Day, May Nineteenth, 1780. [Boston, 1780?]
58. The Vision of John Mills. [No place, 1785.]
59. An Account of the Wonderful Old Hermit's Death, and Burial. [Boston, 1787.]
60. The following is copied from the Journal kept by Mr. Jacob M. Berriman. Suffield, [1799].

This book
was designed and the
letterpress sections printed at the press of
David Godine in Brookline, Massachusetts. The
fine screen facsimiles of the broadsides were all photo-
graphed directly from the originals and printed offset by
The Meriden Gravure Company, Meriden, Connecticut.
The type is Monotype Janson, cast by A. Colish, Inc.
The paper is watermarked Imprint Almanack text.
The binding is by Robert Burlen & Son,
Boston. Of 1950 copies printed,
this is number 1581

Georgia B Burgardner